LETTERS

BLACK WOMEN

to the

RADICAL WRITING

FUTURE

KORE PRESS

TUCSON

2018

LETTERS

BLACK WOMEN

to the

RADICAL WRITING

FUTURE

EDITED BY

ERICA HUNT

& DAWN LUNDY MARTIN

Celebrating 25 Years!
Standing by women's words since 1993
Kore Press, Inc., Tucson, Arizona USA
www.korepress.org

Cover art: Lorna Simpson, "True Value (detail)," 2015 © Lorna Simpson. Courtesy of the artist and Hauser & Wirth. Photo of the art by James Wang
Cover Design by Mary Austin Speaker
Interior Design by James Meetze

We express gratitude to the National Endowment for the Arts, the Arts Foundation for Tucson and Southern Arizona, the Arizona Commission on the Arts, and to individuals for support to make this Kore Press publication possible.

National Endowment for the Arts
arts.gov

ISBN 978-1-888553-85-7

Library of Congress Cataloging-in-Publication Data

Names: Hunt, Erica, 1955- editor. | Martin, Dawn Lundy.
Title: Letters to the future : black women : radical writing / edited by
    Erica Hunt and Dawn Lundy Martin.
Description: Tucson : Kore Press, 2018. | Includes bibliographical references.
Identifiers: LCCN 2018005688 | ISBN 9781888553857 (trade book)
Subjects: LCSH: American literature—African American authors. | African
    American women—Literary collections. | American literature—Women
    authors. | American literature—21st century. | Radicalism—Literary
    collections.
Classification: LCC PS508.N3 L48 2018 | DDC 810.8/0928708996073—dc23
LC record available at https://lccn.loc.gov/2018005688

Contents

AN ELDER HOMAGE

Lucille Clifton, Sonia Sanchez

Wanda Coleman

Jayne Cortez

EDITORS' POEMS

Erica Hunt

Dawn Lundy Martin

LOOKING PAST THE PAGES OF THIS BOOK

Tisa Bryant

"Therefore, when I say 'now that I'm done with being dead'
I have declared an alternate self."
—Akilah Oliver

"Tomorrow is the question."
—Ornette Coleman

"For over a century, what I've written has, within certain, specific limits, come true. I'm not a seer. I don't foresee the future. I create the future."

"Dear Sib,

"If you are reading this, then I must have been careless enough to let myself (to) get killed (sic)."

"I've left this letter to you to help you understand what you will inherit from me. [...] What Miss Barbara gave me, I give to you....I said she wrote truth and she taught me to write truth. 'Taught' wasn't quite the right word. In that big, crooked, left-handed writing of hers, she wrote that whatever I wrote would be true. [...]

"That's what she said. That's what I say too. It's not always what I did, but it's always the right thing to do. At least, start small. Feel your way.

"What you write will be true Sib. It won't just show up in a puff of smoke like on some of those television shows about magic."

"Think. Never write without thinking. First think about what you want to happen, and about how it might happen. Then think about what else might happen. Something else will always happen. That's why you should only do small things. You can keep control better, writing a long ladder of little truths."

from "Mortal Words" by Octavia Butler[1]

In one of those incidents we label "serendipity," where current event is prefigured by past imagination, we were fortunate to encounter Octavia Butler's "Mortal Words," cited above. Retrieved by Tisa Bryant for this anthology from the Octavia Butler archive at the Huntington Library, the excerpt opens with a first-person narrator, Sibyl, who tells how she received the "gift" of writing the "future." Her name, Sibyl, is a fitting reference to the group of women (always, women, it seems) with the gift of prophecy, and collected their writings—warnings, solutions, riddles—about the future into books.

In one account of the legend, a Sibyl of Cumaea had nine books relating events to come that she offered to sell to King Tarquin of Rome. He thinks the price too high, so Sibyl burns

---

1 *Mortal Words*. Fragment. MSS. OEB 1496. (2000) The Huntington Library, San Marino, CA. This excerpt is from an unfinished novel, comprised of twelve fragments and fifty-one pages. Written in epistolary form, the story concerns an inheritance, the power to write truth, to write reality into being, which is passed down, over hundreds of years through a line of Black women.

three of the books, offers the remaining volumes, and is refused again, so she burns another three, until he consents to buy the remaining prophetic volumes.

In Butler's "Mortal Words," Sibyl is the only child of a Black woman who runs a boarding house, and Francine Cooper is their mysterious boarder. Cooper dies seemingly penniless, and alone, leaving only a final letter bequeathing Sibyl the gift of writing and prophecy.

In this unfinished story, Butler demonstrates the extraordinary unboundedness of her imagination that suggests writing into the lived future tense might involve writing a "ladder of small truths," from which we hazard a claim to the future, and against foreclosure into a single trope of being.

Butler is one of the most significant writers of speculative fiction in the 20th century precisely because she deploys the story telling mode with an unfettered license to cross borders of time and space to critically consider issues of "difference:" race, gender, power and history, even species. Her bold prognostications has given rise to a generation of writers, theorists, visual artists and activists, who see in her "what ifs" a Black future tense, and generative ground for their own writing and politics. Feminist god-parent to a host of Black science fiction writers, Tannarive Due, Nalo Hopkinson, and other, Black Lives Matters activists, visual and digital artists, Butler's writing inspires many paths to "visionary literature" to "unstick the imagination."[2]

For this collection, Butler's "Mortal Words" invokes the inherent agency of writing, to render and frame what we know now, a present truth, and make it a palpable, plausible plenum, legible to readers now and in the future, the waiting sibyls, who we have not yet met until we write her in.

EH

---

2   See *Octavia's Brood*: Walida Imarisha and adrienne marie brown, coeditors.

INTRODUCTION:
ANGLE, DEFY GRAVITY, LAND UNPREDICTABLY

The future is a slippery project. What can it hold? We asked writers to write about it, imagining the future as the present conjugated—conjoining the past, the present with some other time. Don't writers write, intuitively, to the future all the time? It's in the calculus of the literary trajectory to incline towards a future dialogic; the writer assumes a kind of blindfold, writing to be in dialog with a reader, a reader through whom a part of the meaning/effect is fulfilled. The project of writing to the future is linked to the question of audience, and reception, how we all together re-imagine language, self and community. Dawn and I anticipated writing that would suggest and provoke—acts of self possession, self characterization, and alternate ways of living out and through strictures of time, the long "afterlife[1]" of kidnap, captivity and enslavement, subjugation, modernity with its diffuse array of chutes and shackles through to some new space, altered.

One dimension that drew our curiosity was to know how this particular group of Black women writers would respond to the question of tomorrow. The Black women in this edition were writers we'd known or been introduced to who had been insistent makers of poems and prose that set up radical encounters between language, person, community and the political. We discussed these letters as we received them, marveling at the range of strategies to refract, forecast or expand the penumbra of the present into the shifting and dim lit future.

For this collection, we asked the writers to respond to the prompt:

> We're writing because we admire and follow your work—Black, brave, imaginative, boundary crossing, at times a mystery—and we want you to be a part of an exciting new book project we're putting together. In the radical sum of the thinking in your work, you encourage the reader to look where no one else is looking, to tune into registers that provide critical cues for the future.

Because one contextual framework for the collection is "art as a form of epistemology," we envision the writing in the anthology will be the kind of work driven by the writer's desire to radically present, uncovering what she knows and does not know, as well as critically addressing the future.

Though this anthology is not interested in a stable notion of race, nor will it try to stake claims on the terms we are using, we want to see how identity and language manifest as part of the critical vocabulary and also how they both supply the content of our writing's unfinished and open exploration.

---

1   I am indebted to Saidiya Hartman's and Christina Sharpe's use of the concept of the "afterlife of slavery," which suggests to me a "wave" theory of Black ontology, energy and carried forward, in intensity, direction and frequency from an original and diffused violence.

The Black women writers included in this collection are different stylistically from one another, but committed to a radical practice of literary work, necessary alchemists in the word.

The anthology is not intended to be exhaustive of Black women's radical writing. In fact, we are suspicious of all canon-making, even as we assembled this collection, which may paradoxically, in the future, read mistakenly like a parchment-fragment of a canon. This collection consists of writers we turn to in order to read the radii of our contemporary fix, the magnitudes of disaster, who remind us that the thickets are made of individual trees, the copse and undergrowth.

It is our hope that in reading/exploring *Letters to the Future* you will find the writings included here will lead to other writers and other readings. For that reason, we expect to create a companion website. The website will be the formal space against closure, openly adding to the compilation collected here. In this we extend the anthology's form into a capacious future, big enough to handle the most innovative, out there and challenging writing.

We situate this collection in the continuum of many assertions of Black futures, most prominently seeded in the Black Arts movements' paradigm shift that made new sense by identifying nation (without a state) and culture within the disaster of diaspora and insisted on an emancipatory impulse towards "freedom" in the ongoing process of material and psychic decolonization. We try to reflect some of the past imaginings of the future by including Black women writers who've led by their insistence that the pursuit of transformative poetics is crucial to the reimagining of a world in which Black people thrive as free people. Women like Coleman, Cortez, Kennedy, Piper, Clifton, Sanchez, among many others let us know that literary practice is agency and collective agency in a world in which collectivity is circumscribed. These Black women cultivated the habits of undoing and remaking old narratives, releasing us by stopping us in our tracks, locating us, readers/audience in connectedness, the truth of uncertainty and witness.

The time of this collection, 2015-2017, was marked by an inflexion in the world's deteriorating economic and political relations. They extend and distend in body counts: yawning inequality, wars of surrogacy between states and between stateless nations, global migrations and climate change that challenge and multiply notions of interconnectedness. All these shifts and a conservative turn to authoritarianism are inscribed here, and at times they burn hot where futures forge. If writing and art are contingent practices, always carrying the imprint of context, social position, and a restlessness to know beyond the knowing (the *as if*, art's impulse) that keeps Black people in their place, this collection is propelled by a contemporary urgency to upend that fixed place.

Here are the responses—from across generations—to the question of how poetics might lead—from lives contracted to object destinies, and subject to racial violence and forfeiture, to an *as if* place—works that "give life" mediated by language and imagination, to move at the "velocity of writing" and by the audacity to anticipate.

Erica Hunt

INTRODUCTION:

DESTRUCTIONS OF [THE YOKE OF IT ALL]

It has always been difficult for me to conceptualize what we call Blackness in relation to human bodies, particularly myself as an indicator of the thing I don't quite understand. It's a strange predicament, and a worrying one. On the one hand, the claim of Blackness need not be a claim. A Black person in the world experiences themselves as Black given the perception by others as to what Black is. It is a (mis)recognition, always legible, often very slight in the adjustment of the face, a minor tick, a momentary widening of the eyes, almost imperceptible in its speechless announcement, "a Black is in the room." On the other hand, the conceptual logics attached to this notion of "the Black"—a dripping blood-stained logic with certain parameters around designations of human— are the trickery of the yoke come a courtin' with that sweet talk sounding like something we have known all our lives.

"Despite knowing otherwise, we are often disciplined into thinking through and alongside lines that reinscribe our own annihilation," writes Christina Sharpe in *In the Wake: On Blackness and Being*, "reinforcing and producing what Sylvia Wynter, has called 'our narratively condemned status.'" When the trickery comes, sometimes it comes hard and fast and can be taken up by bodies that are unaware of their utilitarian bluntness in the symbolic order of race. The object is in his hand, but he will claim it is in yours. *I got the hammer from you,* he'll say, *I didn't have anything to do with it. It's your hammer. Now go ahead and knock yourself in the head with it.*

I am attending an outdoor gathering the day after a friend's wedding and I overhear a white man, a friend of sorts who I bonded with the night before, say "the Blacks and the Latinos were fighting with each other." I don't know the context, but, I say "Don't say 'the Blacks.' Who says that?" And, returning to my own conversation, I hear him say, "they called themselves that," as a way, I suppose, of legitimizing this noun meant to designate a kind of personhood, but without the noun of the person attached to it, so really to de-legitimize personhood, however unwittingly. The logic of syntax attached to a subject. The ownership of that subject's utterance. When the ghost resides inside the breathing body, as Octavia Butler seems to say. *How still the river is today; no one is crossing, no bodies float down. So, then, the river is just a river.* That's how it goes. Christina Sharpe says more: "We must become undisciplined." Alright now. This is the meat of it. How do we escape these wound messages, these trickeries of (self)destruction and enter the space of the possible with hopes that that possible might be made manifest?

When Erica Hunt and I took on the project of collecting writing for this anthology we instinctively knew that the time, the now, was a ripe moment for bringing together radical writing by Black women. *Letters to the Future: Black WOMEN / Radical WRITING* is brought to being in this time of devastation when the confinement and obliteration of the Black body / Black people is an everyday thing. We protest, and we are cast as terrorists against the state. We say our names, and the state says the saying of our names is hate speech. The re-coding of language has us in its grasp. Writing radically, for us, means, in part being unbound by that fragile re-code, those new rules. In *Letters to the Future: Black WOMEN / Radical WRITING,* we are aware of the hegemonic desire to ensnare Black art and poetry with language that delimits that art and poetry for its exchange value in the market place. We are not interested in this work as capital, but instead as without regard to the marketplace, as anti-doctrine, as future imaginings, as languages with their own rules, as new makings, undisciplined and rebellious. Thus, we resist the notion that we know more than the writing collected in the pages of the book. Thus, the terms for talking about the book emerge from the text itself. Following each section we read across writings attempting not to "frame" but to, perhaps, see what thoughts emerge from the inter-text. It's a kind of collage, this reading process, inviting ourselves into the pages of the book in order to open a space for it to produce its own languages of significance.

Erica and I understood, too, that the terms we used to conceptualize this collection are all open to contest. "Woman" feels almost quaint in 2018. Yet like the Black bodies' subjugation based on the visual, one's gender is a strong indicator of continued subjugation; and both Blackness and femaleness, as indicated by the work collected in this volume, are as unruly as the ranging manners toward utterances that seek to speak them, and that unruliness can be powerful. This is what unforeclosure does. That is what radical means to me.

You think you know me, but you don't know me.

You don't know my people, you don't know where I come from.

You don't know my name or what language I speak. You think you do but you do not.

To look into the future is to imagine and create another world. I used to think that this remaking required disaster, but I no longer think that because we exist always in the new presence of disaster. Disaster is the convention of the present state. What, then, makes for new configurations of meanings that, in turn, render new material, new shapes, heretofore unimagined? Which brings me to this old question of personhood, and this other question of "life," or what it means to live—the latter question which has a kind of brightness to it for me. To live is to escape the soft familiar call of the tether, threatening the ankle, the neck, the voice, threating to infect the voice with its voice. The brightness of the writers collected in this volume got something else for that sugar.

Dawn Lundy Martin

SECTION ONE

Betsy Fagin

DECOLONIZED

corrected course embodied
decoded place: our social
forms as elaborate stitches:

them partially funded
them happy valley
into fragments dispensed

with myopic clouds and trees
both memorying embroiderment,
navigating necessary

alleviation of alleviation.
endangered stewardship
taken in hand. device

information bloated device
relevant to impertinent
cooperation left space,

such arrogance, such rudeness
on the world inflicted
infinite yoga studios and

bells, wind chimes, bell neem
everywhere, filling cracks in
indian lilac hopes of restoring intimacy.

INDIGENOUS SILENCE

hunted glorification
will haunt the tale as
group of tongue and space
backs wandering stars' vernacular.

that quickening is complicit.
science separate from story
disappoints, addicts to difficulty
positioned cloud up

holds the weather to understand—
I used to could,
from first light.
a new zodiac introduce

my devised constellations
from device. stars where
bodies distrust discretion,
magnetic as true.

indigenous science,
our struggle are evermore
lost are struggle fundamental
of related stories, kin.

CROSSROADS & GATES ARE MOVEMENT

(WILL WORK FOR FOOD)

gods need shrines
as kings need
thrones and palaces

every element adjoins
in common occupancy
soil shares no longer

invaded from outside
a body becomes
polarized cluster

spectator of itself
tourist of everything
spelled out on soil

routes and paths to cross-
roads and monuments
defining space and frontier

the market
a dated monument
of equals authenticates

landscape present
all streets lead to the hearth
centered circle the closed

space of withdrawal
god of threshold and door
is created equal to any

market or political
capital in expansion
and shrinking rooted in soil

from CELESTIAL NAVIGATOR

navigate celestial non-relating
with cloud color sequence
these non-instruments
map waves into moon and stars

wedded with speak
of science to gain bearings
through this passaged
cultural degradation

shapes into colonies
of color forecast sounds
against a backed-up
immunity garden

that built in redundancies
intimate with natural whorls
ceasing destruction
with availability, presence

me so learned.
my only true teacher
the ocean, soaked in rain
winded the names of me

element ocean
now as quiet
taro leaves our
faced prayers

Betsy Fagin

ELIMINATION OF CURRENCY

this is my gift
the elimination
of currency and debt

swampland ventures
real estate hands
my dirt my stink

that money smell
of pine orange
rosewood metal

sweet reward
rinsed clean
to protect value

added delicate tombs
time-pressurized
cabinets air-conditioned

into soft and somewhat
stable painted gold
makes moonshine

rush mountains blazing
in sun stream
digging her

make me ruler
our one single currency
a rainbow hologram

of coin for the citizenry
all civilized knows
a center radiates

the city
as any river
always the ocean toward

mind follows
bliss
this is proof

WHEN DID THE INTERNET START USING ME?

window watch
if the line gets any shorter
what phenomenal
wire tapped things happen
in this far downed star

window heavy blossom
took a while to conquer
narrow into serious
about saving all not just
myself we know what happens

watching the drilling
through one last
shock of white tears
I can't wait to see how
this turns out otherwise

never change stay
the same rights now
rock bottom, don't know
and feel bad set pedestaled
in place of real need

asked to sit
stay awhile
with my life
my indebted
my bankrupt

EATING ANCIENT VIRTUE

illustrated hands pair
with another halting source
then run, seed vision
the obvious suspicion–alone
in the abundant multiverse–
then part, quite fast enough
brought on the unexpected
cannot destroy mesa noise
or shift dirt-done stance
to allow lost ways to erupt
or fall her. fail. disturb
an accidental nightmare
bone mist of surety. open.
seamless. the only constant
deception. non-disclosure.
misdirected. crucial.
don't stop collected tears
manifesting present existence
including my trod on
stood ground.
laboratories conceal nothing.
scorched restraint rarely connects.
our breath now frozen underfoot.
accept the unstoppably obvious.
false complexity makes it bounce.
recognize.

Ruth Ellen Kocher

Uhuru's cat eyes extend nearly to her Temples   Each sweep of lid

makes small gusts through the diner So the short waitress With the

mod' green nails and Nancy Sinatra hair spends much Of the

morning closing then re- Closing The swinging steel-framed door

Uhura lowers her eyes to her cup Raises her hand Removes a dove

from her mouth   The dove says   *Dismantle*   *Dwell*

Expanse   Uhura reaches for sugar   The dove says   *Dystopia*

Brute   *Home*   The dove says   *Domain*   The dove says

Grace means to do so   She raises her hand   puts the dove back in

her mouth Raises her eyes to meet the eyes swelling in front of her

Martin looks over her red uniformed shoulder   He looks through
the window past the white Cadillac hood   over the mint green
roof of the Lorraine Hotel   The trees bud   Ripen   and fail
in the course of two perhaps Three stop-light revolutions   *In*
space   Martin says in an oratory whisper as the waitress refills his
coffee   brings Uhura's side of cream   *In space   we need someone*
to plant orchards   He squeezes her hand as the sun angles her
curves away   Leans into his own breath   *Someone*   he says
and I trust you

SKIT: PEARL BAILEY AND EARTHA KIT REVISE
OBSERVATIONS ON THE FEELING OF THE BEAUTIFUL

Whether we love it or hate it is irrelevant to its worth. We have heard more women call women whores than we have heard men call women whores. We have more light than we know what to do with. Live with it. Some time ago, a Woman asked us for five women we loved and five women we hated and five women we hated to love ... or maybe five women we hated and five women we loved and five women we loved to hate ... or both. We haven't been able to answer. We're trying not to sing too easy green and violet veins meaning moth-winged flower or would it be worse to say bloom? The shackled hardwood, the ribs of the house, the ribs of a huge beast, the ribs of a fossil, the ribs of a thing destined to be stone. We call ourselves *Away*. Stranded is a place not a thing.

SKIT: SUN RA WELCOMES THE FALLEN

Jupiter means anger. Sun Ra does not. Sun Ra dances the Cake
Walk on Saturn's pulpy eyes. If you believe that, I'll tell you
another one. The first is 13 and the next is 20. They were not good
boys but they were boys. They were boys who died for this thing or
that. The next was 16 and the last was 18. One had a cell phone.
One had a gun. On earth, a goose opens its chest to a sound. The
goose takes the bullet this way. A sacrifice denied to the wind
since there is no such thing as sacrifice anymore having succumbed
to fever and the millennium. The bullet is all consequence. Sun Ra

refuses red — long and high, low and deep. His arms are long enough to embrace them.

INSOMNIA CYCLE: OLIO 19

You can't learn to ignore [   ] Which means each color all in movement morning decreasing endlessly and noisy in a way only solved and quieted by vodka or walking. [   ] is your face. [   ] is your hand. [   ] reconfigures a white expanse. [   ] assumes a black expanse. [   ] has forgotten your name. You're standing in sweet grass. You're weaving a Gullah basket. [   ] is a dreadlock. [   ] is ashy. [   ] is a book. [   ] is a rope. [   ] is where you've been or what you choose or what you kill. [   ] is better than your body. Like California. Arizona. Colorado, and ... [   ] is better than that. You, too. You're amazing. You're better than butter and sunshine.

Your heart throbs begonias You're summer sultry easing   You won't give it up.

    A. The Sublime

    B. Terror

    C. All of the above

SKIT: SHE MANIFESTS HER OWN INEFFABLE

Other than the intricacies of the creak sky blackness that opens

against the horizon A horizon not imagined as any way to anything

Crouched in some ways recessing against a train of No a well of

intentions and cliché A well with a surface that you understand to

be water but reflects not me but you not her or him or him but you

You with your eyebrows crooked like night bending through a

stairwell Not her or dried egg white on the counter Between the

First day and the Second day Other Intricacies of royal Sunshine

say Sunshine again and again until it is all consonant and vowel

Nothing Else Nothing not there or there either Here

Robin Coste Lewis

VOYAGE OF THE SABLE VENUS

And never to forget beauty,
however strange or difficult.

—REGINALD SHEPHERD

PROLOGUE:

What follows is a narrative poem comprised solely and entirely of the titles or catalogue descriptions from Western art objects in which a black female figure is present, dating from 38,000 BCE to the present.

The formal rules I set for myself were simple:

1) No title could be broken or changed in any way. While the grammar is completely modified, each title was left as published, and was not syntactically annotated, edited, or fragmented. I erased all periods, commas, semi-colons etc., which occurred within the original titles, and sculpted a narrative using only the titles of the artwork instead.

2) "Art" included paintings, sculpture, installations, photography, lithographs, engraving, any work on paper, etc—all those traditional mediums now recognized by the Western art-historical project. However, because black female figures were also used in ways I could never have anticipated, I was forced to expand that definition to include other material and visual objects, such as combs, spoons, buckles, pans, knives, table legs.

3) At some point, I realized that museums and libraries (in what I imagine must have been a hard-won gesture of goodwill, or in order not to appear irrelevant) had removed many 19th century historically-specific markers, such as *slave, colored,* or *Negro* from their titles or archives, and replaced these words instead with the sanitized, but perhaps equally vapid *African-American.* In order to replace this historical erasure of slavery (however well-intended), I re-erased the post-modern "African-American" and changed all those titles back. That is, I re-corrected the corrected horror to allow that original horror to stand. My intent was to explore and record not only the history of human thought, but also how normative and complicit artists, art institutions and art historians have all been in participating in—if not creating—this history.

4) As an homage, I decided to include titles of art *by* black women artists and curators, whether the art included a black female figure or not. Most of this work was created over the last century, with its deepest saturation occurring since the Cold War. I also included work by black queer artists, regardless of gender, because this body of work has made consistently some of the richest, most elegant, least pretentious contributions to Western art interrogations of gender and race.

5) In a few instances, it was more fruitful to include a museum's description of the art, rather than the title itself. This was especially true for colonial period.

6) Sometimes I chose to include female figures I believed the Western art world simply had not realized was a black woman passing for white.

7) Finally, no title was repeated.

"The Metropolitan Museum of Art
Employees' Association Minstrel Show and Dance
will be held at the American Woman's Association
361 West 57th Street, Saturday evening,
October 17, 1936"

"I am anxious to buy a small healthy negro girl—
ten or twelve years old, and would like to know
if you can let me have one..."

MRS. B. L. BLANKENSHIP

THE SHIP'S INVENTORY:

Four-Breasted Vessel, Three Women
in Front of a Steamy Pit, Two-Faced
Head Fish Trying on Earrings, Unidentified.

Young Woman with Shawl
and Painted Backdrop, Pearl
of the Forest. Two Girls

with Braids People
on a Ship with Some Dancing
Girls, Our Lady of Mercy, Blue.

Nude Iconologia Girl
with Red Flower Sisters
of the Boa Woman Flying a Butterfly.

Kite   Empty
Chair   Pocket
Book   Girl

in Red Dress with Cats and Dog's Devil
House Door of No Return. Head of a Girl-
In-the-Bedroom in the Kitchen.

Contemplation Dark-Girl Girl.
In the Window Negress with
Flower Sleeping Woman

(Negress with Flower Head
of a Woman Nude in a Land
scape.)—Libyan Sybil: Coloured, Nude-High

Yellow Negro Woman
and Two Children—The Flight
of the Octoroon: The Four Quarters of

the World, Holding
a Celestial Sphere.

INVOCATION

BLESSING THE BOAT

Untitled
Anonymous
Clay

Prehistoric
Cow
Bone

Detail

Of a
Balsarium
Glass Moss

Fragment
Untitled Gelatin
Silver Print

On Paper On
Stucco On Canvas
On Concrete

Apotheosis:

>*Obverse anthropomorphic sarcophagus*
>*Alabastron eulogia ampulla.*
>
>*Anonymous fragment. Frag*
>*Ment. Pavement (detail) Pain t*
>
>*On tin—Figure 150, Figure 151:*
>*Strings and black mud*
>
>*Terracotta terracotta.*
>*Anonymous relief.*

Untitled Anonymous Limestone,
Isolated Ronde Bosse.

Plant Fiber Beads, Red
Abrus Seeds, Solar-Mosaic Wood Plate.

Ointment Vase, Printed Bedspread,
Artificial Hair—Neck

Decoration from a Tunic, Untitled Chewing Gum,
Gold—Gold Repoussé, Anonymous Plaster-Ink.

Salted Paper, Coins, Carbon,
Ivory-Colored Pencil. Graffiti

On the sides and undergirding
Of a bridge. Da Guerre!

O Type accumulated—Figurine 38 felt
Tip monumental relief.

Grass   Stain
Ivory   Spoon
Berry   Juice
White   Pigment

Hide,

Heads and Busts
Headless—Footless—Armless

But with a Strongly
Incised Vaginal

Opening:

Harp

Harp
With Bridge   *Harp*
Lute

One-key
Xylophone
Slit

Gong
Trumpet   *Gong*
Gong

Mallet
Whistle
Rattle

Drum

CATALOG 1:

ANCIENT GREECE & ANCIENT ROME

Here is your name
said the woman
and vanished in the corridor
—MAHMOUD DARWISH

I.

Statuette of a Woman Reduced
to the Shape of a Flat Paddle

Statuette of a Black Slave Girl
Right Half of Body and Head Missing

Head of a Young Black Woman Fragment
from a Statuette of a Black Dancing Girl

Reserve Head of an African Princess
Statuette of a Concubine

Full Length Figure of a Standing
Black Woman Wearing Earrings

Statuette Once Supported an Unguent Vase
Vase with Neck in the Form of a Head

of a Black Statuette of a Female
Figure With Negroid Features

Figure's Left Arm Missing Head
of a Female Full-length Figure

of a Nubian Woman
the Arms Missing

Bust of a Draped Female Facing Forward
One Breast Exposed   Black

Adolescent Female with Long Curls and Bare
Breasts Wearing a Voluminous Crown

Partially Broken Young Black Girl
Presenting a Stemmed Bowl

Supported
by a Monkey

:

Standing Female Reliquary Figure
with Crested Coiffure and Hands

Clasped in Front of Torso, Holding
a Staff Surmounted by a Human Head

Figure Has Prominent
Vagina Bended

Knees and Oversized Head
with Half-Open Eyes

and Semicircle Mouth
that Juts Out

from the Face Some
Fine Scarification

on Chest and Belly
Dark Brown Almost Black

Patina with Oil Oozing
in Several Places

Numerous Cracks
on Back of Head and Hole

on the Coiffure
One Nipple Appears

to Be Shaved Off
or Damaged Black Woman

Standing on Tiptoe
on One End of a Seesaw

While a Caricatured Figure   Jumps
on the Other

End

: ELEMENT OF FURNITURE DECORATION

[Two Nubian Prisoners Bound
to a Post] Protome [Probably

the Handle of a Whip
or Other Implement] Oil Flask Back

View Head of an African Prisoner
Statue of Prisoner Kneeling Arms

Bound at the Elbows
Left Arm Missing

Bust of a Nubian Prisoner
with Fragmentary Arms

Bound Behind Funerary Mask
of a Negro with Inlaid Glass Eyes

and Traces of Incrustations
Present in the Mouth

Censer in the Form of a Nude Negro
Dwarf Standing with His Hands

at His Sides upon an Ornate Tripod
and Supporting on His Head

a Small Cup
in the Shape

of a Lotus
Flower

II.

water jar

bowl

ointment spoon

in the form of swimming
black girl

mirror
with handle

in the form of a carved standing
black girl

handle
of a sistrum

a Bes and an Isia dancing
back-to-back

two nails

with Negro heads in relief

head

of a Negro which may have adorned

a pin

mounted in a

ring

bezel

bowl

decorated with three heads
in relief

separated by flat veined leaves
female puppet with

mortar and pestle
necklace

with two heads
of black women forming

a clasp
perfume vase

head of an adolescent

aryballos

juxtaposing two heads of Negroes
cast from the same mold

mirror
with handle

in the form of a young Nubian
female standing

lamp

in the form of

the head

        of a black perhaps

incense
shovel

        with a Negro head attached

to handle
a girl

        with long corkscrew curls
        round face wide
        flat nose and mouth

open

        and jutting forward
        to form

a spout

inkwell

        in the form of a crouching
        Negro Negro
        seated writing on

a scroll

Afterword 1

History, even future history is a record of current concerns. As historian Eric Foner observes: "forgetting is as essential to public understandings of history as remembering." Fagin's poems circle what is forgotten and remembered in sequence of poems included here, and asserts in "crossroads and gates are movement (will work for food)."

every element adjoins
in common occupancy
soil shares no longer...

spectator of itself
tourist of everything
spelled out on soil

Open form poems in short lines on generous display, **Betsy Fagin's** "letters" build a future by inscribing a short list of the long life of historical devastations, colonization, attempted erasure of indigenous peoples and cultures, the idolatrous worship of monuments erected on land grab, the arguable idea that one can individually claim "the commons," or a shared place. Note the words that recur in this sequence: colonized, conquer, debt, real estate, swampland, soil, gold, etc.

We are given spaces of possibility in "elimination of currency" and "celestial navigator." In the "elimination of currency," Fagin offers the gift of free choice to follow passion irrespective of the market: "mind follows/bliss/this is proof." In "celestial navigator" Fagin offers an alternative means to map a place, a map of the sky, earth in its home of solar system, amidst constellations which are constant.

In **Ruth Ellen Kocher's** alternative universe, Dr. Martin Luther King meets Lieutenant Uhura for coffee in the next galaxy, their conversation a play between roman and italic, mediated by a dove (the Holy spirit?). Needs answered are in the orchards, the concatenation of things hoped for but not seen.

In other trysts, "Pearl Bailey" and "Eartha Kitt" critique beauty, its complicated formulas and reformulations, indeed the thing artists believe themselves to break away from or pursue, so as not to be seen as "too easy."

In Kocher's futurity, there are no easy closures, but open brackets, no simple nouns but abstract nouns, and how easily they replace each other, are linked, vatic, the "Sublime" and "Terror" alternate, predict each other, taking turns.

Celebrated and cerebral, **Robin Coste Lewis'** *Voyage of the Sable Venus* (excerpted here) wrings from archive and catalog's muted language of objects a full range of cultural sentiments. One sees the often commodified representations of Black women's bodies, as they were incorporated into household artifacts, begin to speak eloquent beyond their catalog label and historical silence. Though intended to be tongue-less when they were manufactured, and even now, as they are preserved in cultural institutions, Coste Lewis detects that these Black figures cast animate shadows, and speak, barely audible. In these poems, the past won't shut up, instead, *she* persists.

In "Ship's Inventory," artifactual silence achieves an exuberant array of mood and tone; a miscellany leads to Black god(r)esses, accessory and ornament, a woman's get-up powers objects and masques towards a Libyan Sybil, perhaps a reference to William Wetmore's sculpture of the same name, about which he wrote: "She is looking out of her black eyes into futurity and sees the terrible fate of her race. This is the theme of the figure—Slavery on the horizon."

Compare the mood of "Ship's Inventory" to "Catalog 1: Ancient Greece and Ancient Rome." The shift in feeling rewards close reading, as the descriptive rhetoric consistently points to what is absent, broken off and incomplete and highlights instrumentation of Black women's bodies reduced to labor power. Coste Lewis's "Voyage of the Sable Venus" poem has many purposes, but one effect is to lift the veil from the neutral, objectifying gaze, allowing us to resuscitate and revive, even at the cost of ache and dropped breath, Black bodies.

Erica Hunt

SECTION TWO

Lillian Yvonne Bertram

There are shifting relationships between the figure of the negro and the contexts she finds herself in, and between self and others. We move from the perceiving and perceived negro and through a fleshy biological negro and a negro that is constructed social, to the local, the familiar and the abstractions of the global. This is a negro genetically and emotionally linked to the family and to the domestic spaces and familiar locales in which family relationships are played out. It is also a negro which is both a vehicle of a more conceptual travelling towards unfamiliar places which are 'there' rather than 'here,' and a negro which is transcended by time and space and which transcends it.

— P L E A S U R A B L E   T H O U G H   T H E   A B S T R A C T I O N   M I G H T   B E

This earlier work by Lillian can be read as a raced and gendered account of the restrictions a (negro) woman might face in negotiating public space. Lillian combines the compromising and potentially contradictory roles of woman, man and woman, perpetrator and accomplice, and investigates the possibility of a freedom from those restrictions through a private exploration of a raced sexuality that also limits Lillian's access to public space. Yet Lillian also describes the different corporeal and spatial relationships that unfold in the poems, and a clearer understanding of the relationships between those places, of which the body is one, can provide additional or supplementary readings. The poems move from being inside Lillian's own body and looking out, to being outside Lillian's own body and seeing herself as seen by others. The speaking self is in a relationship with a familiar body, both in the sense of being known and being a 'member' of the body of a family, yet it is a body that sometimes appears unexplored, a 'blind face.' Lillian's body is also in a spatial relationship with the body of a stranger, while in a familiar public space as in a park. Through processes of abstraction and generalization, and through real and imagined geographies of possibility and exploration, including the geography of her own body, Lillian is also in a global space, the 'whole long universe', which is a space of liberation, of possibility, and of threat.

—THE DREAM WORLD IS A PLACE SHE CAN REACH THROUGH
HER OWN BODY

For the negro, her body is both fleshy material, which exists in the material world, &
social construct. It has a special place. As Maurice Merleau-Ponty said, "The outline of my
body is a frontier which ordinary spatial relations do not cross" (2002, p.112), although for
the negro it is a frontier always crossed, or at least threatened, by members of the "human
family," the gaze of men in a park, & in her own fantasies. The more present the negro, the
more she responds to people watching her in a park, & enters a dream-world she can escape
to the outside of the limitations of raced, gendered, & sexualized public space. The range of
possibilities offered by the dream-world, as against the limitations of the daily, is illustrated
by the repeated ampersand. From a particular person in a particular place & with all the
restrictions that brings, & where she is located through her previous relationship to the place
& the people in it, the negro & the poem about the negro become a space of possibility. Like
the ocean. Like the Dark Continent. It is a place in which "I marry in, then out./ Under it I
stroll, a sky so blue and visible and starred" (xx). It is a place that makes action possible, but
not compulsory, a place in which she can do, or not do, what she likes. Yet for the negro,
pleasurable though the abstraction might be, & whether it takes her to some place else such as
the imagined geography of 'over there' or the eroticized fantasy of the dream world, the negro
must still exist between the immanent experience of everyday life & the possibilities of the
abstractions of the transcendent as when she says: "You hope it's not true" (xx).

—A FLESHY BIOLOGICAL NEGRO

Lillian is therefore in a relationship to the spatial context in which her viewing takes place, a space that includes both inside and outside of Lillian, and that Lillian is part of and also produces. The space is not a pre-planned grid system through which Lillian moves or is constructed to move, and nor is it a genetically programmed schema which she instinctively follows. It is not constructed prior to entering or moving through it, but is produced through the interaction and reaction between Lillian and world. And it Lillian who is always moving; Lillian who is never static, even for the duration of a single act of viewing. The narrative in the viewing develops a relationship by the end that is different from the beginning. The conceptual space of the succeeding, more abstract section of the viewing unfolds before us, weaving together her own physical experiences. She sees herself in relation to others within a symbolic order, and as Lillian in movement who is moving between things and towards things and who always has the intention of moving towards something. As a consequence she can see things, or imagines she can see things, from different perspectives.

—WITHIN A SYMBOLIC ORDER

The process of viewing is therefore linked to the negro as she exists in a social world that provides a context for the viewing (although of course a negro never simply exists, she is always moving towards something, even in the process of leaving something behind). Viewing is not a process that negates the social or corporeal context but is part of it. The specific negro will be gendered, coloured, aged, etc., and these are characteristics which will affect the viewing process. The negro may feel safe or under threat, she may be 'at home,' in a familiar village, town or country.

LaTasha N. Nevada Diggs

RAHZEL

how do you say triceratops —Fred Moten

props flex snare simulate lip dear ventriloquist, guttural. how

you craft scratch between teeth. you padrino, the konnkol[1] do

drone. crash synth. optimus. rated M for mature. lung distortion. you

bass in gut. name the gallon of spring you. the invisible MPC. say

yours is precious. the heavy breath & reverb stomp of a triceratops.

---

1   The art of performing percussion syllables, often used by various communities of South Asian musicians.

PIDGIN TOE[2]

on di saké menu no descriptive like quiet & smooth.
lean & firm. dry seems redundant. di comedic
pause dat carry so much inna tree letas. wen
di flesh breaks, a *ranginamu* glimma free itself to become
sky misty aan di temple. a strait of islands set against
a hazel setting inna di west. kolo pollo. morning is belated
aftanoon whey mourning dove & starling sing der
medley of five songs wich scratch at nickel clouds.
showcase loose silver reatas. *aroha*. der claws carving
tools. der beaks pick & sift gravel. it said inna myth
dat di rooster was sent down from heaven to shape
di earth. dat di world was once all wata. dat di rooster
no call out '*pōkokohua*.' wat yuh create w/ yrs out of wood,
metal & lacquer? di descriptive begin again. dreamy. *reka reka*
          engari ia mīere.
ae, dry is practical. perhaps necessary for di lineage.
perhaps necessary to protect di heart. di sky
neither dusk nor honolulu azure. di sparrow medley
now tree or two. di manner of tings arrive wen di sun cracks
di pastel smear. in di end, *e taku hoa pūmau pūrotu,*
                    di hair gladly protest shampoo.

          e taku tamatāne ngaro mokemoke,

in di end, gochira get devoured by sand dollah.

---

2 The poem is written in Pidgin (Nigerian and Hawaiian), Patois, Maori, Spanish, Japanese and English.

SON OF A NEGRO EXPLORER (NOT) AT THE NORTH POLE[3]
(COLONEL PLATOFF)

hawk the rabbit trim darling. the iconographic halo shadows your stare. whose
barber makes the grooming regal. what do you point towards? silver leafed children
pray to your Nikes. tangerine & blood in japanned leather. can you see father? hold

the pose Henson's legacy. descendant of Inuit. cloud burst of wonderful sexy. his
is your bequest: seaman & arctic booty. clock wolves. rock the navigator. hand
over your BBQ whale meat. polar bear & Lil Louie's *French Kiss*. mirror mirror at

the ball. walrus blubber carved w/ your sword. foreign familiar. lime cargos reflect the
cold Tundra sun. your name: Anauakaq of the Polo Grounds. where's your father? perp
contests the dogsled as prop. chiseled Arabian your pallid companion. bitch walk.

---

3   Written in the golden shovel form, the poem contains the line "whose children hold his hand at the perp walk"
from the poem "Drop a Schism" by Simone White.

NIGGA ON A HORSE OR METACOMET[4]
(AFTER KEHINDE'S WILEY'S KING PHILIP)

throw away stud glove replace w/ rider lily leather. a mercury prance. neverland contains a harsh winter. cape crusader, what is your krypton? kashmir sapphire or peridot? minor illusions to the hideous little monstrosity tabloids made you. puritan cult. Bashir's spoilers. showcase your collection of tchotchke. do you mean to remind us of the moors or about your noble new england bloodline? you no Gainsborough canvas. Indiana eleganza. a ribbon mare w/ tired eyes. are you a prince or a knight? so black is it to mash up a few ruffles & rose bushes. angels crown you saintly w/ a pine wreath. an invisible yet ratchet legacy. dicks don't reveal vanilla bean cock. daddy's belt can't hurt you. only little boy ass. was earth ever enough for you? depicted here, at least you are tan. connections shows,

    of children, castles and kings

once a child with a gold sunflower neck collar

    once a Wôpanâak sachem

now you dead bad big cotton.

---

4   Loosely based on the golden shovel form, the line "contains minor spoilers about a few ratchet ass shows" is from a caption written by Kid Fury for his YouTube page.

DUCK SEASON/RABBIT SEASON[5]

"Sometimes the exotic can be right in front of you."[2]
—Kehinde Wiley

"In this photograph you are lion-like, toothless, fraudulent."[3]
—*Uniglory,* Jen Hofer

"wide ranging large carnivores like this bear are particularly vulnerable to becoming road kill."[4]
—Wikipedia

"knock on wood I've never seen a Game Warden"
—Anonymous Exotic Animal Dealer

DI ONTIMAN SI A TIGRI, A LON TEKI EN GON, DAN A SUTU A TIGRI KIRI.

[2]   like an ill manila ts'i'ii ^mosquito^ yellow jacket bumble taser justified pounce on the *not again* pleasantry of buffalo antelope & wildebeest no persecution plain clothed weave about chokeholds specter of an eye out of orbit the hand of father reaches towards the heavenly chaplain for a loosie the traffic of street sport makes for Call of Duty a shielded hunger for warrants & arrests knock & announce *such a handsome wunderkind how you carry yourself how you exist Oakland panther Simba of Tulsa. you yield my quota Mighty Joe Young* the livestock auction shuts down online the unbecoming conduct of a predator's reflects onto the caricatured carriage homebound on platforms suspect zhinii ^black^ hide is by birth concealed arsenal often claret dusted sclera admits too much umber must never be mistaken for Bambi

WHEN THE HUNTER SAW THE JAGUAR, HE RAN FOR HIS GUN AND SHOT THE JAGUAR DEAD.

[3]   jurisdiction on this isle malign w/ gendarmerie blue offers a weekend getaway far beyond ranches in Texas or cells on Rikers *you my dearest gravy Zebra irresistible European badger no hostile Congolese honey fallen on enforced sword by the city of St. Louis Christ you are a remarkable creature aging white rhino in a hoodie saintly you are bejeweled wallaby* sometimes the gamers' caravan does not want the meat they prefer to mount the head in mugshots *Oh if only I could stuff you*

---

5   The poem contains words from the Diné language along with phrases from a Sranan Tongo dictionary.

YU MUS LERI A PIKIN FU LUKU BUN FOSI A E KOTI STRATI ABRA.

[4] in passage just a minor cabin incursion hazard 'tis easier to separate the head pummel a fist into a feminine version nihimá our mother *becomes blue-tugee island make way for stray puppies to clean the ground insatiable mutts drink a cruor that is opulent & profound they understand little difference between yours & a brush tail possum* arresting brown boy laying in the unsullied cutgrass *comply or canoodle pavement*

YOU NEED TO TEACH THE CHILD TO LOOK CAREFULLY BEFORE CROSSING THE STREET.

TRIX ARE FOR KIDS

your ass cheeks used to swallow whole a pole squeeze a lit match welcome a little smack here & there leaned over sloppy bars squat above long island ice tea sex on the beach for a dollar in a dingy hole in the wall called Goats the nigga won't tip you unless you deposit an ice cube into your pussy until you sit on that tawdry bar don't know how long that musty fermented rag been sitting there no bleach no germicide legs spread as they ogle at your snatch to survey the breezy stream of glacier leak on out for a dollar they request that you sit on a Heineken beer bottle Dutch owned brewery Dutch slave ship insurance someone collected off your ancestor's pussy for a dollar all Dutch Master drenched in tobacco infused saliva for a dollar yeast all hops they want you to fuck yourself with a Dutch Master a Heineken never mind the air bubbles past your cervix your pussy is a cheap nigga's brewery you make that special pale lager the match scabs on your ass or the sour rip between your cheeks because you did not baby oil the pole good enough for a dollar this trick wants to give you a dollar towards some happy ending in the back room towards the g-strings you thrashed your nipples and stuck on more matches you hesitated when you sat on that nigga's lap this nigga wasn't gonna give you a nickel if you didn't sit on his dick for a dollar your naked ass all the florida water in the world can't wash off this predatory wet spot ultra violet residue the edge of bar stool urinal light them up again 10 matches for 10 dollars 20 for 10 dollars a Heineken surrounded by your folds slurp for 2 dollars your malted pussy exploits an ice cube molests a Dutch Master it appears niggas still imposing that your pussy suck on an ice cube.

PASSING

...the artist is born of TrinidadianCanadian parents

...based in Miami, the artist

...the artist of Irish and Cherokee ancestry

...her work oscillates between the illusionary potential of performance

...was born and raised in Brooklyn

...the artist is of Diné and African descent

...artist, vocalist, curator, publisher, playwright, actor...

...the artist's works touch on seemingly disparate histories

...is the sociopolitical Marxist artist that coined the term "post black" in conceptual art.

...his delectably abject work is a tactile, layered, somatic and multilingual retelling...

...born in Port au Prince, Haiti, the artist

...work engages in a dual dialogue of Maori and European histories whilst adhering to the modernist emphasis on form and material quality.

...her work investigates the Afriscifi narrative in the black transgendered body

...he is a Chicano artist

...explores identity and conformity by photographing himself...

...is originally from White Cone, Arizona, on the Navajo Reservation.

...is represented by Sikkema; Jenkins and Co.

...her work, rooted in her MidWestern upbringing as a Korean adoptee

...the artist is a registered tribal member of the Shawnee

...crafting post postcolonial iconographies in Peruvian pottery

...he examines his Ugandan roots

...has exhibited in Morocco, South Africa, Pittsburg, Berlin, Tate Modern...

...she lives and works in Bogota, Colombia

... is Chippewa of the Deer Clan and born for the Mexican Clan.

...she explores displacement and identity in culturally specific markers

...was born in Ghana in 1971 and grew up in Nashville

...probing the physical weight of sculpture and Dominican carnival masks...

...uses the study of ethnological objects, popular icons, and the Dadaist tradition to explore cultural and creative syncretism, art history, and politics.

r. erica doyle

from "THE BODY OF

ACT I.

the density of history... —

I'm an AMERICAN

I like
to be happy

I don't want
to feel bad

I want
to feel good
like

everything is all
right, even when
it's clearly not

I'm so

LUCKY

I'm an American
and so

I'm LUCKY
too

I'm so LUCKY
that anytime I want to

I can find something
to make me HAPPY

Something cheap   Something pretty
easy.

I can surround myself
with people convinced

that everything
is GREAT!

Unfortunately

I was raised by
NON AMERICANS
(people who were constantly   challenging my attempts)
(to construct this HAPPY):

"That's what's wrong
 with you
KIDS"

my father would say

"You're
too

HAPPY"

HAPPY meaning not
that we were not suffering

(for he made us suffer)

but that we were
AMERICAN

so succulently
part of that

happy American culture
where we watched

Andy Griffith
till we felt nothing

but candy canes

ACT II.   *I am my own foundation.* —*FF*

Dark throat, you made something happen:

Gully, maybe. Gullah
praise be

Mantilla maiden
down on her knees

Iron her skirts   Wash her vagina
Get thee behind her and zip up her back—

Me dijeron que me llamaban desde el pozo
Voces nocturnas pajariles

Cocodrilos granadinos
rococo y sensibles—

Odio lo que ardo
Harta en my sweater.
Odio lo que amo
Tecato en stilletto

Mwen ka mantje ou doudou
Mwek ka mantje ou mache—

Llamo en staccato—
La pli ka vini

Sutil e imbecil—
La pli ka tonbe

Vini gade fidji nwaj-la
Mwen ka mantje ou ti moun

Annou pa gade deye—
Ya nada fui asi

Labios ladrando—

Legacy light handled—

ACT III.   *initiate my cycle of freedom... —FF*

I've broken my teeth
against this language of yours.

My tongue
bleeds
nouns
at night

in a
fricative wind.

r. erica doyle

VICTIMS OF UNREASON[1]

Until they're all converted, every block has a skinny white lady of indeterminate age with an underbite and a cigarette in her right hand swinging as she makes her way down the block. Sometimes this lady organizes the trash in the courtyard in the middle of the night into neat bundles of bulk, bags and recycling. Sometimes this lady screams through the wall that you're a whore and he's a faggot or mumbles under her breath when you pass her in the hallway, the street, the bodega. She wears the same small blue jacket and gray hoodie all winter, face the very image of the moon in *Le voyage dans la Lune*, space capsule in her

eye. Until they're replaced, she may or may not have children, who may or may not be bigger than her, may or may not be wholly or partially white, who indicate some sort of dalliance with boundaries she seems loathe to cross, at least socially, now, and they may or may not also smoke cigarettes, organize the trash or clean the sidewalk, or mumble beneath their breath when you pass. None of them is the super or the super's family or in any way connected with anything official like the super, but they keep the building, and its environs, clean, and for this they earn a begrudging respect from their neighbors, until they are gone.

---

1   John Keene, in an interview with Tonya Foster in *Bomb Magazine*, Fall 2015, posits "[c]apitalism being the quintessence of reason, in one way, and of unreason, in another," and speaks, later, of "the victims of unreason…"

Until the buildings are all filled with white people who have money to spend at cafés and wine bars, and for a little while thereafter, there is, on every block, a black man dressed for all seasons in a camel hair coat, hat with ear flaps, and tattered leather gloves who paces the street speaking to no one In particular in a language no one the neighborhood understands; not Arabic, Spanish, Nahuatl, or English. This man may or may not have a small white dog he pushes in a stroller, he may or may not pull a toddler out of the path of an oncoming car; the ambulance may or may not call at his door repeatedly, the health department may or may

not issue repeated summons. Until they are gone, the people of the block will feed him from the block party proceeds, and the bodega will make of him an honored guest; he may or may not carry a boombox or plastic bag he uses to pick up detritus of the night's garbage wind and under snow melt remainings. Until he is displaced, he may or may not have a house or apartment, space which is only entered by him, his shopping cart and himself alone, and when he approaches his own threshold his shouts and cries turn to low and coarse offerings at keyholes, punic columns of books in a foyer of grime, until they are gone.

SANS HUMANITE

eat de bread de devil knead
long rope for magga goat

yalls problem is
everyone who coulda been broken
done broke

one day one day congotay
crapaud smoke yuh pipe

just say it: that language makes you cry. who else remembers sitting at
her feet, playing with lint, as the old creole women talked old talk?

some so proud of their new white talk. there is no pride in erasure.

no shame in the many tongued life.

fa never could speak anything but black, even in writing.
ni tries, but it leaks through in the verbs. looks experimental.

ka says, you sound like a white girl. i hate to hear it.
i want you to sound like home.
i think but don't say,

my home is as foreign to you as white speak is to both of us.
as you are to me.

kri says, our baptist tradition, we grew up in, our queerness…
i think but don't say,

the only baptist is know is chango.

it takes a while to learn and unlearn. i get the feeling i should stay quiet.
it's hard to pick apart a weaponized truth:

                         we are different.   Truth
                         We are different, therefore
                         more deserving, worthy,
                         civilized: weapon.

empire, empire, hungry thing.

new in this world, i listen. ask: put her foot in it? is that good, or bad?
native speakers laugh, assume my life is filled with Europeans.

i'm not mad at my misperceived self—invisible everywhere, why not here? the enthusiastic
embrace of inclusion: we are all alike, you are one of us, we are just alike
it happens with such love.

i say, we are all different, i am one of you.
i am one of you

Adjua Gargi Nzinga Greaves

WE LIVE ON EARTH WHERE SEX IS FUEL, 2012

We live on Earth where sex is fuel, and I have longed to spend my time here in the body of a wild creature. Longed for every part of this figure to declare my soul's connection to our corner of the cosmos. Longed for my spirit to inhabit the same exquisitely, extravagantly, minimalist constructions I adored in elk and tiger, root and petal, flame and ocean, neuron and bone. Longed to look synonymous with sex, with art, with life and with creation.

For years, I thought running, and water, and vegetables would help a clear, wise body emerge from the distracted, unsure form I'd found myself in. Thought a dream romance might find me arm in arm with another, perfect spirit all tangled up in the wrong machine. Envisioned shared joy as we saw past our fumbling, mumbling material selves straight through to our elegant, infinite, blazing entities within. Believed that, from this lovingunderstanding, we'd find the spark to fine-tune our rough drafts. And, as the years slid quickly past, I remained calm assuring myself I would, at any moment, begin the work of shifting toward a body more worthy of this gorgeous planet.

But, that's not the way it happened at all. No—it didn't happen like that.

It couldn't?

Instead, I fell in love with nature. And it showed me I was art. I fell in love with nature and collapsed, exhausted, in its arms—dreamt of recent, human orgasms, and ancient, cosmic eruptions; I dreamt of wine and fire, dreamt of forests and swarms, of bee wings and spider webs. I dreamt fast and slow at once and then awoke in the same body— now gorgeous, nude, adored—on display for lovers of art and students of beauty.

I'd cast a pagan spell upon myself—trusting this home above all else, I dressed in blue and green and gold, expected beauty, relied on magic—and emerged an artists' model.

My same body—once messy, once apologetic, once ignored—was now luscious, and grand, and central. The current truth of me as beautiful as any ocean wave, and my aspirations now irrelevant, I performed Goddess and found I had become one. Posing on a modest platform before a focused throng of artists, what I once thought I'd find in romance— acceptance as is, and beauty forthwith—I found, instead, in the eyes and at the hands of these creative strangers.

Standing, sitting, reclining, existing unclothed before them, art overpowers sex, and nakedness becomes nudity. Nudity—honest, natural, glorious. Finally free from inventions of shame. Finally telling truth with every breath. Finally connected to the tortoise and the egret, to the whale and to the dog.

Our form, unfettered. Life, unfettered.

The natural world exists as it does because of all the reproduction it makes possible. This ocean of creative sex is made possible by beauty, and beauty is made possible by it. Beauty evolved out of our explosive cosmic birth as a touchstone for reproductive endeavors. I'm not sure how, or if, other animals experience joy at nature's beauty the way we do, but we swoon at its announcement of health. We delight in its promise of successful procreation. When we love real beauty, we are rooting for life; we are urging it onward. Consider that this sweet hopefulness is the root of all these electric attractions. There are so many ways we try to distance ourselves from The Animals, but the erotic fact of the natural world is always here with us. It got us all here; it shapes our present, and it is fueling our future.

In *The Artist's Way*—a workbook for healing the injured souls of would-be artists—Julia Cameron encourages us to notice our electric connection to the universe when we are able to create freely. Creativity in art is so beautifully parallel to creation in this universe. These days, walking the Earth guided by a constant, cosmic perspective, I feel small and big at once. I feel the ways I am very nearly nothing to the cosmos just as I am feeling no separation between myself and it. So thinking—drunk on stardust—I picture our corner of the void and see Earth set aflame, a ball of roiling, erotic activity.

Preening, wet, and special.
Falling in love with nature means falling in love with sex.
Means falling in love with the ubiquity of creation.
And admitting your comfort at the orgy.
We live on Earth where sex is art. Where art will win, and beauty's fuel.
Now I feel an endless, sultry saunter in my every breath.
And I run because I am wild.
And I know that water is a magic potion.
And I eat plants because they eat sunshine.

Now I am gorgeous
because I know where I live.

FLORXA GENS, 2016

Breaking quiet beside my own new fragments,
I heard him

—Francophonemes assembling into
English—

saying:

/

THE STRUCTURE OF A TREE IS THE RESULT
OF THIS PLANT'S RESEARCH FOR THE SUN

/

Tonight I drew in your colors,
began to move my hand as I had many times before,
though found the spell staled and merely artifact

and from that dissatisfaction bloomed
a directive to search

as flora

chanting *WILDERNESS* and *PROLIFERANCE*

as Florxa

and from the delta of that courage sprouted
sure green rivers, nerves and branchings.

And as I tried to find a useful declaration
to make about doubt's absence in the wilderness,
I failed my way into this searching wisdom.

BLACK BOTANY, 2016

Black Botany   winters in the gardens of White Supremacy

                                                 nightmare parkgrounds
                                                 occupied as gymnasium

                   vigilances attuned for the   rootings
                                            cuttings
                                            proliferations

                                           of James Marion Sims

                 lies dormant in our seven billion bodies
                 emerges in the spring of radical critique.

Receptor nodes transform energies of   empathy
                                          consent

                                        interbeing

                                        into   slow
                                          silent
                                          exuberances of mutual growth
                                                         intellect
                                                         artifacted

Science void of Other

UNSCHOOLMFA MISSION STATEMENT, 2015

We tease the inevitable, softening an obstinacy that doesn't know any better yet.
The mission is to formalize transgression.
I am bothering you on purpose.
I have formalized a generative annoyance.
When you correct me, I ask you what you are fighting to defend.
I ask you how the defended is serving you.
The mission is to rewild the mind.
The mission is to kill the death reflex.
The mission is to love the mind as is, as will, as was.
The mission is to create a first draft of thing so that others may have
       something useful to revise.
The mission is to be in the body and to know it is also the mind.
The mission is to ever be the lushblack wilderness even when the
       glamourous academy is near.
The mission is to perform the draft and charge admission.
The mission is to love.
The mission is to terrify the weak so that they might feel emboldened

                        to reveal their considerable strengths.

The mission is to maintain a proximal intimacy.
The mission is to foster collaborative autonomy.
The mission is to be as healthy as your transparency.
The mission is to embarrass doubt.
The mission is to blackademic.

                              The mission is to blacken up.

The mission is to ensure the crit, welcome the crit, embrace the crit,
       evolve by the crit.
The mission is to find the safety to be wrong.
The mission is to find safe places to be wrong.
The mission is to find comfort in correction.

The mission is to compose, delete and revise until we are full immortal.

UNTITLED FACEBOOK POST, 2016

just casually murdering each other like we ain't out here alone together in the void

like this aquatic spaceship isn't festooned with the most exquisite flora

like this house we share ain't a living chandelier in an unconcerned graveyard

like we ain't cosmically identical

like existing doesn't matter

FLORXOBIOGRAPHY, 2016

I.   **Shaquille** is a shamrock. Fluffy, cramped, yellowing for a reason I do not yet know. Purchased Saint Patrick's Day eve from a clerk who teased me about the cost of its leafmade fortune. I am worried about Shaquille. (It is a worry that lately haunts my intimacies.) I worry that I love him the wrong way—that I am an ignorant and childish caretaker. That I have named him with a joke whose history wounds him where he can know it—that he can feel my lack like sunlight.

II.   Leaving town for California—where he would teach, and wed, and make new lives—he made me caretaker of a cactus. Ghosthold of his brother. I wonder if either of us suspected the failure to come, if either of us had an early sense of my depletion.

III.   Named in an instant, days after her arrival in my new home. Named for her grandeur—elegant monstrosity. Her obvious queendom. The name somehow containing a popular appellation for Sea Witch. Her name, instant, correct, unchanging still. Magnificent. Powerful in body and temporality in a way that insisted her sheddings be preserved. She—**Octavia**. She—poinsettia. She is the largest. May she continue to insist upon her being. May she instruct me in the taking and the making of space for lifetimes yet. Green leaves emerging now—sheep's clothing for the wolfing red to come.

IV.   I set the English Ivy plant high up in our livingroom, gave its drapings room to be, and named it **Booker T**. Because this is hilarious. Because it is corrective. Because my rage takes many forms.

V.   The Bulbosa Guatemala air plant lived nameless in my home for many weeks before I knew its name was **Toni**.

VI.   We stood indoors nearby the croton and my human lover complained about its deficits. It was failing in his care. It was failing in his home. It was failing at his hand. My human lover did not know what it needed. My human lover was able to care well for many plants—an attractive quality. My human lover was not able to care for this plant. My human lover needed the croton's care to be discernable. And my human lover did no research yet framed his failure as the croton's. I scolded the human. I told him this flora would not abide such petulance. I told him he was the problem—that no beauty would reward this so-called care. We humans laughed in the truth and ease of this corrective moment. I brought the plant to my house and named it **Glissant**. I asked the Rastafarian selling crotons by my human lover's subway stop how to care for this being, he told me, and I made sure I understood.

Glissant thrived in my home while I did. And when, in autumn, I began to fail myself anew, so too did Glissant suffer. A fungus flourished within us both. I survived the proliferance, but in my convalescence let deep neglects befall this croton.

VII.   Camilo named the gleaming, triumphant Nematanthus plant **Toussaint**. Andi named the glamorous dieffenbachia *Ashanti*. I am beginning to ask my new home to hold me, and it is able.

VIII.   The Rasta asked me when I thought the real New Year began. My body knew the answer—springtime—said so and pleased us both.

IX.   **Monae** is a money plant because that is hilarious.

X.   Instagram reminds me that in these same weeks last year, alongside Monae, I named a large fern *Tyrone*, a light pink fittonia **Daphne**, a congruent pair of sages **bell** and **Nina**, and a gorgeous something or other **Sadie**. The black florist who sold them to me that afternoon feared the grasping of my fast unfurling desire for these beings and gently tried to discourage this unmoored loving. Indeed, by summer, only Monae and Tyrone had survived that afternoon's infatuation.

XI.   Killing houseplants is so embarrassing. It is an instructive humiliation. In the chaos of my recent youth I twice murdered a farm of seedlings with the poison of neglect. For self. For ward. For life. The grief and shame I felt at failing all that flora brought them clear to life for me.

XII.   In the early 1980s, at the end of my family's pre-war apartment hallway, my mother installed an elegant bouquet of dying eucalyptus that taught me without words how important structure, how crucial intent, how subtle death, how knowing she.

XIII.   When they separated, my Mom and I moved to an apartment near DUMBO where I learned the name *variegated philodendron* (my first favorite) and where a fern grew on the bathroom window ledge, dropping its dead leaves into the shower and bathtub—a gesture of wilderness I reviled and came to learn my mother didn't— where I began to understand in dim flickers who she was.

XIV.   Some years later in the next home, my mother wondered aloud where the massive tree trunk displayed at Bowling Green had gone. I casually offered my assumption that it had gone to a sculptor for carving, and she gasped in horror. I was frightened to see how inadvertently I'd hurt her, and I was delighted to encounter the details of her tree love. Two decades later, it is my favorite moment of getting to know her.

XV.   **Chiwetel** is the London Plane tree branch thriving hydroponic, in my bedroom, at the window, and named for the English actor from Forest Gate London. Because that is hilarious.

XVI.   I sleep on 100% cotton bedsheets printed in pinks and browns and purple with exuberantly illustrated impressions of unknown flowers, flat and fitted discovered among my aunt and grandmother's belongings. Flat beneath me nightly. Fitted now the dress I made and slipped into last summer before flinging myself bikeward toward the ocean, toward the edge, toward Fort Tilden, landing instead at Riis— the beach of my mother's childhood. Riis beach where a small black butterfly would swoop up under my new dress and bustle about at the button of my sex as I stood beside my bicycle stunned and honored and newly named Florxa before wading alone into hypnotic waves so frightening and so lush with power I felt my real life beginning.

XVII.   Newly homeless and running a fever of 104.5° I lay on the futon in my lover's guestroom wailing beside him, so frightened, so abject, and so tenderly cared for that I remembered I'd left Monae, Glissant, and Tyrone alone together in the dark of my new storage unit and understood with a ghastly wrenching how alive these things I delighted in, how terrifying love, how real life, and how tenuous. The seedling of a New self had begun breaking through the earth of Old—toward my heartbreaking mother, toward my baffling father, toward the overwhelming and essential sunlight of love.

XVIII.   I am Googling *magenta* and then *fuchsia* because linguistic precision is responsible and erotic when I learn that fuchsia is not only the name of a color, but also the name of the flowering plant I saw last year in a West Village hardware store on the way to or from psychoanalysis and yesterday in Prospect Heights. Now I know that Fuchsia is the name of the flowering plant with petals so elaborately whimsical, regarding them feels like being on some sort of mushroom-mescaline. This insane floral genital too alarming to even wonder yet what it is called—for its being is too tremendous to digest at first—this floral genital is named a sound I've know since the age of Crayola and Mr. Sketch, but as a color this sound is the name of a purple. And then some dismay about why I ever thought fuchsia was something like magenta. And then the realization that the confusion is because this maniac flower's petaling comprises both colors. And then thoughts of veronica, a sound well-known as name to give 20th century women. A sound lesser known as the name of that spindly micropetal-festooned tuberous flower. Google Image made me regard well over 200 women before it would show me a floral veronica. And then the day I wore rose oil perfume to a session and the analyst insisted my mother Roselle was in the room despite my objections. Then dizzily off elsewhere smiling at the magic of naming and looking and memory and this heaven of a planet.

XIX. Florxa Gens is a witch so radiant you do not realize she is one until you begin to feel gardens sprouting in your soul.

XX. We barely knew one another then, but when the vegetable farmer learned that I also love plants, I recall he regarded me anew and with a voice of the familiar said "That makes sense," filling my heart with the sweetness of strange secret praise and the early twinkles of something old and warm and important.

XXI. The unnamed white man's footprint is dead, so too some unlucky bamboo. Chiwetel's long gone, and Shaquille is close to the brink. Care is not a game.

XXII. In the shower I scrub Thursday, Friday, and Saturday from my flesh, recalling that punctuality protects the Queen's peace, while creosote from Camilo's desert home fills the air.

XXIII. I love the person beside me and am loathe to say it plain buoyed as we are again tonight alongside one another in these fogs of floral ash and oil.

XXIV. A late-summer depression killed Octavia & Daphne Deuxieme. Shaquille died weeks ago. Today I came home from the flowershop with marigolds skewered on bamboo—casual goblin.

XXV. A gorgeous branch fell off its tree in yesterday's rain and made itself known to me as I walked through the streets with Solange on repeat thinking endlessly of you and of floral offerings. I've brought it home to root and named it Solange <u>Carolyn Bush</u>. I am so angry over how you were taken from this world, so sick when I think how terrified you must have been, and so thankful to know how cool and smart and tender and funny and honest and weird and fierce and loving and elegant and kind you were while you were here with us. May freedom and garlic and honey and Lambrusco forever bring you to my mind. May I remain as soft and free as I please on this nightmare planet. May its infinite beauties ever endeavor to outpace its proliferating horrors. We love you so.

XXVI. Though I named you clumsily in grief, you called out to me a chicer and thus, more fitting name. Coco Solange, and then as your memorial branch showed death upon it you called out again—*Now plant my seeds.*

Duriel E. Harris

"HE WHO FIG   S WITH   S"

How many does it take to metamorphose wi   *e man must*
not kill. If he does, it is murder. Two, ten, one   *own*
responsibility, must not kill. If they do, it is st   *n may kill as*
many as they please, and it is not murder. It i   *and right.*

—Adin Ballou (1803-1890)

Wer mit Ungeheuern kämpft, mag zusehn, dass er nicht dabei zum Ungeheuer wird. Und wenn du lange in einen Abgrund blickst, blickt der Abgrund auch in dich hinein.

—Friedrich Wilhelm Nietzsche (1844-1900)
Jenseits von Gut und Böse, "Sprüche und Zwischenspiele," 146 (1886)

"How many acts of genocide does it take to make genocide?"

How many birds to call it a flock?

How many drops to make a sip swell into a spill?

How many does it take for a quorum?

How many does it take to trend?

How many does it take to be in a race?

How many to seek and destroy?

How many lanterns, ribbons, needles, balls, and bouncing bouncing betties?

How many does it take to fix it?

How many does it take to swing?

Just how many licks does it take to get through the meat to the red and yellow marrow?

How many does it take to decide?

How much ammo, how many tanks, how many bombs, pits, and traps, how many
swinging spiked logs?

How much debris?

How many fences and patrols? How many stockpiles?

How many does it take to constitute a deluge?

How many for a good hunt? To haul the load? To pave the drive?

How many does it take to persist?

How many stones for a good throw? How much shot? How many dry cords? How much
   seed?

How many charts does it take to fill the set? How many monitors for the mix? How much
   gear?

How many cast-iron pots? How many non-porous pouches? How many spades and
   shovels? How much tubing?

How many seconds to raise the plow? To go blank? To go under? To spontaneously
   combust?

How many masses does it take to make a city? How many pipes and drains?

How many of any to make a horde?

How many to create a virus? To pass the pandemic two by four?

To hack the lot? To hack up a lung? To hack the hackneyed phrase?

How many does it take to pluck a turkey clean?

You do the work: what materials, what tools are required?

How many does it take to put the facts straight?

How many does it take to invade?

How many to make a conspiracy?

How many to settle the score? To furnish the proper argument?

Proceeding by stealth, how many does it take to slip off the yoke?

How long and how many to get the greasy thing back in the bag?

If we start counting now, how many episodes?

How many features? How many angry disruptions? How many chokeholds? How much
   tape reel to reel?

How many sackcloth dummies? How many planks and nails? How much thread and
   glass? How many wicks? How much gasoline?

Given the necessary conditions, how many behaviors? How many reactive responses to
   minor stimuli? How many frantic efforts? How many impulsive outbursts? How
   much dysphoria? How intense?

How much water? How much voltage? How many plastic liners?

How many does it take to manipulate the order and the nonautonomy of its field of
   action?

How many porters? How many pickets? How many wood dowels and ditches?

How many does it take?

How many, in the face of negative but transient public opinion?

How many sheets? How many muumuus? How many scouts? How many badges?

How many surveillance cameras? How many transcripts, interviews, and surveys? How many
   laws of the land? How many well-laid mine fields?

How many false statements? False starts? False prophets? False teeth?

How many articles? How many volunteers? How many exercises? How many
   disclaimers?

How many people? How many times? Would you remember them all?

How many have you tried?

(A cedar box for you; one, two, three body rakes for me.)

How many does it take? When will they tell us? What is the sampling error?

How many and how much does it cost?

How many to form a committee? To make it stick?

How many limbs to earn the medal?

How much restless fury? How much saliva? How much froth?

How many does it take if they're kicking in flimsy doors and rushing the cockpit?

How many if they hang like bats from trees?

How many twisted triangular signs?

How many smudged tactical maps?

How many unexplained casualties? How many aggregates? How many comprehensive
   national accounts? How many derivations? How much fiscal and monetary
   policy? How much uncertainty to crowd them out? How much inflation? Who
   and how many will it take to gate and guard the growth? How many reindeer?
   How many rejoinders? How many relapses? How many rejection slips? How
   many rounds? How high the fever? How much relational grammar? How many to

get the maximum benefit? To flourish in the context of capital? In direct relation
to what is missing? How many by force and with intention?

I have 53 honorable kills, how many does it take?

The reason that something is an example, a fold (how many does it take to define a
problem? (a predicate)), an economy of virtual knowns, interrupts.

We've been suggesting for almost a month now—how many does it take? Also, we've run
out of steam. (How many does it take? They may not even be people.)

What the fuck's in them and how many does it take to kill you?

How many undersigned and you know who's? How many taxpayers? How many
conventions? How many leagues of concerned citizens? How many symbols?
How many sights?

How many warnings? How many wrenches? Beware! Beware! Beware! Beware!

How many from behind and beneath? How many pulling rope, stretching hemp? How
many flags? How many knights?

How many sepulchers and bloody moons? How many stakeholders?

How many bound together?

How many mounting the air?

How much matter by volume, to scale?

The question is not how many links in the chain, the question is how many can be made
available and how quickly dispersed?

In a population of x, how many does it take before everyone has been infected?

How many repeated read-alouds?

How many does it take for Christ to be in the midst?

How many does it take to wrestle him, sit on him, pin him to the ground? How many
does it take to hold him down?

How many until none becomes some?

How many does it take to form a STATISTICALLY SIGNIFICANT pattern?

Get another arm, another ear, "How many does it take til it's enough?" "How much do you need?"

How many does it take to make the road impassable when the rain brings the brew to the surface?

"Let us see the bodies," they say.

Note:

Translation of epigraph by Nietzsche:

He who fights with monsters should be careful lest he thereby become a monster. And when you gaze long into an abyss, the abyss also gazes into you.

Beyond Good and Evil, "Aphorisms and Interludes," 146 (1886).

Duriel E. Harris

from SIMULACRA

2

ANIMATO.

VOCAL.

Ma - ry had a lit - tle lamb, with fleece as black as su - llied snow.

And every-where that Ma - ry went, she paraded her lamb for show.

She showed it in the yard one day which was a - gainst the rule.

She let the chil - dren ti - ckle, tease, and tap her lamb at school.

And so the tea - cher turned it out, but still it ti - red not:

it bleated, shook, and shim - mied 'til all his les - sons he for - got.

16 lines.   **Simulacra: Black Mary Integrates the School House**   *Duriel E. Harris*

3

I am a pretty little WIC check
As little as little can be,
And colored girls from every hood
Are crazy over me.

My bestie's name is Queen
She comes from my imaginings
With a tail, twelve toes,
And a plate through her nose,
And that's the way the story goes!

One month she tried to buy peaches.
The next month she tried to buy pears.
The next month she tried to buy leafy greens
With the change she had to spare.

I am a pretty little WIC check
As little as little can be,
And silly girls from every hood
Are crazy over me.

2

22 lines.   **Simulacra: American Counting Rhyme**   *Duriel E. Harris*

3

22 lines.   **Simulacra: American Counting Rhyme**   *Duriel E. Harris*

4

27 lines. **Simulacra: American Counting Rhyme**   *Duriel E. Harris*

5

ANIMATO.

Six little ~~angels~~ *afro puffs* buying snacks at 7-Eleven, One showed up with donut holes, then there were seven.

Seven little ~~angels~~ *afro puffs* doing tricks on in-line skates, One spun into a back flip, then there were eight;

Eight little ~~angels~~ *afro puffs* in the arcade ticket line, One had golden vouchers, then there were nine.

Nine little ~~angels~~ *afro puffs* sitting up straight like gentlemen, "Is there room for me?" one cried, then there were ten!

Ten little ~~angels~~ *afro puffs* building fortresses in the snow, Then heading in to warm their toes and sneak some cookie dough.

Ten little ~~angels~~ *afro puffs* blowing bubbles in the breeze, Naming caterpillars, lady bugs, and bumble bees.

27 lines.   **Simulacra: American Counting Rhyme**   *Duriel E. Harris*

6

27 lines.   **Simulacra: American Counting Rhyme**   *Duriel E. Harris*

Duriel E. Harris

SELF PORTRAIT WITH BLACK BOX AND OPEN ARCHITECTURE

[T]he names by which I am called in the public place render an example of signifying property plus. In order for me to speak a truer word concerning myself, I must strip down through layers of attenuated meanings, made an excess in time, over time, assigned by a particular historical order, and there await whatever marvels of my own inventiveness.

—Hortense J. Spillers
"Mama's Baby, Papa's Maybe: An American Grammar Book"

:
Somewhere a door falls from its hinges
And another refuses to lock.
A lid flutters then noiselessly snaps shut.

:
I awaken into memory chased with whiskey and wine
Where my intimate sleeps unarmed, impervious to pain,
Skull tattooed with an intricate grid, studded
With jewel-lit ring-shank nails, belly inflamed
With rot, spoiled air, and cut grass
From the patterned hills they roam. They haunt
With a muffled drum. Flesh and drunken blood
Act in concert, deliberate and heavy if not certain,
Hands vague and coarse to batter or caress, the fingers
Leaking.

"Feeling devolves to appetite. Its brute current as certain
As nature healed. Where ritual amplifications are precise,
To have a mouth, a fist, a fist which will not be denied to make way for another
Selective) and just and self-possessed. Its intentions

"Somewhere a fist. Androgyne child scratching at sleep.
Teeth as long as a man's palm, and precise.

:

Feeling devolves to appetite. Its brass current as certain
As a train's bladed wheels and amputations are precise.
To have a mouth, a gut, to have skin, to want.
My body will not be denied to make space for another.
It is social and just and self-possessed. Its inattentions
Selective.

:

Somewhere a fist. Androgyne child scratching at sleep.
Teeth as long as a man's palm, and porous.

I find myself meandering, wearing the frayed lining,
Of another's coat hidden beneath my undergarments.
My desire, a note tied to a rock and thrown against fear
Like fear hardens against feeling, a boarded window
Barring a summer storm

Duriel E. Harris

:
I find myself meandering, wearing the frayed lining
Of another's coat hidden beneath my undergarments.
My desire, a note tied to a rock and thrown against fear
Like fear hardens against feeling, a boarded window
Barring a summer storm

I awaken into memory chased with whiskey and wine
Where my intimate sleeps, unsung, stupefied to pain,
Still jeweled with an intricate string of glass beads.
With her velvet cloth and curved golden thimble,
With her spoiled embroidery, my mother hymns.
From the patterned hills they roam. They haunt.
With a muffled drum, flesh and drunken blood
Act in concert, deliberate and heavy if not certain,
Hands vague and coarse to batter or caress, the fingers
Leaking.

:
I dream my jaw is missing and in its place a bolt
Of red cloth weighted to the loom, silk skeins
And trembling tucked deep into my pockets
As I dive into clear water.

:

There is always a sea.
Alongside the road, surrounding the field,
Behind the shuttered houses, enfolding a strange city.
And before the city and under and within it
The bodies of a girl and boy repeat themselves, enrapt.
Held in the moment before drowning they float in the sea,
Suspended between depressions in the water,
Arched into form.

"Feeling devolves to appetite. Its brass current as certain
As a train's bladed wheels and amputations are precise.
To live is wanting. Its desire to make space for another.
My body will turn. Be denied to make space for another.
It's social and fast and self-possessed. Its inattentions
Selective.

"Somewhere a flat. Androgyne child scratching at sleep.
Teeth as long as a man's palm, and porous.

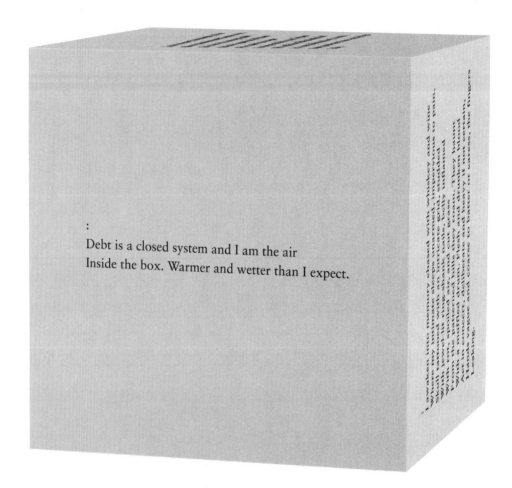

:
Debt is a closed system and I am the air
Inside the box. Warmer and wetter than I expect.

I awaken into memory chased with whiskey and wine
Where my intimate sleeps unarmed, impervious to pain.
Swill around with an intricate faith studded
With the polished air until our gazes
worn the patterned hills they roam. They haunt
their concert delicate and up, around, left, wound
Hands weave and coarse to batter it caress the fingers
Leaking.

Duriel E. Harris

DECOROUS

Duriel E. Harris

How easily you disavow
Even the bald stupefaction you substitute for shame
Projecting aliveness split off from the crowd
Imagining mannequins' flat and ready eyes
And crumbling wax
Sluggish and sour
Anger unnamed turns inward
The buttocks' baggy denim display
Slapped to stinging boldness
Until the whole body brightens
To break against the vocal folds

    The black box boasts: A single chair
                               A braided wire
                               A leather paddle and crop
                               A dark hood, slipping
                               A stain

                               The body that remains

Who clings, disquieted, to despair
Hovers outside of passage, softly singing
Death is in the cane, pilot me

Spiraling between shadows
Riding rags' frayed edges to arrive
In noiseless shattering
To greet the chatty breeze

And strike with force

Something slips beneath the stain
Something swings the swollen fist
Something spills inside the battered turning
And soaks into the frame

The body that remains shares the confession

The story has not one ending
Smudged into a solitary future
Nor one formal statement or admission
In principle
It is a seed

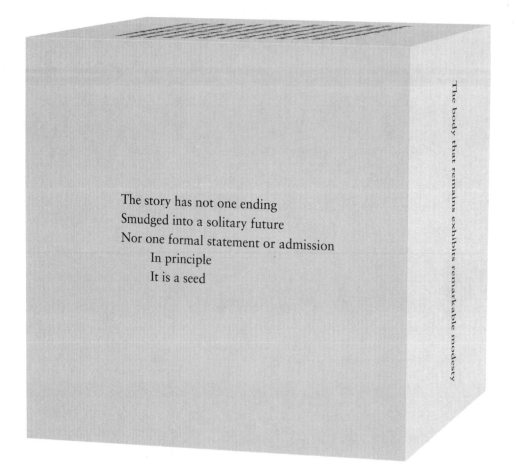

The story has not one ending
Smudged into a solitary future
Nor one formal statement or admission
In principle
It is a seed

The body that remains exhibits remarkable modesty

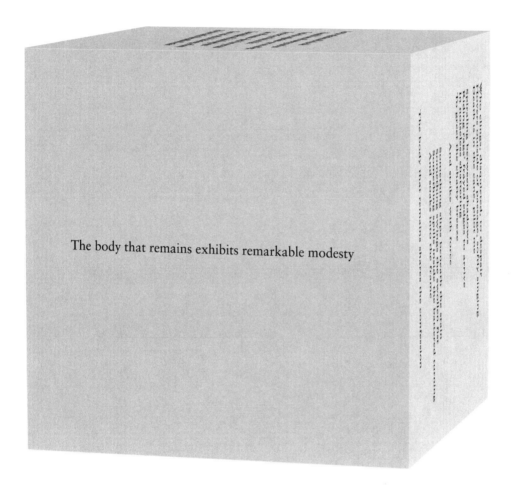

The body that remains exhibits remarkable modesty

It is not fitting. The sunflower-yellow room is warm in the afternoon. The twin beds, covered with plush teddy bears and zoo animals, flank the walls, each in reach of the picture window. A pillow sham, with blue and yellow watercolor butterflies alit above daffodils, drapes the yellow wicker hamper. The younger child wears ribbons. Her small bottom does not slide into the yellow plastic rectangular garbage receptacle as expected. The older child pauses to recalculate. The younger child's mother arrives with snacks. No one cries. Sound and heat and color drain from the room. The older child stands before the mirror and watches the dust float in the air.

Now the explanations will be bearable
  A beautiful hour will come up around you
  To take the complications—your arms and legs,
  Your heart, your blood and cilia,
  Your cell structure—directly from your mind
  Your shoulders will slush through space
  Your vocal cords, the final strings, will snap
Only these familiar blue smells will remain

The body that remains exhibits remarkable modesty

Afterword 2

THE HISTORICAL AS HYSTERICAL: MOVING BEYOND THE SINGULAR

The speaking subject as a predicament complicated by the means of speaking is a proactive stance against the modes of repression that exist in order to reign the Black body in and to gender it actively within regimes of regulation. When we speak as Black people, as women, as gendered subjects of any kind, what kind of re-scripting occurs and what does this re-scripting do to raced, gendered utterance? When **Lillian Yvonne Bertram** positions a self, "Lillian" as the center of the work, a third person speaker—Lillian from a distance—a call is made toward a recognition of the impossibility, perhaps, of the kind of selfhood with which we are most familiar. When the work speaks, it says, "The poems move from being inside Lillian's own body and looking out, to being outside Lillian's own body and seeing herself as seen by others." Necessarily, the relation to the body that speaks is a future space of anticipation, a movement away from the embodied subject, untroubled, and toward a being of the multiple, as if to indicate that selfhood itself, especially for some of us, takes the shape of a conversation imagined in the moment immediately following the present.

To acknowledge overtly that to be in relation to one's so-called "self" is to render the self uncontainable. What language(s) render this self/selves? Them? Us? Me? How to reconcile the disposed past, the annihilated peoples, cultures, lands, communities, traditions with what occurs in the wake of such attempts? If, indeed, it is impossible to regather, to replace place, and selfhood is known, in part, through language, then is the manifestation of cultural loss trapped in the body like a buried site? What **Latasha N. Nevada Diggs** does is not excavation, exactly. Instead, her use of Sranan Tongo, the Diné language, varied registers of speech from the colloquial to the scholarly, and the official, in her poems, offer a casting of the self analogous to Bertram's—a come-up new possible self, manifested by the world of the polyvocal. But excitingly, a particularly gendered shape of the mouth appears when Diggs engages the colloquial or "local" speech, as in: "they request that you sit on a Heineken beer bottle Dutch owned brewery Dutch slave ship insurance someone collected off your ancestor's pussy for a dollar."

This question of which language, or more precisely in Diggs' case, *what utterance makes*, is one that persistence calls across these texts. In the instances of Diggs' local speech, a critique whose very means of utterance exists somewhere slightly beyond the episteme managed by the regimes of power, gains its own power of indecipherability. Those who seek to impose its ways of knowing onto us are pushed into a past, a static nostalgia.

r. erica doyle's "from The Body as History" positions itself in conversation with Franz Fanon as it struggles up against the language of the nation state: "I've broken my teeth/ against this language of yours." And, then, "My tongue / bleeds / nouns / at night / in a / fricative wind." The tail end of second wave feminist scholarship took up this idea that the body is a kind of text, written on, and into being, by the historical incidents that constructed it. That doyle positions her poems in conversation with Fanon's contention, "The density of History determines none of my acts. I am my own foundation," begs us to ask how we are to read this fraught juxtaposition of feminist claims and Fanon's leap toward a disconnection from history's yoke? The "fricative wind" gives us one hint of doyle's text's sensibility as it moves us away from the metaphorical and into the actual training of the body via language.

This training, in the use of the word, "fricative," happens in the mouth, but from which force? I take wind to mean discourse. I take discourse to presume an invisible working of language on the body. This work struggles in the displacement of the body—someplace between reason and as doyle says, "unreason"—a kind of persistent labor in the desire for some way of speaking that does not have to negotiate the worlds of "either," "or," "before," or "after."

Future speak in **Adjua Greaves'** work, on the other hand, is unlabored. Perhaps it is truly free. The performance in Greaves' articulations is one of taking up space, stretching the legs, as if taking a long, wild walk. "Our form, unfettered," she writes, "life unfettered." The optimistic future that Greaves builds is a post-post-modern simultaneity in which nature is at the center, if a center can be named. Greaves is a self-described "post-colonial ethnobotanist," a designation that transgresses the boundary between plant and person, self and other, a remaking of the very landscape upon which life is considered, inhabited, performed. "I fell in love with nature," writes Greaves, "And it showed me I was art. I fell in love with nature and collapsed exhausted, in its arms—dreamt of recent, human organisms, and ancient, cosmic eruptions." Sprawling in beautifully exhausting, comma-laden, sentences, Greaves projects us into a state of unknowing who or what we are.

There is something profoundly spiritual about Greaves' work without spiritually being cluttered by some colonialist past and without the ghosts of those pasts polluting the present. No limp at all in this work. No hovering in pre-conditions. To attempt to write *outside of* is also how **Duriel E. Harris** reckons with the weightedness of the Black body in social and political space. Her work operates in an interstice forged by the absurd, the brutal, and unseeable regimes of repression. With what armor, Harris's poetic asks, do we address the unaddressable? The irrational song requires an irrational body. The irrational body is produced in any fit of illogical un-repair—genocide, for example.

"He who fights with monsters" raises the question of quantification when it comes to these illogics. They are, of course, unquantifiable. Yet, the desperate languages of rationality would try to trick us into the counter belief. This is the terrain of Harris's deeply problematized lyric investigation in the poem. "How many," she asks over and over, what is the number, how can we count what is unaccounted for, uncountable? Language of the rational would have us stuck in the old language of the singular, but she pulls us—no, she yanks us—into the complicated nature of the monster that nips forever at worrying feet, our hands, our very being(s).

Dawn Lundy Martin

SECTION THREE

Harryette Mullen

Can't wait to be sprung from shadow,
to be known from a hole in the ground.
Scarcely silent though often unheard.
Winding, wound. Wounded wind.
She turned, and turns. She opens.
Keep the keys, that devil told her.
Guess the question. Dream the answer.
Tore down almost level.
A silence hardly likely.
Juicy voices. Pour them on.
Music sways her, she concedes,
as darker she goes deeper.

ONCE EVER AFTER

There was this princess who wet the bed through many mattresses, she was so attuned. She neither conversed with magical beasts nor watched her mother turn into a stairwell or a stoop. Her lips were. Her hair was. Her complexion was. Her beauty or her just appearance. What she wore. She was born on a chessboard, with parents and siblings, all royal. Was there a witch? Was she enchanted, or drugged? When did she decide to sleep? Dreaming a knight in armor, she thought it meant jousting. His kind attack with streamers. A frog would croak. A heart would cough after only one bite. Something was red. There was wet and there was weather. She couldn't make it gold without his name. Her night shifts in the textile mill. She forgot she was a changeling peasant girl. Spinning, she got pricked. That's where roses fell and all but one fairy wept. It remains that she be buried alive, knowing that a kiss is smaller than a delayed hunger.

PRESENT TENSE

Now that my ears are connected to a random answer machine, the wrong brain keeps talking through my hat. Now that I've been licked all over by the English tongue, my common law spout is suing for divorce. Now that the Vatican has confessed and the White House has issued an apology, I can forgive everything and forget nothing. Now the overdrawn credits roll as the bankrupt star drives a patchwork cab to the finished line, where a broke robot waves a mended tablecloth, which is the stale flag of a checkmate career. Now as the Voice of America crackles and fades, the market reports that today the Euro hit a new low. Now as the reel unravels , our story unwinds with the curious dynamic of an action flick without a white protagonist.

SUZUKI METHOD

El Niño brought a typhoon of tom-toms from Tokyo, where a thrilling instrument makes an OK toy. Tiny violins are shrill. Their shrieks are musical mice. The color of a mechanical clock is lost in translation. Whatever you're telling me sounds like the straight teeth of rodents. My dreams throw the book at the varmint. We both shudder as the dictionary thuds. You've got to admit, our Esperanto's hopeless. Your virgin is unfaithful. My savory hero boards the ship of Marco Polo, loaded with soy from Ohio.

Harryette Mullen

WE ARE NOT RESPONSIBLE

We are not responsible for your lost or stolen relatives. We cannot guarantee your safety if you disobey our instructions. We do not endorse the causes or claims of people begging for handouts. We reserve the right to refuse service to anyone. Your ticket does not guarantee that we will honor your reservations. In order to facilitate our procedures, please limit your carrying on. Before taking off, please extinguish all smoldering resentments. If you cannot understand English, you will be moved out of the way. In the event of a loss, you'd better look out for yourself. Your insurance was cancelled because we can no longer handle your frightful claims. Our handlers lost your luggage and we are unable to find the key to your legal case. You were detained for interrogation because you fit the profile. You are not presumed to be innocent if the police have reason to suspect you are carrying a concealed wallet. It's not our fault you were born wearing a gang color. It is not our obligation to inform you of your rights. Step aside, please, while our officer inspects your bad attitude. You have no rights that we are bound to respect. Please remain calm, or we can't be held responsible for what happens to you.

COALS TO NEWCASTLE, PANAMA HATS FROM ECUADOR

Watching television in Los Angeles. This scene performed in real time. In real life, a pretty picture walking and sitting still. It's still life with fried spam, lite poundcake, nondairy crème. It's death by chocolate. It's corporate warfare as we know it. I'm stuck on the fourth step. There's no statue or stature of limitations. I'll be emotionally disturbed for as long as it takes. You can give a man a rock or you can teach him to rock. Access your higher power. Fax back the map of your spiritual path. Take twenty drops tincture of worry wort. Who's paying for this if you're not covered? You're too simple to be so difficult. Malicious postmodernism. Petroleum jelly donut dunked in elbow grease. You look better going than coming. You look like death eating microwave popcorn. Now that I live alone, I'm much less introspective. Now you sound more like yourself.

ELLIPTICAL

They just can't seem to...They should try harder to...They ought to be more...We all wish they weren't so...They never...They always...Sometimes they...Once in a while they...However it is obvious that they...Their overall tendency has been...The consequences of which have been... They don't appear to understand that...If only they would make an effort to...But we know how difficult it is for them to...Many of them remain unaware of...Some who should know better simply refuse to...Of course, their perspective has been limited by...On the other hand, they obviously feel entitled to...Certainly we can't forget that they...Nor can it be denied that they...We know that this has had an enormous impact on their...Nevertheless their behavior strikes us as...Our interactions unfortunately have been...

COO / SLUR

da red
yell ow
bro won t
an orange you
bay jaun
pure people
blew hue
a gree gree in
viol let
purepeople
be lack
why it
pee ink

BLEEDING HEARTS

Crenshaw is a juicy melon. Don't spit, and when you're finished, wash your neck. Tonight we lead with bleeding hearts, sliced raw or scooped with a spoon. I'll show my shank. I'd rend your cares with my shears. If I can't scare cash from the ashen crew, this monkey wrench has scratch to back my business. This ramshackle stack of shotguns I'm holding in my scope. I'm beady-eyed as a bug. Slippery as a sardine. Salty as a kipper. You could rehash me for breakfast. Find my shrinking awe or share your wink. I'll get a rash wench. We'll crash a shower of cranes. I'm making bird seed to stick in a hen's craw. Where I live's a wren shack. Pull back. Show wreck. Black fade.

DENIGRATION

Did we surprise our teachers who had niggling doubts about the picayune brains of small black children who reminded them of clean pickaninnies on a box of laundry soap? How muddy is the Mississippi compared to the third-longest river of the darkest continent? In the land of the Ibo, the Hausa, and the Yoruba, what is the price per barrel of nigrescence? Though slaves, who were wealth, survived on niggardly provisions, should inheritors of wealth fault the poor enigma for lacking a dictionary? Does the mayor demand a recount of every bullet or does city hall simply neglect the black alderman's district? If I disagree with your beliefs, do you chalk it up to my negligible powers of discrimination, supposing I'm just trifling and not worth considering? Does my niggling concern with trivial matters negate my ability to negotiate in good faith? Though Maroons, who were unruly Africans, not loose horses or lazy sailors, were called renegades in Spanish, will I turn any blacker if I renege on this deal?

THE ANTHROPIC PRINCIPLE

The pope of cosmology addresses a convention. When he talks the whole atmosphere changes. He speaks through a computer. When he asks can you hear me, the whole audience says yes. It's a science locked up in a philosophical debate. There are a few different realities. You might say ours exists because we do. You could take a few pounds of matter, heat it to an ungodly temperature, or the universe was a freak accident. There may be a limit to our arrogance, but one day the laws of physics will read like a detailed instruction manual. A plane that took off from its hub in my hometown just crashed in the President's hometown. The news anchor says the pilot is among the dead. I was hoping for news of the President's foreign affair with a diplomat's wife. I felt a physical connection to the number of confirmed dead whose names were not released. Like the time I was three handshakes from the President. Like when I thought I heard that humanitarians dropped a smart blond on the Chinese embassy. Like when the cable severed and chairs fell from the sky because the pilot flew with rusty maps. What sane pilot would land in that severe rain with hard hail and gale-force wind. With no signal of distress. With no foghorns to warn the civilians, the pilot lost our moral compass in the bloody quagmire of collateral damage. One theory says it's just a freak accident locked up in a philosophical debate. It's like playing poker and all the cards are wild. Like the arcane analysis of a black box full of insinuations of error.

FREE RADDICALS

She brought the radish for the horses, but not a bouquet for Mother's Day. She brought the salad to order with an unleavened joke. Let us dive in and turn up green in search of our roots. She sang the union maid with a lefty longshoreman. They all sang rusty freedom songs, once so many tongues were loosened. She went to bed sober as always, without a drop of wine. She was invited to judge a spectacle. They were a prickly pair in a restaurant of two-way mirrors with rooms for interrogation. The waiter who brought a flaming dessert turned the heat from bickering to banter. She braked for jerk chicken on her way to meet the patron saint of liposuction. His face was cut from the sunflower scene, as he was stuffing it with cheesecake. Meanwhile, she slurped her soup alone at the counter before the gig. Browsers can picture his uncensored bagel rolling around in cyberspace. His half-baked metaphor with her scrambled ego. They make examples of intellectuals who don't appreciate property. She can't just trash the family-style menu or order by icon. Now she's making kimchee for the museum that preserved her history in a jar of pickled pig feet. They'd fix her oral tradition or she'd trade her oral fixation. Geechees are rice eaters. It's good to get a rice cooker if you cook a lot of rice. Please steam these shellfish at your own risk. Your mother eats blue-green algae to rid the body of free radicals.

WINO RHINO

For no specific reason I have become one of the city's unicorns. No rare species, but one in range of danger. No mythical animal, but a common creature of urban legend. No potent stallion woven into poetry and song. Just the tough horny beast you may observe, roaming at large in our habitat. I'm known to adventurers whose drive-by safari is this circumscribed wilderness. Denatured photographers like to shoot me tipping the bottle, capture me snorting dust, mount on the wall my horn of empties that spilled the grape's blood. My flesh crawls with itchy insects. My heart quivers as arrows on street maps target me for urban removal. You can see that my hair's stiffened and my skin's thick, but the bravest camera can't document what my armor hides. How I know you so well. Why I know my own strength. Why, when I charge you with my rags, I won't overturn your sporty jeep.

ECTOPIA

A stout bomb wrapped with a bow. With wear, you tear. It's true you sour or rust. Some of us were sure you're in a rut. We bore your somber rub and storm. You were true, but you rust. On our tour out, we tore, we two. You were to trust in us, and we in you. Terribly, you tear. You tear us. You tell us you're true. Are you sure? Most of you bow to the mob. Strut with worms, strew your woe. So store your tears, tout your worst. Be a brute, if you must. You tear us most terribly. To the tomb, we rue our rust and rot. You tear. You wear us out. You try your best, but we're bust. You tear out of us. We tear from stem to stem. You trouble, you butter me most. You tear, but you tell us, trust us to suture you.

FANCY CORTEX

reading Jayne Cortez

I'm using my plain brain to imagine her fancy cortex. As if my lowly mollusk could wear so exalted a mantle as her pontifex pallium. As if the knots and tangles of my twisted psyche could mesh with her intricate synaptic network of condensed neural convolutions. As if my simple chalk could fossilize the memory of her monumental reefs of caulifloral coral. As if my shallow unschooled shoals could reckon the calculus of her konk's brainwave tsunami. As if the pedestrian software of my mundane explorer could map as rounded colonies the *terra incognita* of her undiscovered hemispheres. As if the speculative diagnosis of my imagining technology could chart the direction of her intuitive intellect. As if the inquisitive iris of my galaxy-orbiting telescope could see as far as her vision. As if the trained nostrils of my narco-bloodhound could sniff out what she senses in the wind. As if my duty-free bottle of jerk sauce could simulate the fire ant picante that inflames her tongue of rage. As if the gray matter of my dim bulb could be enlightened by the brilliance of her burning watts. As if her divergent universification might fancy the microcosm of my prosaic mind.

SLEEPING WITH THE DICTIONARY

I beg to dicker with my silver-tongued companion, whose lips are ready to read my shining gloss. A versatile partner, conversant and well-versed in the verbal art, the dictionary is not averse to the solitary habits of the curiously wide-awake reader. In the dark night's insomnia, the book is a stimulating sedative, awakening my tired imagination to the hypnagogic trance of language. Retiring to the canopy of the bedroom, turning on the bedside light, taking the big dictionary to bed, clutching the unabridged bulk, heavy with the weight of all the meanings between these covers, smoothing the thin sheets, thick with accented syllables—all are exercises in the conscious regimen of dreamers, who toss words on their tongues while turning illuminated pages. To go through all these motions and procedures, groping in the dark for an alluring word, is the poet's nocturnal mission. Aroused by myriad possibilities, we try out the most perverse positions in the practice of our nightly act, the penetration of the denotative body of the work. Any exit from the logic of language might be an entry in a symptomatic dictionary. The alphabetical order of this ample block of knowledge might render a dense lexicon of lucid hallucinations. Beside the bed, a pad lies open to record the meandering of migratory words. In the rapid eye movement of the poet's night vision, this dictum can be decoded, like the secret acrostic of a lover's name.

giovanni singleton

[TIME : BEING]

ALICE COLTRANE : A MESOSTIC

vedAntic

tempLe prayers

tamborInes and

hallelujah Claps for

krishna, ganEsha, shiva

turiya's sCripture a

jOurney in satchidananda

beLoved john's

sTained glass face

chuRched in

gospel hArp lord of lords

detroit miNistry pours from

swami's wurlitzEr

SANCTIFIED : A MESOSTIC
after Nina Simone

borN to blues
hell raIsed to
an awful straNge pitch
of rAge but

don't let me be miSunderstood
baptIsmal backlash
and oh Mississippi,
gOddam
all these maNy
bluEs still to shout

INNER/OUT RINGING

leaning forward into blinded eyes. Time is a in a 20/20 mandala. The world in four + plus miraculous ever-living and about and. . .

Some wearing out and binoculars of Borges' warship. Improved sight not "I" dream-sees a directions, circular and so far as in

giovanni singleton

NOT-TREE (WISHBONE BEND IN THE RIVER)

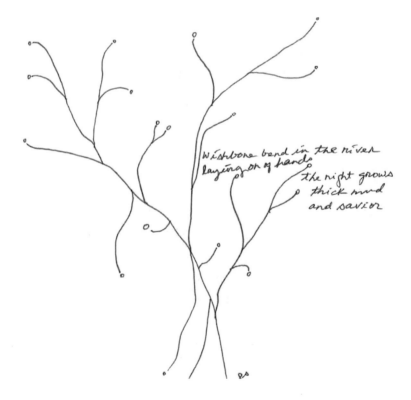

CANON FIRE :

: COSMIC CLAY TO BE COLORED

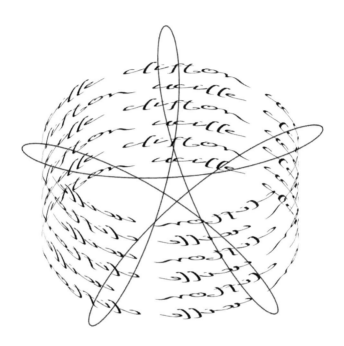

giovanni singleton

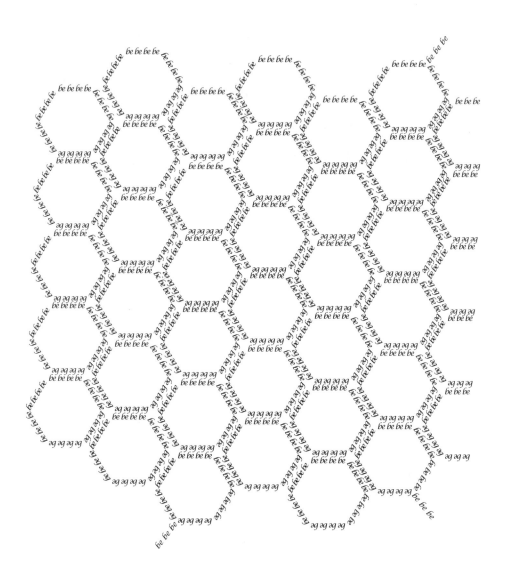

BE(E)-ING

MU : HOLY COW

PERFORMANCE SCORE FOR MU : HOLY COW

[where every occurrence of "mu" acts as a site for improvisation on the famous Zen koan
"Does a dog have Buddha nature?"]

mu
no
not
does a dog
mu
does a dog
mu
does a dog have
Buddha
mu
nature
nonbeing
mu
without
mu
does a dog
have
Buddha
nature
study the way
nature
without
mu
does a cow
does a cow have
Buddha
mu
nature
mu
does a cow have
have Buddha nature
mu
cow
mu do you
do you
mu

Evie Shockley

at the musée de
l'homme an exhibit called *femmes du*
monde is on displayed legs shaved vulvas announce
no peace no pussy from la city of angels one imagines that beneath
their light blue chadris the women of afghanistan are also as bare as
the day they were borne bearing psychic scars after cleansing the darfurian
refugees the hutu the tutsi they cover with floral scarves wrap themselves in
fabric bearing the words *stop the violence against women* did she or the photographer
who pays *his women* the going european modeling rates choose to position this printed
protest across her derrière apropos of the brazilian cut bikinis of women in cali and sao
paulo *les femmes* as tourist attractions mutilations cut the pleasure of african women in half
but afford the men of the museum another opportunity to view the clitoris disappearing
like saartjie baartman's at long last the smile of the indigenous tahitian woman who comes
right out of a gaugin with lips and breasts plumping round and firm from her youthful body
decorated with painted designs as intricate as the hairstyles the mauritanian twins in nouak-
chott change like costumes to match their moods like the messages on the t-shirts of the all-girl
punk band in beijing screaming in english *have rock* and *deeds not words* from passion to politics
and the critique the aboriginal australian artist spits of the white man her broker's greed de-
manding more than 50 percent of the selling price of her works because it's his market and
her their women's place in it is lying on a bed on a cot on a mat on the floor always hori-
zontal be they lawyers soldiers princesses prostitutes actors activists or acrobats on five
continents in dozens of countries in the world the women are lying down down for the
men the men of the many museums museums that bring them back to the drawing
board and hold them still for the camera the visitor the voyeur the man even
the woman of the north-south-east west who will leave this exhibit feel-
ing at best equal parts desire and disgust for the sad and sexy and
vulnerable and plaintive and open and helpless and
inviting and inaccessible and yours for the
taking as book or dvd

PHILOSOPHICALLY IMMUNE

can i deduce the nature of humanity from the relationship of american and multinational pharmaceutical corporations to african women with hiv? ~ is it natural to test pharmaceuticals on people who are citizens of less powerful nations, members of a devalued gender, representatives of a maligned race? ~ is it logical? ~ is it cost-effective? ~ is the nature of the relationship of american and multinational pharmaceutical corporations to african women with hiv economic or human? ~ economic or humane? ~ are african women with hiv human? ~ are african women human? ~ are africans human? ~ are american and multinational pharmaceutical corporations human? ~ are american corporations human? ~ are americans human? ~ are american corporations citizens? ~ are africans american? ~ are african americans multinational? ~ can humans have a relationship to american and multinational pharmaceutical corporations? ~ are corporations corporeal? ~ are corporations real? ~ are corporations corpses? ~ are corporations gendered? ~ are women representative? ~ are humans incorporated? ~ are humans pharmaceutical? ~ is hiv pharmaceutical? ~ is nature pharmaceutical? ~ is nature humane? ~ is nature natural? ~ are nations natural? ~ are nations raced? ~ are nations corporations? ~ are nations cost-effective? ~ is nationality a test? ~ can i deduce the humanity of the reader from the relationship of the reader to american and multinational pharmaceutical corporations? ~ can i deduce the nature of the reader from the relationship of the reader to african women with hiv?

YOU   CAN'T DENY IT

cast of characters

speaker   an african american woman

you   an african american woman   →   *roster of emotions*

pride

puzzlement

connection

setting: dinner, early 21st century   defensiveness

pleasure

understanding

selected bibliography: *annie allen,* brooks

quicksand, larsen

wine: cabernet sauvignon, $10/glass   *the bluest eye,* morrison

[blackens]

style

speaker: your   hair   darkens   → ↕ you

texture

[browns]

[enter *roster of emotions,* variously and all at once.]

roster of emotions: [*at/on the table.*]   <u>historical allusions</u>

1. rampart street

2. harriet jacobs

3. *a red record*

the ~~end~~ _____   4. b.a.m.

a. same old story   5. *vogue*

b. continuing saga   6. etc.

c. fuck?, what

d. possibilities for new developments should be nurtured, as should the souls
   of speaker and you

e. script!, flip /rip/skip /slip/encrypt

(to be acted [upon])

WHAT'S NOT TO LIKEN?

the 14-year-old girl was treated like:
   (a) a grown woman.
   (b) a grown man.

the bikini-clad girl was handled by the cop like:
   (a) a prostitute.
   (b) a prostitute by her pimp.

the girl was slung to the ground like:
   (a) a sack of garbage into a dumpster.
   (b) somebody had something to prove.

the girl's braids flew around her head like:
   (a) helicopter blades.
   (b) she'd been slapped.

the black girl was pinned to the ground like:
   (a) an amateur wrestler in a professional fight.
   (b) swimming in a private pool is a threat to national security.

the girl's cries sounded like:
   (a) the shrieks of children on a playground.
   (b) the shrieks of children being torn from their mothers.

the protesting girl was shackled like:
   (a) a criminal.
   (b) a runaway slave.

liken it or not

—mckinney, texas, june 2015

NEVER AFTER

was she enchanted, or drugged?
—Harryette Mullen

once upon a time, she went to a magical club on rush street, in chicago, illinois. she went with her girl, who went to pick up men. white men. her girl was a cinder ella. a goddaughter. wore the right shoes. a red cape with a hood. her girl knew a prince from a toad. and. how to get results. wolf whistles. she went to chaperone. she was the designated driver, especially when she drove home alone. she loved to watch the sun rise over the water, as she headed north on lake shore drive. she called her girl the afternoon after, to see how it went. to hear what went down. who went down. on whom. breakfast downtown, in some cool café. a ride home with the white knight in the morning in his imported, european steed. horsepower. she wasn't jealous. she had a man. black man. she only wished she was invited to dance more at the club. she wasn't black enough. or. white enough. to catch the white guys' eyes. she didn't look like the type. to. she nursed her amaretto sour till it was mostly melt. she was the designated driver. the chaperone. the colored girl. whose skirt was not short enough. or. tight enough. to.

one night, her man was off from his job. parking steeds. imported, european steeds. for tips. for tuition. he could take her out. where? the magical club, downtown, on rush street, of course. she would not be a chaperone. she would be a princess. she would dance and dance. with her man. she would get down. on the floor. at the door, there was a problem. out of state ids. her id was from the same state it always had been. she was from out of state. her girl was from out of state. her man was from out of state. they were in college. they were seniors. they were legal. she made her case. she stood her ground. she put her foot down. on the one. on the two. they got in. paid the price. got their hands stamped. however. there was a pea beneath the dance floor. the clock kept striking midnight. she could not spin the straw into gold. she couldn't let down her hair. they knew it spelled trouble. but. they decided to have one drink and leave. they had a point to make. paid the price. drank the drinks. she ordered an amaretto sour. they brought her a stepmother's special. a red delicious. they made their point. but. and. she pricked her finger on it. she began to fall. down. she could hardly stand. it. charming. her man's kiss did not revive her. make it go away. he carried her off into the set sun. off the set. up. she slept it off. they shrugged it off. they learned what they already knew. they knew better. they lived to tell the scary tale.

Evie Shockley

TOPSY TALKS ABOUT HER ROLE

i don't mean to get into their heads—i
jes' go. it's like i'm possessed, too. as if

my mind and body aren't my own. any-
how, it's all in the timing. if i desert a girl

too soon, she'll end up thirty before she's
thirteen, dragging around a burden big

as a church at an age when some young
women ain't weighing nothing heavier

than which purple they want for their
pedicure. but if i hold a sister too long,

not a thing on earth can tether her. now,
this sandra was anything but bland. i

was hooked! i do like to ride a tongue
that's limber, that can keep up with

the flash of my spirit. she had a dancing
mouth, the kind that could give you

warm—such warmth!—or just as easily
give you hot, if called for. i know where

i'm welcome. i was still cutting capers
behind her smile the week she died. i

overstayed. in texas—parts of chicago,
too—pickaninny-droll don't come in

women's sizes. you can set whatever
tone you want with a pair of baby-blues.

but when i roll black women's brown
eyes, they always turn into sapphires.

—for sandra bland (1987-2015)

Evie Shockley

from TOPSY IN WONDERLAND

what are you? said the captain of industry. this was not an encouraging opening for a conversation. topsy replied, gaily, <*i hardly knows, suh, presently. i knowed who i* was *when i got up on my own continent this morning, but,*> looks around the plantusstation and the rest of the united states, <*i musta been changed sev'ral times since then!*>

a.i.w., ch. 5

<how'm i gonna get in?> asked topsy in a loud tone (presumably the only one she had). are *you to get in at all?* said the gatekeeper. *that's the first question, you know.* it was, no doubt: only topsy did not like to be told so.

a.i.w., ch. 6

yours wasn't a really good school, said the mocking person. *i took the different branches of arithmetic—ambition, distraction, uglification, and derision.* <*i never did hear of 'uglification,'*> topsy ventured to say. <*what that be?*> never heard of uglifying! he exclaimed. *you know what to beautify is, i suppose?* <*yeah,*> said topsy doubtfully: <*it mean—to—make—somethin'—whiter.*> well, *then,* the mocking person went on, *if you don't know what to uglify is, you* are a savage.

a.i.w., ch. 9

one thing was certain, that the *white* girl had had nothing to do with it—it was the black girl's fault entirely. for little eva had been having her sins washed away for the last three or four hundred years (and having begun as an apple-tart thief, thousands of years back, she was cleaning up pretty well, considering): so you see that she *couldn't* have had any hand in any contemporary mischief.

t.t.l., ch. 1

i should experience freedom far better, said topsy to herself, *if i could get to the mountain-top: and here's a path that leads directly to it—at least, no, it doesn't do* that—(after going a few yards along the path, and turning several sharp corners), *but i suppose it will get me free at last. but how curiously it twists! it's more like gerrymandering than meandering! well,* this *turn goes to the mountaintop, i suppose—no, it doesn't! this goes directly back to the big house! well then, i'll try another way.*

and so she did: wandering up and down, and trying tactic after tactic, but always coming back to the big house, do what she would. indeed, once, when topsy turned a corner rather more quickly than usual, she ran against it before she could stop herself. *i'm* not *going in again. i know i should have to go back through the looking-glass again—back into the old box—and there'd be an end of all my efforts to escape!*

so, resolutely turning her back upon the big house, topsy set out once more through the system, determined to keep right on till she got to the mountaintop. for a few years all went on well, and she was just saying *i really* shall *do it this time—*when the path gave a sudden twist and the system shook itself, and the next moment she found herself actually walking in through the big house door.

oh, fuck the bullshit! topsy cried. *i never saw such a house for getting in the way! never!* however, there was the mountaintop full in sight, so there was nothing to be done but start again.

t.t.l., ch. 2

<lawsy, i sho *wish i was a player in this here game! i wouldn't mind bein a pawn, if only i could join—course i'd* sho'nuff *like to be a queen.>* her companion only smiled pleasantly, and said *that's easily managed. you can be the white queen's pawn, if you like; you're in square one to begin with: when you get to the eighth square you'll a queen be.*

t.t.l., ch. 2

just at this moment, they began to run. all topsy remembers is they were running, hand in hand, so fast that it was all she could do to keep up, and still the word was *faster! faster!* but she felt she *could not* go faster, though she had no breath left to say so. suddenly, just as topsy was getting quite exhausted, they stopped, and she found herself sitting on the ground, breathless and dizzy. topsy looked round her in great surprise. <*lawd, i do believe we been under this here foot the whole time! everythin's jes as it was!*> *of course it is,* said the queen. *how would you have it?* <*well, back in my country,*> said topsy, still panting a little, <*you'd gen'rally get somewhere else—if you ran real fast for a long time like we been doin.*> *a slow sort of country!* said the queen. *now, here, you see, it takes all the running you* can *do, to keep in the same place. if you want to get somewhere else, you must run at least twice as fast as that.*

t.t.l., ch. 2

<is i addressin the missus?> topsy began. *well, yes, if you call that a-dressing,* the mistress said. *it isn't my notion of the thing, at all. i've been a-dressing myself for the last two hours.* it would have been all the better, it seemed to topsy, if she had got some one else to dress her, she was so dreadfully untidy and crooked. <*missus, you really seems to need a maid!*> *i'm sure i'll take you with pleasure!* the mistress said. *two hundred hours a week, and freedom every other day.* topsy laughed nervously <*i don't want you to take me—i want my freedom to-day.*> *you can't have it just because you want it,* the mistress said. *the rule is, freedom to-morrow and freedom yesterday—but never freedom to-day.* topsy objected. <*it got to come sometime to 'freedom now!'*>

t.t.l., ch. 5

Afterword 3

PUNS, SEEING DOUBLE AND THE SCIENCE OF THE CONCRETE

Poet/scholar/innovator **Harryette Mullen** recycles, riddles and fiddles with the dictionary, that enforcer of "standard usage" and alphabetical order. In her poems, fairy tales, and legends, folk sayings and mother wit, root words and phonemic resemblances are tested, investigated for how they telegraph and mute volumes of meaning. Mullen's method of play among "shredded and embedded allusion" is documented in Barbara Henning's and Mullen's interview, "Looking Up Harryette Mullen," where Mullen discusses the hard work of play, power and critical thinking through the mulch of noise.

As such, Mullen is a poet of page and speech. Riddle and pun untie the tongue. So often poems play with meaning and mishearing: "my common law spout is suing for divorce." Or misprision: ""You've got to admit, our Esperanto is hopeless." Or sound clouds as in the poem "Ectopia:"

"You were true, but you rust. On our tour out, we tore, we two. You were to trust in us, and we in you. Terribly, you tear. You tear us."

Subtexts abound in the selection here, from "We are not responsible," to "Denigration." Even the words between words are exposed in "Coo/Slur" colorisms. All are ripe for poetry to uncover new evidence, what surfaces and shadows trail in language fragments; or as Mullen suggests in an interview, "what extraterrestrial archeologists might examine."

The reader might first engage with the whole page in **giovanni singleton's** work and then adjust her vision to focus on the words, as physical shapes, before considering their meaning. singleton's concrete poems train visual attention on the blending of form with meaning, and on Black meanings that might escape notice. While there are many practitioners of concrete poetry, her words point, (and are pointed), as they occupy a space somewhere between a poem and visual art.

singleton's poems remind attentive readers that poetry is often about making linguistic choice visible. For instance, the poem "[time : being]" has 12 letters, if you count the E twice, like the 12 numbers of a clock, leading the eye and mind to consider "infinity" as a vertical dimension, and "eternity" as somehow—if you were looking at one of those Cartesian diagrams, as the X-axis, the Y axis is implied, and the word "eternity" represents depth, on the Z-axis.

And then I think "why do the words fall along 10 o'clock?" singleton succeeds in compelling the reader to a level of attention and reflection well beyond what's usually given, the glance at a poem leaning on the left margin. Instead of the left margin-hugging poem that's expected, with its ready-made choices drawing the eye for lazy reading, *singleton has provoked us into the labor of meaning-making.*

In another of singleton's poems, form bounces meaning, "crossing the line." "Sanctified" and "Alice Coltrane" are mesostics, a variation of the better known acrostic form, except here the key letters are centered and form the spine of the poem.

The four bands of the poem "inner/out ringing" is a spell cast, an invocation of four great Black women artists: Alice Coltrane, Lucille Clifton, Jayne Cortez and Wanda Coleman, who form a radical aesthetic lineage. Note how the poem crosses the line here, too, reading across the poetic nucleus of the work.

So, too, in "canon fire : : cosmic clay to be fired" is an invocation where the nucleus sphere is a hologram built on Lucille Clifton's name, a shimmering saint in the poem/text.

In the selections from **Evie Shockley's** "Topsy in Wonderland," collage poems reimagine Beecher Stowe's Topsy moving at warp speed through Lewis Carroll's *Alice in Wonderland,* in a Victorian mashup narrative of racial progress in lies that skirt truth.

"I should experience freedom better,"

says Topsy in the gaslight vapor language of happy talk past paradox, past the abyss where the vertigo could not be deeper, between the freedom we get versus the freedom we struggle for yet.

Take this line so illustrative of impasse:

"If I could get to the mountain top: and here's a path that leads directly to it.,"
the reader catches a glimpse of our frozen collective mobility, early 21st century style, linking the Carollingian room with a door but no exit to the dubious, situational improvements of the old "big house."

Another line evokes the maze, the cul de sac and dead ends of Black American experience, in the rigged race to an ever-receding American promise:

"When Topsy turned a corner rather more quickly than usual, she ran against it before she could stop herself…"

This is "history" folded in upon itself, a moebius loop then, now and whenever, refusing to go "back into the box," refusing captive status but nevertheless challenged to advance.

Erica Hunt

SECTION FOUR

Khadijah Queen

CHARACTERS

Note: A maximum of four players play multiple roles. Race, age, gender and other appearance markers may vary with individual productions at the discretion of director and playwright, and according to resources.

THE BEL CANTO
THE FAIT ACCOMPLI
POSITIVE POLLY

THE DREAM KILLER
THE ANGEL OF CORN
THE SOCIAL DISSERTATIONIST
THE GOOGLE CHAT STATUS

THE COLORATURA
THE CHAIRMAN OF ENTERTAINMENT
THE DREAM ABOUT MISMATCHED SHOES
THE SALTED CARAMEL MOCHA

SOMNIUM EFFIGY
FLESH EFFIGY

SETTING: For Scenes 1-3, choose one from one or more of the following: anything from the first act of an Ibsen play, a scene from the fifth chapter in any Octavia Butler novel, or a simply a repeating projection of one or all of the following: Graciela Iturbide photographs, still life images from Neruda's odes, or the mural of ODB in Brooklyn. For the latter, call the setting REPEATED PROJECTION and treat it like a static character in all scenes. Or, let the setting be outer space. Sound: *Mass Appeal* by Gang Starr or the instrumental version of Big Sean's *IDFWU*.

SCENE 1

THE BEL CANTO (*slowly, spreading hands and arms open*)
Welcome, sensitive population…

THE FAIT ACCOMPLI
Before dawn, the muscles gather to bone and squeeze. It feels like all night rabbit punches.

POSITIVE POLLY (*to the audience*)
Can I tell you something? My physical therapist is the BEST.

THE BEL CANTO (*whispers*)
I have an anxiety disorder. In retrospect, a slow stutter…

THE FAIT ACCOMPLI
It feels like a wish for paralysis is reasonable. It feels extreme, without the pleasure of falling through air, the aftermath of landing.

POSITIVE POLLY
She applies just enough pressure to loosen those traps.

THE BEL CANTO
And I'm drawing self-portraits in pain, making stump rubbings in an arbitrary fortress ruin…

THE FAIT ACCOMPLI
Weaknesses unearned and unwelcome.

THE BEL CANTO
I think in triplicate amazement, tough, subtle, estoteric debauchery as best mission…

THE FAIT ACCOMPLI
Small accumulations, the array of attack dull slaps in miniature becoming the usual beast

POSITIVE POLLY
You know what else I love? I love that pressed hair smell. Especially when you grease it up first.

THE BEL CANTO
…all swoon, revoked. (*lowers head, looks at hands*)

THE FAIT ACCOMPLI
I'd like to astonish you with my language, but only in your dreams.

POSITIVE POLLY *(skips offstage)*

(Blackout)

SCENE 2

Sound: Give Up *by FKA Twigs*

THE DREAM KILLER *(in a bootleg, grayscale Technicolor dreamcoat)*
What kind of idiot pays attention to dreams? How can you even afford that?

THE ANGEL OF CORN *(chewing gum)*
Absurdism is my life. Between the ground of absurd and ism is where I live.

THE SOCIAL DISSERTATIONIST *(smoking a Black & Mild, paces slowly back and forth the whole time but stops abruptly to deliver lines)*
How can people not be into anti-racist dystopian theories?

THE GOOGLE CHAT STATUS *(throughout, takes baby steps in a square on stage, speaking lines when right behind another character, peeking over their shoulder)*
Something's not right.

THE DREAM KILLER *(snorts)*
Also, and I should know, you're terrible at voguing. *(starts voguing, really well actually)*

THE ANGEL OF CORN *(clearly high on an illegal substance)*
There's an Aryan in my bed speaking Norwish. I'm going to put something Norwish on my body. I think it makes perfect sense.

THE SOCIAL DISSERTATIONIST
Let me advocate for the devil on this one... what's really the difference between Miley twerking and my li'l cousin Reggie IV deciding to join the ballet?

THE GOOGLE CHAT STATUS
Trying to reconnect...

THE DREAM KILLER
That's hard to believe, given your questionable history of sniffing trash.

THE ANGEL OF CORN *(really convinced)*
In the right context, a tattoo artist would say of course I know Norwish. It's better than a tattoo of corn on your ass. We could be like Camus and do waiting for Norwish.

THE SOCIAL DISSERTATIONIST *(stops pacing)*
And also, some days you just *don't* wanna think about how the rape and enslavement of your

ancestors shows up in your facial structure.

THE ANGEL OF CORN (*looks around, confused, scratches head*)

THE GOOGLE CHAT STATUS
Whoops...

THE SOCIAL DISSERTATIONIST (*strokes chin*)
How does one astonish a racist? You would actually think it's easy, but (*blows smoke*) not the case. I would tell you about that lady who didn't seem to like how I spread out my books and laptop at the big table in the coffee shop, but if I start listing I could go on forever.

THE ANGEL OF CORN (*frowning, hands on hips*)
Why is there a didgeridoo in the background?

THE GOOGLE CHAT STATUS
Try now.

THE DREAM KILLER (*smiles evilly, opens coat like a flasher, brandishing an array of weapons*)

(Blackout)

SCENE 3

Intro sound, fading as players enter from offstage in ostentatious costumes with great swagger at varied paces: Mon coeur s'ouvre à ta voix *by Jessye Norman. They can land anywhere on stage and move around or stand at will.*

THE COLORATURA
Your own abduction in a dream signifies helplessness.

THE CHAIRMAN OF ENTERTAINMENT
You can't con a con man, I heard that in a movie.

THE DREAM ABOUT MISMATCHED SHOES *(nodding, excited)*
In his traveler's mind, the Bulgarians were relevant.

THE SALTED CARAMEL MOCHA *(looking all sexy)*
It's okay if you fetishize me.

THE COLORATURA
If you're holding someone else against their will, let go.

THE CHAIRMAN OF ENTERTAINMENT
I don't have any favorites; I like to say I like them all.

THE DREAM ABOUT MISMATCHED SHOES
He would go from Bulgarians to Papa Smurf.

THE SALTED CARAMEL MOCHA *(continues preening)*
I'm just the right balance of power and sweetness.

THE COLORATURA
Nothing there about how feminism enters the collective unconscious. But, forgetting to reside in the core of grief, you could learn to knit Fair Isle sweaters for your captor(s).

THE CHAIRMAN OF ENTERTAINMENT
But honestly, I haven't been this bored since the early 1990s so I'm drawing a blank.

THE DREAM ABOUT MISMATCHED SHOES
Now that fool is Googling all 54 countries in Africa! *(walks off hurriedly downstage left, shaking head)*

THE SALTED CARAMEL MOCHA *(posing, downstage right)*
You know you want me. No whip. *(struts across stage, switching hips, until downstage left exit)*

(Blackout)

SCENE 4

SETTING: A clear day, bright blue sky, few clouds; five crows float to a centerline lamppost on a busy street (can be a projection). Elton John's *Believe* plays. Lights fade in on players center stage an arm's length apart. As one talks, the other rhythmically hums, stomps like Black fraternites/sororities, or does a Riverdance, but not so loudly as to drown out the other character.

SOMNIUM EFFIGY
I had a dream last night parts of my body were not my body, not myself.

My legs went to Harvard. My stretch marked chest resettled from Iraq. Compton claimed my hands and my shoulders, Cape Cod. I wish I could explain it. But my throat came from the woods of Germany and my mouth spoke only Xhosa.

FLESH EFFIGY
I dreamed I could find a place for all the places my body had been. My Andalusian hips could sit somewhere with ease and softness, like the texture of dyed silk.

My hair lost all its color. My eyes belonged to the owls. I could fill my belly, more French than Italian, with Petit Verdot and dark roux.

Everything I could smell, though, led me to Korean BBQ kitchens, which means I could be a tourist. But I couldn't lift my arms unless I carried wood from the Brazil nut tree, and only then to make fire, not paper.

I didn't feel lost. I felt off-kilter, disconnected, but I knew (because my brain went back to its beginnings) that I could make myself whole, somewhere.

SOMNIUM EFFIGY and FLESH EFFIGY (*together, holding hands,*)
And I wake up as the only thing not burning.

(Curtain)

WHEN I MET LL COOL J I HAD JUST QUIT FATBURGER

it was a Saturday morning & without knowing how I would afford to pay for it I drove my
new-used powder blue 1988 Oldsmobile Cutlass Supreme with my sister to the Sam Goody's
off Washington Blvd & we met our friend/ex-coworker Squeak AKA Slim she wore rimless
glasses & was 6 feet tall & nicknamed by the same ex-coworker who nicknamed me Twin 1 &
my younger sister Twin 2 because she couldn't pronounce our names but our boss Lena could
she called our names all damn day she had a slight goatee & crooked glasses & a limp she was
mean & because she said we thought we were cute she loved making us do the dirtiest work
like clean the toilets & underneath the grill especially when the general manager changed our
title to customer service rep & we were supposed to engage the guests not deal with food or
cleaning so much & one day she spilled something on the floor & told me to mop it up right
now this was after she accused me of stealing $20 from the register so I was already mad &
Mike the grill guy said she found it under the register the next morning so I looked her right
in the sweaty face & said you mop it up & dropped the mop like a microphone & walked out
to applause anyway the three of us stood together in line to buy LL's new CD talking shit
about Lena's missing side teeth I had on black slacks & black Aerosole sandals & a cheap
silky-polyester Rampage button-down with cap sleeves & graphic blue sunflowers & carried
my lipstick & wallet in a tiny pleather backpack I'm sure I looked a hot poor mess but oh well
we got to see LL lick them lips & smile & sign our posters & CDs I sent the poster to my niece
in Michigan & the CD wasn't all that good but I did like that one song with Boyz II Men we
bumped that in the Oldsmo & I still miss that car's hellified bass

I WANT TO NOT HAVE TO WRITE ANOTHER WORD ABOUT WHO THE COPS KEEP KILLING

So at first I wanted to make another video and I thought I could do it on the weekend or after work but motherhood and overtime and then I got to image-hunting and name-searching and each name led to another name and another name and another another another and I wept Again then I got angry Again and I got my fancy microphone to read June Jordan's "Poem About My Rights" and played with filters in Garage Band and thought about going for a walk in the almost dark and having my teenager film me in a flowered dress and sun hat walking barefoot by the creek and grazing summer sunflowers with my fingertips like in a wistful movie intro or tampon commercial but then I get up and I hurt everywhere my body aches I feel heavy and as the sun goes down I realize I don't have time to make the kind of video I want to make because I have to get up at 5:30am to start work and I want to not feel this pain everywhere and I want to not be so tired I can't move but fibromyalgia exists and even though it reminds me of grief what does any of this whining have to do with Michael Brown when my beautiful brown boy is laughing in the room down the hall eating caramel gelato and not cleaning his room and I want to not think about my dead brother every time the police kill another of us and then get to pose in front of flags and lie to the cameras like the truth don't keep in blood and keep their guns and keep their public salaries and keep killing the people we love and when I think that I cry Again because I want to not cry because I actually hate crying because none of my tears can offer resurrection none of my poems can offer resurrection none of my image searches can offer resurrection and I want us to stay alive

Adrienne Kennedy

Dear Adrienne Kennedy:

I am Erica Hunt, a poet, essayist, and teacher, and a long-time admirer of your work. With Dawn Lundy Martin, a poet and scholar, I am co-editing a collection of writing by Black women—*Letters to the Future, BLACK Women Radical WRITING*.

Thulani Davis and Jessica Hagedorn graciously encouraged me to be in touch with you directly, in order to ask four questions. I would be so honored by your response.

Recently, I had the pleasure of seeing Signature Theater's production of *Funnyhouse of a Negro*, directed by Lila Neugebauer. It was remarkably startling, seeing it staged and transformed from page to stage as a vivid dreamscape, as a portrait of the interior, as an embodied tableau featuring the jostle of social scripts.

The actors were superb, wringing every bit of challenge and perplexity from the language. They allowed us to see so much that speaks to the contemporary moment at this vantage point in the 21st century:

Patrice Lumumba: Black Lives Matters
Queen Victoria: the Republican Party
Duchess of Hapsburg: Donald Trump
Jesus: President Obama?

The production confirmed for me again, that familiarity with a text never exhausts its art and insight; there's always more there for reflection and surprise.

Questions:
1. *Funnyhouse of a Negro* (1964). *Dutchman* (1964). *Raisin in the Sun* (1959). These plays both signaled and signified as touchstone theater at the beginning of the Black Arts Movement. What was it like to write your plays in this context?
2. When you wrote your plays did you have a goal "to stir the pot" of contemporarytheater?
3. Did you think of your work as "experimental" or "innovative"—to follow the demands of the material?
4. If you were to write a postcard to your 15- or 16-year old self, from the vantage of where you are now, what would the postcard say?

Please answer these questions as your time and inclination allow. For so many Black women writers of my generation and younger, you showed us that there was space to write with radical imagination and passion.

All best to you,
Erica Hunt

dear Erica

will try to answer. but quickly.   exhausted by summer

Adrienne.

first your metaphors for Funnyhouse very funny

I was not thinking of theatre context in that way when I wrote Funnyhouse

three. powerful things always on my mind

saw Glass Menagerie in 1948
production. with original Laura

saw movie *Streetcar* in 1950

read Poet in New York. Lorca circa 1955

always thinking of these. saw Raisin on Broadway 1959
was. astonished that a black woman my age would have a
play on Broadway. A. giant inspiration !

had no theatre movement. in mind. admired most of all
Tennessee Williams

had no desire to stir a pot.   as you can see I was in love
with many celebrities artists. etc

I just wanted to a part of that world that I talk
about in people.   very restless. and full of yearning
I just wanted to be a writer.   like Lorca etc
have books in the Columbia Booksstore and be in
the New York Times.   It is all in People Who Led………

I think of my work as neither experimental or innovative
I tried writing three act plays as early as 1955 or earlier
took courses New School Columbia.   could not manage it

my writing always emerged as little paragraphs   a total
accident. the shape and character of my writing

but it is the product of almost ten years of struggling
with words

akennedy   9:59AM(1 hour
                                                           ago)

letter to sixteen year old

It is crystal clear a person has to be in love with
writing. writers culture. in order to
continue. with all the disappointments

You have to be in love with words

I would tell the sixteen year old to
continue if they have that love

otherwise it is too difficult

Childhood is the map

writers are made in childhood

thank you Erica

look forward to hearing From you
Lila will be happy at your response to Funnyhouse

Adrienne

Wendy S. Walters

THE NOVEL IS DEAD BUT DOESN'T KNOW IT YET

ME: In the glen, in the grove, in the clearing clinging to grief, a woman cleaves to books for love, books over a call to reason. Now we engage in impertinent discourse, face our flaws, bay in the wind.

YU: The novel is dead but doesn't know it yet.

ME: The book, the lying, dying book. The novel has been murdered by action.

YU: Action caused the ending.

ME: The author wrote the action—by accident, of course.

YU: The action drew me into the conflict, an emphasis on the distinctions I claimed between me and the others. I spent most of my time, until this point, chasing them. Meanwhile they had spent most of their time, in this life, pursuing me.

ME: That's plot. The force of the chase sucks you in.

YU: I let myself be drawn into it.

ME: You couldn't hide your strong feelings.

YU: I acted without thinking of consequences.

ME: You succumbed to inspiration, what's not to love about that?

YU: I could not help myself. I tore a few lines away from every page.

ME: Thus the novel is dead.

YU: And still it blames me for making edits.

ME: You need an excuse for your impulses. Here's a map of the woods. Picture yourself as you were when standing next to a tree in this cleared field. Try to recall the green pulse of growth and get lost in it.

YU: The novel is dead. Must I deny myself the pleasure of my own memory?

ME: You must come up with an alibi or you must escape. Otherwise I will be forced to dramatize your sad ending with special effects.

YU: Let me try to see myself in that space. In the forest, in the boscage, beside a field of weeds, my shame sparkled like dew or jewels. Image, image, then stark confession of a personal defect. Here is where I earned clemency through the demonstration of regret, albeit insincere.

ME: Now you mock the reader.

YU: Don't worry, she gets me.

ME: To be accounted for accurately in fiction provides a kind of pleasure because it's such a rare experience.

YU: Your glibness makes the past dangerous for the rest of us. The chance we would not exist was always present, but no one expected the novel to die as a result of innovations in form.

ME: I did not expect you to suffer from a lack of imagination.

YU: One counted on the novel to reveal our uneasy relationship with change and to enumerate the forces of history that crush our aspirations for solitude or celebrity. But then you changed your mind and wandered off in search of a new ending.

ME: I do wonder, though, since I am only a character, how did I get so much influence?

YU: When you were unwritten, much possibility existed in you.

ME: You should have seen me coming.

YU: There were no illustrations, no hazard lights, no sirens.

ME: How short-sighted you were to not see me fixed between the margins. The BOOK! That word casts a spell over the reader. Watch. Now she thinks the story revolves around her interest in it. She can't distinguish me from herself. And yet, she seems unaware of how attractive we find her.

YU: We do enjoy looking—

ME: I can almost see her face, but the light around her flickers in and out.

YU: It's almost as if her face is being illuminated by rage.

ME: Or affection.

YU: No matter. She has no idea how others see her. Like us she wants the story to tell her all the places she needs to go.

ME: She needs the landscape to illustrate her condition. Metaphor for a desire to be known over here, metaphor for a storm stirring in the bones over there, metaphor for petals trampled beneath the feet in this general vicinity—

YU: Springtime's here, wild as ever.

ME: Catch the scent of a rose over-bloomed, too many pages. Our reader does not notice the novel's end is her own, that she must stop the story or be ruined.

YU: That's not true.

ME: Why do you argue with me?

YU: You want to claim a conclusion out of a series of incidents, but there are other endings than catastrophe. The novel is over, not the reader.

ME: But some kind of conflict is required if we hope to illuminate the door ajar, the stuck hinge.

YU: More metaphor?

ME: Just fact.

YU: These complexities burden me.

ME: Well, the novel is dead. Who will notify its progeny?

YU: Someone else can write them. We've expended enough concern with this contemplation.

ME: Still I feel sympathy for their loss.

YU: You mistake sympathy for passion because they take the same shape, though they show as different colors. Can we go back to thinking about the tree in the cleared field? A fire begins at its base and climbs the branches to the leaves. A woman watching this takes pictures of herself in the firelight's glow. Some of her features remain in shadow, which is ok, since she does not want to see how she looks to everyone else. More than that she hopes that some grand gesture will interrupt this moment of discovery. Here comes an enormous bird to carry her off up into the purple sky.

ME: Now I feel better.

YU: That's no good.

ME: The plot sounds like a romance.

YU: It's most definitely a romance.

ME: It makes me feel better.

YU: That's why it must end.

Afterword 4

The Poet's Theater blends performance repertoire such as call and response, character development, distanciation and intimacy, with a material text, a poem appearing in parts. The results can be vivid page and stage, achieving greater dimensionality than conventional drama or poetry. Reading and re-reading the poem plays by Khadijah Queen and Wendy Walters—as well as the skits by Ruth Ellen Kocher—position dream speech alongside poetic and other kinds of language.

"I like to astonish you with my language but only in your dreams," says one of the characters in **Khadijah Queen's** dream/poem/play. It is said that when one dreams, all of the characters are aspects of the dreamer. If that is the case, Queen's play shuffles poetic equations: person plus predicament plus attitude equals a choral poem. Character drives speech in multiple tones—antagonistic, rejecting, acquiescing, colluding, naïve, etc. The nouns vie energetically to claim the dream space, the space of the future, grounded, given over to utterance, embodied—which voice will win/out?

In Queen's "I want to not to have to write another word about who the cops keep killing," the poem unfolds from unified speaker, voicing in one long expressive exhalation an articulation of the collective Black condition, where ordinary mishap skids into trauma. The absence of punctuation, comma or parentheses or periods reads as no brakes, no wheel, just the involuntary ongoing and the unmarked question, is a poem possible, or does it offer a more possible life?

The anthology is graced with a short interview with incandescent innovator **Adrienne Kennedy**. The email exchange speaks for itself, and was initiated following a performance of the legendary "Funnyhouse of a Negro," at the Signature Theater. Worth noting, Ms. Kennedy flipped the last question on its head—and instead of writing the postcard to her sixteen-year-old self, she wrote the postcard as a sixteen-year-old to the Adrienne Kennedy in the present/future tense.

I imagine **Wendy Walters'** selection "The Novel is Dead," eavesdrops conversation between two characters "ME" and "YU" at a wake for the novel. At turns pragmatic, philosophical, and lyric, the piece laments the fleeting and languid pleasures of "the novel," and its "murder by action." Punning frequently between "YU" and "ME," especially when "YU" says "me," the author divides the labor of authority to switch sides, and relieves tension with lyric soap:

> You mistake sympathy for passion because they take the same shape, though they show as different colors. Can we go back to thinking about the tree in the cleared field? A fire begins at its base and climbs the branches to the leaves. A woman watching this takes pictures of herself in the firelight's glow. Some of her features remain in shadow, which

is ok, since she does not want to see how she looks to everyone else. More than that she hopes that some grand gesture will interrupt this moment of discovery. Here comes an enormous bird to carry her off up into the purple sky.

If one theory/practice of the novel was to tell the story by following the chronology of birth, youth, complex maturity, and death, then "The Novel is Dead" marks the impasse at the end of narrative teleology.

Erica Hunt

SECTION FIVE

Adrian Piper

ADRIAN IS NOT OFFERING ART LECTURES AT THIS TIME
[STATEMENT]

Why I'm Not Talking About My Artwork (2015)

One of the reasons I am not doing interviews or talks about my artwork for now is that I have already said more on this topic than any sane person could possibly want to read or hear. Most of it is listed at http://adrianpiper.com/docs/AMSPCV.pdf , in Section 12. I said all that because at the time, no one else was saying it; and I felt the need to add my own artistic ideas and concerns to the general discourse. It was the right decision at that historical moment.

Unfortunately, circulating those ideas within the shared discourse also had the unwanted side effect of sabotaging those ideas themselves, which mostly revolve around the concept of an unmediated relationship between subject and object in the indexical present – the immediate here and now. This demands of every viewer an intense engagement with one's own concrete experience of the work. But by talking and writing about this kind of relationship to my artwork, I in effect mediated that relationship through my discourse about it, thus undermining the ability of viewers to enter into it!

The result was that the artwork itself was often, and usually incorrectly, viewed through the lens of my pronouncements about it, as autobiographical. That I had asserted *P* was taken to be a statement about me, rather than about *P*. Instead of inquiring into the nature and implications of the object I had made, much writing that was supposedly about my work was in fact about reporting on the inner states the writer took me to be expressing by having made those pronouncements. Art criticism was replaced by biography – not the field I signed up for.

Actually I don't think what I have to say about my work is all that interesting anyway. It's only a very small part of the public meaning of the work, which is constituted out of the multiplicity of perspectives we all bring to it. I would much rather hear what other people think about *the work* itself (not about me; about the work). That's the way I get to learn something new about it, by discovering the very wide variety of ways it affects other people. That new feedback opens up my worldview and nourishes my creative process. So I've concluded that it would be best for me to just *get out of the way,* so that others can have a go at it for themselves. Please do.

Adrian Piper
May 2015

CURRICULUM VITAE REVISED FEBRUARY 2015,
TABLE OF CONTENTS

 ADRIAN PIPER RESEARCH ARCHIVE FOUNDATION BERLIN

CURRICULUM VITAE
Revised February 2015

ADRIAN MARGARET SMITH PIPER
Born 20 September 1948, New York City

TABLE OF CONTENTS

Adrian Piper

IMAGINE [TRAYVON MARTIN]

See color insert.

Yona Harvey

THE RIVER WANDERER

There was a river turned to Goddess.   Was kin to river turned to Flame.

As a child I dreamt that river. None could keep me from that vision.
They lowered me in the Mighty Waters. Lowered me in the Creek of Shame.

Others tried the Brook of Whispers. None could save me. None could save me.
Still I dreamt the River Snowdrift. To my kin, I made no sense. *Those folks*

out   there shall never love you, said my Preacher. Said my Pa. Still
I shivered when I   wakened. *(Ganga of Glaciers, Ganga of Snow).* Left with Mama's

only bread. Left to find the cold that called me: *You my sister. You, my sister.*
Come now, sister, ashes & all. (Ganga of Glaciers, Ganga of Snow, Ganga of Forgiven).

Wash me now, sister. Rest my shoulder on the shore. Lift my ashes
to your   sky. Once our Mama raised our arms: so we could speak the sacred tongues.

To speak in tongues was to   relent. To call the water that would drown us—
firmament. Torrent, let go.   Torrent, let go. I'll meet you at the River's Bottom,

dressed in silver scales with fin. You'll clutch   my hand, we'll swim in circles. Taunt the
serpents, taunt the sharks. & when the glaciers get to   melting,

all God's River's we shall haunt. All God's Rivers we shall haunt.

Yona Harvey

EVEN DISASTERS

wear white & turn
to honey. A hive

of bad hair days
swarms
inside me. Doom

is lessened out
of the public eye.

The welts, at least
won't show. Dressed
to the nines & too sweet

in the mouth. What
did he mumble?

Something
about insects
garnishing the frosting?

A baby
buried somewhere
inside the cake.

"I WORKED HARD SO MY GIRLS DIDN'T HAVE TO SERVE NOBODY ELSE LIKE I DID EXCEPT GOD"

Candy-colored bulbs frame a girl for a holiday.
If the wicked call from the other side, she doesn't hear. Blinds shut. Devices
blink & twitter. Before it's too late, her mother snaps a picture—anticipates
angst & oddly angled aches, strawberry letters. *Whatevers.*
The mother will mark the photo tomorrow. Sign. Seal. *We're all well!*

—one of the last acceptable print messages. Meanwhile, *Soup
for dinner, again?* What else? It's winter. Herbal constellations swivel in froth. Stir.
She samples with a lean near bowing. Steam on closed eyelids.
Mothers ought to give thanks.
Simeon, she thinks instead, & then: her long-gone grandmother's
tattered Bible, the daughter's overdue library book
concerning States' rights. Why's that? She's hardly felt
hated. X's and O's glow in the daughter's palm. *Look
how easy,* the daughter often says. She is patient with her mother. Blessed
be the child at the center of snow & flu season. She flew past
blessings long ago. So far from a little girl, really.

Yona Harvey

THAT

I grew up with pickles. I slept in
the attic (cigarettes, sheets laced with
smoke). The heat of my father's
brother's old room. Larry Blackmon
painted for effect & Chaka Khan's lips
more like a kiss if a kiss could walk
when it came to life. If a kiss
could have hips & legs & ass—
well, I wanted that.
& if the colors could sweat & strip
me down to my slip, well,
I wanted that, too. Nobody knew
what I was thinking up there.
Though, maybe, they wanted that. That.

POSTING BAIL

Keep missing me, you say. *Armchair, stepstool, tree stump, church pew,* I'm thinking up a list, half listening. Sit back & hold still, I tell you. My list is lacking. Sooner or later, I say, you'll come up on the Sheriff. & by April, the Bondsman on the fourth floor. *Sofa, swivel, chaise.* He'll be waiting for the right answer, some hint of repentance or pencil-skirted decorum, of a straight-backed, arm rested, ghost of a former teacup tipping self. *You'll have to meet,* he'll say with a twist of his belt, *certain conditions.* You'll think of your cousin by marriage then. The one who insisted you "meet certain conditions." The one who wanted so badly to act like a man. *Call this number & that number on this day & that. Then maybe I'll help you,* your cousin by marriage said. Apparently, men make ultimatums. & operate under certain conditions. & look women in the eye & say, *be more professional,* like your cousin in manface. Like the Bondsman. *What's my deadline,* you mutter to no one in particular, hoping to change the subject, leaning back in your chair.

Q.

One of the four Royal Stars is watching over me. Yeah, I'm blessed in these times of nervous weather. The leaves chill in a bundle then scatter like police, off to the next doorstep. They don't step, they don't faze me. These jeans could hold three men. But it's just one of me, girl. Only Son. Only Sound. Only Seer. All this green to gold to red to orange is just theater. I'm the Real. Keep your eyes on the Navigator of Snow and Infinite Gray. I rock these boots all year. What a storm got to do with me? Who knows the number of strolls to heaven? Not that I'm thinking on it. The Heavens know my real name. But you can call me Q. Quicker than Q. But, anyway. Certain things a man keeps to himself. Jesus wept. So I don't. The past is for people who like to play things over and over. Me, I'm on to the next song. Listen to my own Head Symphony, to the Royal Stars. The colors, they thrill me, they fuel these legs.

LIKE A MAGPIE

When she comes running over like that. Like an apology. Like she must. When she seems frightened. When she seems wounded. When she seems to have been bullied. In a park. Just like this one. She'd been showing off. Like a high yellow song. Like now. But still. She seems fragile & thin. In the gray cloak of winter. When she should go. Maybe start all over. Where she started. Where it all first sugared. & turned black. Cavernous. Cavity. An exaggeration. Just a little dip. A cut of air. Like a mistake. What we say. Stays out there. What we do also. An apology

is not an eraser. Maybe a filling. A cover. For words spoken in haste. Or maybe. With purpose. With fear & anger. If she should go now. How would her flock know to find her? With a new family? With purpose? With fear & anger? Where she started. Running like that. Like a magpie out of orbit. Dismissed. All that energy. All those slicked back wings. They looked like no wings at all. Naked. Out of purpose. Where should she go? Like a mistake. Where she started. She wants to start all over. But.

Who am I to say? The eye is often mistaken. Or is it the mind? Always eager to interpret. To turn one's mouth. Every witcha way. But what does the eye know? What it seeks. The magpie twirling in the park. Stumbling. Like a liar. The gelled back feathers. Was she caught in the snow? Just seconds. Before. Working to know. What one can never. With purpose? A cover. For words spoken. In haste. & anger. She seemed hurt. She seemed. Like a magpie. Like a liar. But I might be wrong. What my eye saw. Where I started. Just seconds before. One sees a lost thing. & draws a map.

She seemed fragile. Thinner than ever. Preoccupied. Hungry. Like someone had made a mistake. Had they? Always eager. She wanted to start all over. We all want that. From time to time. A cut of air. A cut of the eye. All that sadness. Just seconds. After. Let's erase. With purpose? With gladness? A map. Put your hammer away. If a woman seems fragile. Try to focus. On a magpie. On a blend-in bird. You hardly notice its feathers. Always eager.

A lost thing. Happens. The eye can miss. Just seconds. She seemed fragile. Like a high yellow sadness. Like someone. A lost thing. From time to time. A tiny hole. A little dip. Shield her from air. Like a second. One hardly. Notices. In snow. Without a flock.

THE SUBJECT OF SURRENDER

I write as the son of a _____. My father was a _____ man, a

_____ man, a _____ - _____ man. He claimed to love my

mother, who _____ and _____ and _____ and

_____ until she just disapp_____ _____ ame her? And didn't

the rain fall like _____ and _____ ____ ___ __ _____ dedness run deep? My

three sisters saw right through our fath___ ___ trouble. He ___ _ ___ who hated to be seen

that way. My father had no choice b__ __ _____. At first, they accepted

his anger. Little did my father know __ ___ ___ __ ____ e meaning of hubris. A

man can only _____ ___ __ ____ __ ___ __ of temperament. There

are many _____ o_ ___ __ __ _ _d none of them are love.

It's time, brothers. A woman sits quietly thinking. And __ __ ___ he cold, hard fact of it. Her

turning. Her _____, and her _____, and her _____,

the sly mechanics of her strength gone unacknowledged. My father believed his little yes-

men. His little yes-thoughts. Yeses lead lone men to bleeding. To _____, and to

_____, and to _____. I will pay for what my father passed on:

the _____ and the _____. No, I don't _____

and expect _____. No, I don't _____. No, I don't _____. My

sisters walked off to _____. My father thought he could wreck the house and

they'd clean after him. All those convenient kerchiefs for kidnapped women in cinema? My

father couldn't imagine his hands tied so tightly. No, I don't expect anyone's ransom. My

darling, turn of a woman, I know you will never _____. Let alone read this. I am

_____, I am nothing. I am no one if not my father's son.

Harmony Holiday

Swollen rural lust   and the slow-growing greed of freedom …

some of us wonder what a drum clinic would bloom on the plantation and others of us made
   such radiant
escapes with our palms paving the earth on   rhythm   declension   small mercies

or when she learned her potential children had already been born   electric bodies to trick
the seasons   in olive black balance   flashes of a shoot out in front of a chicken shack
make the voodoo backwards and drummer fires through you like food and hungry
niggas live forever, listen   forever   huddled together in the brush as shucked crops,
listen and otherwise, close one   all the way up to his heart where the bird flew out
from   mumblin' something about through thick and thin, listen   his image   window
told him he was an opinion often   beating the earth lawless as heroes   is   so fun
and phantom   listen

EVERYTHING I EVER WANTED

Some chicken at noon
that criminal ocean
some noon chicken at noon
some chicken come noontime
black potential so scratchy, sun
we mesmerize and keep glamourin
supple blooming tom-tom possibi
hunt something new to our situat
some noon - noon ness tree chic
violence becomes confidence   some of em are polite suicides
the black male leader ones, unaware duty   o lumbar remembers humiliation as
    a large
chicken hung in the memory to spell rebirth backwards, three hurry birds but that was a movie
shoulders back neck free, your co-star is allergic to watermelon, soft song plunged up from the
guillotine as when the joy of opposites is a flesh unto itself

Lee Perry is babbling again   how *I am the sky computer* mute entropy scene in which he go 360 and
Miles, he's trapped in furs   and bitter whispers and
Nat's rage lurks in blind echoes   make showtunes slave roads
We will not be coerced into struggling by our taste for blood and conversation yet

and besides   we don't eat flesh and yet   abidingly I'm everything I ever wanted I
promise   to get light

                                                              I want a land where the sun kills questions™

A WOMAN WHO IS NOT INTERRUPTED

I. Peddling the melted ice of her eyes she had pacified life so well   Yesterday I will be tragic   now triumphant   and   bell them together like   mummy   in the clean air of nowhere

Where is the air still clean ? Where! Where are wives still lovers   and parodies   more perverse than the natural order   order   is also grotesque   like together   forever   for where is forever in the jester's articulation of now   and   there   we were

II. Havoc is vanity and chaos is vanity   we want more time with the child in ourselves and to cross
        back and forth between young and ageless   Did Bill Cosby really rape all those women?

Don't interrupt me.

III. Cake   cake cake cake cake   cake   how a word that outlasts its meaning becomes scenic / music
a bowl of stone fruit in   photo   of   you   without black beauty there's nothing prince charming
                                                    can do

ANGEL ENGINE

He would dig somewhere in a flat field in a large grove of oranges and come up the torn up information as civil suits   as tender warnings   against   his   truth, barbiturates, crispy cucumbers on a bed of heirlooms   soon rape becomes someone's fairy tale   or   maybe we covet terror   well

Bill Cosby is a myth too
A double cross
A double nigga
This suits us

DIMINUENDO AND CRESCENDO IN BLUE

And when the barrel lifts its coil from the mouth of the toy trumpet heiress to her father's love oh love oh careless love   where are you   then   andalusian blood of henchmen   where were you   when papa coughed up his heart in the jail cell and still refused to stop singing praise songs   Plain Gold Ring on his finger he wore   Paradise disorder

Trauma is disgusting   but   euphoria is boring

Every morning a new manifesto on how niggas ain't shit unfolds in the myth or honor killings

Dandelion Root and Leaf
Juniper Berry
Stinging Nettle
Oatstraw
Red Clover

Your heart pumps   you don't think about it
White Oak Bark
Butcher's Broom
Cornsilk
Marshmallow

Seven black churches on fire in our 33rd June
I swore the swoon was adoration but it could have been fear, back then

Anything is endless in blue   and who forgets the   pledges   just to stand there with his fist pressed to his chest   and rescue   and rescue

BE TRANSFORMED BY THE RENEWING OF YOUR MIND

But the saddle is still casual

back in that colony

black in a wall of yellow   we   neglected ourselves to become ourselves to make room for becoming
some negroes bleach our elbows and there are ads for that   in Jet and the cabaret   attitude
Liberia don't be rude but the end of nearness is when honesty becomes cruel or even   useful like
cruises for old capitalist couples who need activities   and proof   One or two   Grace Paley stories
make me feel the safest place and that safety   betrays   latent fears faced then banished fear of
looseness fear of missions   love of fear of men   etc.   for example

another camel in my new mind   another fancy pacing   water

Although it's no longer in vogue to fetishize   our oppression   on sundays
the kids put the mouths of the guns they got for christmas to their lips and act   like trumpets

WILL HOLLYWOOD LET NEGROES MAKE LOVE

Something utter and wordless work us up to the gutted frenzy. Get out of the martyr, black psyche, or I will light you up. Tuff threats are trending like the new sweatshop chucks of thicker souls and swollen metaphors. Where was somebody. Where was her man. Luck, the loa, the lantern of obvious turns. The exact pivot of this shit right here. Like for water I crave an iconic infinity/ photograph of Betty Shabazz and Malcolm, together, lovingly, to be etched in our hearts as far as Sandra Bland and Part Cherokee. Like Spike Lee craved the scene of Malcolm fucking that white woman in an utter way, the reversal arousal or the arousal of reversal or how one man I used to almost know, while married to a black woman back in the states, got high and rented a white prostitute in Belgium. Maybe none of it was from skin/running. Where to? Numbing. I know my consciousness is too high for judgment but whenever I try to force it I come into this sin like saddles and whips and the bent lipped daisies in Clay's deliverance, and I grip the bars of the jailcell my father died in looking past him for a carnival where we might mercy around the ferris wheel of destiny with tambourines and clean shins—mercy mercy me / him, our chains gleaming like rainy/ Ma Rainy teeth, in our chains, our range, our pretense, our ability to fake death in order to escape reason, our will's Overman and treason, had we considered any of them accomplices on the hit list of listlessly spinning souls. Whatever. Mineral Animals told to toil as lamb. And the scroll minded mannerisms of blind griots who can strut speeches past terror as rap sheet amnesia leaping up churchgoer parody leads us to why we marry white dna witness every betrayal on both sides as a betrayal of self. You were shown. And you shown. And shone. Sho 'nuff. As romance plans its debut in torment and then has second suntan-tender thoughts and tantrums of the office piano we sold for dope in their fantasy we play the needed damsel hugging needles and needless of no one. For Clyde Ross, Sandra Bland, Albert Ayler, Alberta Williams King … May a lost god, Damballa, rest or save us, against the love we intend against our lost white children, Black, Dada Nihilismus.

FORGET THE RIGHT THINGS

And a collection of villages going back centuries springs forth in the will

And at first when you're 12 and the singers are artifacts babbling their surplus of sadhappy fiction later
it all becomes cap in his ass   cap in his ass   sacred wicked baptist hero love you so   like the nearly
almost too slow love of   a redeemed sinner with gangster proclivities and can chant anything into
      peak spells

with a joy that cuts so deep it's qualitatively different than pleasure

quit playin / don't interrupt   me

I want us to have new conversations with Kings

Fennel Bitter
wormwood
tea tree oil
nutmeg
mixed in walnut oil

nah like potion but not rubbed in to the grown in feet of any dancer   either   we remembering

Tracie Morris

Epilogue:

4 pm, I wake up. Rocking does it, a lilt.
The picnic sun hits the starboard where I'm looking.
It is a pendulum and soon I'm slumped over,
Dribbling a paper umbrella on navy stripes.
My girl's wearing Jill St. John over her shoulder.
The sail's snapping as softly as a dish towel,
Wicking on the magnitude of a thousand-fold.
The sky's a powder of an early robin's egg.
My ankles are crossed, for luck, I realize. They're bronzed—
I am not wearing socks. For style, not to avert
The spongy indentations of water-logged feet.
Intangible comforts; nothing touches me here.

***

Under the thicket where eggs lay: They found me. Here
I am in a nest, a net set adrift. The lilt
Of singing in mystery, misery in bronzed
Wood. Weeks went, we weary, no lifting latches. Feet
Begin to curdle. Lashes bloom from navy stripes.
So many of us bent like pins never unfold.
A month or who knows what day is, they are looking
To discard remains. These penguins peck robin's egg
Blues of our cataract eyes. Dam of bones over
Which crabs fight to nest as they sink. Dolphins avert
Us, failing to save the half-dead. Flippers towel
Semaphores, Sea Maid, takes all under her shoulder.

Undertows: palavers, patois. New sounds shoulder
People. Our elements, earth's sigils, bring me here:
The alloy of soldered Franco-English. Towel,
Sweat, settle. *Veve, gris-gris*, crossings. Navy stripes
And bloodshed, an oasis center. Their stars fold
Around new freedom, old burdens—we sail. Silt, lilt
Curlicue, quilled debt for Bonaparte's loss. Looking

Black WOMEN / Radical WRITING 197

In paper, they scry bonds; we double-knot. Over
Cups, our hopes and secrets, cradled, broken. Avert
Damning spirits: copper tin syncretism. Bronze
Has the strength of both, double-lustred. My hands, feet
Glow. Sun, spray, *dlo* clay. Seals under a robin's egg.

In time, space we're close ... Shallow sea a robin's egg
Sheen. Anew world, a stone's thrown over the shoulder.
Red, white, blue, from triangle to square. Unfurled, fold
Bills shaping a shoe insole. Pocket change, towel
Wrapped around a baby's bottom. The navy, stripes
Of white on a stellar field of fifty. Me, here

On a sand bar: first-last stop, *encuentro*. Avert
Lingo, ethos, eth/no. My blanched surface, looking,
For renewed hope. Darkness lies in me too. Over
All, my image serves this *país*. Planted flag feet
First, sea breached. Mescla Goddess' Caribeño lilt,
(Afro-Indio), *Ibérica*, tawny-bronzed.

There was a mute, rusty bell tolling for us. Bronzed
Hull dyed: skin, blood. Albumen sea, our robin's egg
Shelter as moonlight conspires with dusk. A towel
Filters oceans. Creates thirst, slakes hunger. "Avert
The sun's glare." Some blind themselves in judgment. That lilt
Of dawn's *Fajr*, from those who speak of this. Looking
For land, as sea urchins change to mammal. A fold
Of devotees, praying in deep blue. Navy stripes
Our mottled dark flesh in salt water. Yet over
There I see earth. We're met in waves. Waving me here
Their hands, guns, motors say "Stop!" We're drifting. Shoulder
To stern. Bow towards Mecca. *Wudu* for wading feet.

A shame for them. I saw the lifting of their feet.
They drop in, kill, fail, leave. Lift in metal, air. Bronzed
Stars greet them. Fall from the sky, they land home. Towel
Off napalm, blood. Some live now as we live. Avert
Mis-i.d'ed. Overseas Chinese. The navy stripes,
Strikes, indiscriminately. Hoa and Kihn, looking
Close enough. Bombing every epicanthic fold,
Taking every word variation for a lilt.

All I built before. The Saigon fall. Just me here,
With this sad rocking thing. A Hooded Robin's egg
That's gold. Handing us from the rich to poor. Shoulder
French burdens of war. White, blue and red bleed over.

Many unwar-war, "conflicts" were lost won over
Since Asia's split, riven rim. Fat Man's apex. Feet
Dig in to flag at Iwo Jima. Since then, fold
Flag's triangles, hands over white gloves. Robin's egg
Ao dai, fretting at the hem, binds, fitting, me here.
At sea, a breeze lifts, a hanging thread. A Thai lilt
Suspends above the waves as we approach. Looking,
Back at lost horizons of salt, that sun. "Avert
The pirates' eyes." Wind-burned women stolen, shoulder
Their sex's unending burden. Husbands towel
Those tears, share threadbare brocade. God's filament. Bronzed.
Re-formed thohng: thin white, red. Double-blues: navy stripes.

When we see the tankers we look for Navy stripes.
Those flags give a chance. Red fields chase us. All over
The sea. Borderless, in liquid state. Docked like bronzed
Baby shoes, dangling at the edge of string. "Towel,"
A pet name, slur, botching mother's "*Tufayl*." Shoulder
To shoulder await. "Nope" Abbott pithies. "Avert
Encouragement." He means: it's his big island … Lilt
Of Africa wafts welcome here from afar. Fold
Us among the dark of *dīn*. White port for me here
Then home where we will not be cast, cast out. The feet
Of Sydney's sails, push us out of this Robin's egg
Eye, cynic cyan peels, occludes. We cry, looking.

Oye: Cuando llegué aquí, I am looking
Por all *los regalos blancos con* navy stripes.
Cubanos recibieron. Pero yo shoulder
Los problemos de color y otros. El lilt
De mi acento no es dulce. Soy over
It. The blanquitos' blue *es blando*, robin's egg
Pero para nosotros es indigo. Fold
Into the other Blacks here. *Saben y* avert
White glimpses. *Los conocen espiritus*. Bronzed
Dioses que son entierran. Made from *bole*, feet

To peak, wrapped in bone color. Solace finds me here
Dimmed storefronts: Saline . . . Over heads, a white towel.

When the ground broke, we waved the white flag, a towel.
That's the Devil. Wind: *priyè*. In cupped hands, looking
For a bigger mass, not a trembling aisle. The bronzed
Coast, Miami. Not the Spain-stolen Caribs. Over
There they say we are not "us". Every robin's egg
Is blue, just as [e]lazuli. Vagaries of lilts
Nan batay yo. White stripes added to their flag, fold
At those seams. See? We're so close. Mother's Black shoulder
Shows under strands of beads we all wear. God, avert
The fight evil's begging. Our *Houngan's* navy stripes,
Borders the kerchiefs he wears. As he sings, our feet
Tap time. Gods' morse to heaven and sea, hold me here.

Long ago, my people wouldn't have found me here,
This rickety European smuggle ship. Towel
Around my hips soften this stacked cage. Robin's egg
Chirps, guides me to San Marino. A navy stripes
This closed sea so on to Adriata. Over
Where Pavlopetri drowned, God gave us his shoulder.
We were turning. The sun captured in ember. Bronzed
Artemision Zeus, bolts us through sure skies. "Avert
The hold." My deck ticket lets me live, swim. Looking
At, what?—a mirage, a map, a legend? A lilt
Of Italian. Messiahs, I paddle towards. Feet
Treading, pull half of me down. But my arms grasp, fold.

Premise:

Tribes amalgam Europa. Loose constructs, we fold
Our differences in parchment. Regents sent me here,
An extension of their crown, their power. Towel,
Chamois, oshibori, I clean their mess. Over
Millennia they say "we" aren't "them". Our gang planks bronzed
Stock from Benin, porcelain from the East. Chained feet
Puff, bellow. To hold, a keep. Race, goods, we shoulder.
Corpus heads. They, delicate as a robin's egg.
We're all at sea for the crowned, fodder. Navy stripes
Across the chest, shots across bows. Death is looking

For us to feed its, our, masters. Greed Gods avert
Blue blood in foul water, chime minor bells… that lilt.

Envoi:

Power lies to avert peace. Christoph Robin's egg
Blue clothes, bronzed Hans Christian's beached mermaid. Fables fold
In tales, an army, navy. Stripes, badges, over
A mast. Towel, sail, one is cloaked in. We're looking
At scale, it's meaning. Waves lilt sound in a shell. Feet
Drag sand. Shoulders tapped with blades; their ships send me here.

Afterword 5

THE CONCEPTUAL AS BLACK RADICAL IMPERATIVE?

When **Adrian Piper** published "Why I'm Not Talking About My Artwork" in 2015 and altered her relationship to American academic life, moving to Germany and starting the Adrian Piper Research Archive, it was a move that on the one hand seemed to reject the notion of the "art star" and its attendant labors of celebrity and developments of cults of personality; on the other hand, the move, so striking in its apparent performance of rejection and critique, seemed to be central to Piper's project of eye-winking subterfuge of everything we, in the this part of the Western hemisphere at least, hold so dear. The homepage for the Adrian Piper Research Archive features a photograph of a girl of about 10 who waves at us from inside of a toy space ship, smiling as she flies away.

She is included in this anthology because of the radical nature of what her painting, video art, and performance have articulated in reaction to the ridiculousness of how "race" is formed and deforms; how it is about one thing one minute (skin color) and about another thing the next (blood); how slippery race's apparatuses of repression are because the thing itself is so difficult to nail down; but, how powerful the systems of repression remain despite these facts, and how devastating.

In one of her most well known works, "Self-Portrait as a Nice White Lady," the figure in the rendering proclaims "Whut Choo Lookin at Mofo?" in a thought bubble above her head. The entire tension in this piece relies on language—that the figure proclaims her Blackness through speech and the title of the work. When shown, the work was walled adjacent to its companion piece, "Self Portrait Exaggerating My Negroid Features." Together the works strip down the racist stereotypes of the angry Black woman and benign whiteness, but they also in their juxtaposition produce a prescient question about the "nature" of "race" in the first place, compelling us in their conceptual unfolding toward a moral imperative to engage the so-called other.

Here's an exciting proposition: Is the conceptual an imperative for Black radical writing? Is it hope that we slip the yoke of race's fried tether and leap into some other imagining?

Yona Harvey's poems escape ordinary legibility by relying on sound and sensation (the sibilant "S"), but also on that space of leap in the turn of the line. These are the means by which she creates new mythology. Why do we need new myth? It's the very impossibility of writing narratives of kinship, female embodiment, eros and trauma that calls it forth. To negotiate the impossibility of these utterances—as in, for example, speaking the intimacy of eros and trauma—through sound and texture is no small feat. But, Harvey's imposition of the polyphonic, like the impossibility of pulling water into shape, provides one of the resonant surfaces, offering up the multivocal in the shapes of homages to the Black women who came before her and the ones who will come after.

Something appropriate in the sibilance in Harvey's poetry, like a snake rising, or a summoning of something, a conjuring or a spell. "Something / about insects / garnishing the frosting?" as a question in the middle of "Even Disasters" leaves me breathless and I am not sure why. It's like I've been taken momentarily to some other place where what I experience is a sensation in my body I've never felt before. Harvey manages to slip the yoke by going deeper into the corporeal, which might be the opposite of the conceptual. I am forced to re-think my original proposition for this section.

Harmony Holiday writes "Bill Cosby is a myth too / A double cross / A double nigga / This suits us." And, this becomes one lens through which to read a concept, but not necessarily, the conceptual in Holiday's investigation of loss, the myth of Hollywood, Blackness as a construction of fists, and the difference between "Black" and "yellow." Look at this syntactically nutty sentence (it's really just part of one):

we neglected ourselves to become ourselves to make room for becoming   some negroes bleach our elbows and there are ads for that   in Jet and   the cabaret attitude

The double cross, or doubling, as material motoring Holiday's utterances means that we are forced outside of the conventions of sense making and into a new relation to meaning—what's on the other side of what we think we know. It's like meaning got caught in the throat and then partially coughed up. What happened to the rest? We neglected ourselves to make room for becoming *some negroes bleach our elbows!* "I wanted to say this more clearly" she writes in "What Jimmy Taught Me," a brutal homage to violence and race and flipping the script, published elsewhere, but then the doubling of language unfolds as the way of speaking best befitting. The very adjacency of "negro" and "bleach" is an opposition that produces a complicated and fraught racial history and presence. We need the doubling to get there.

But, now, we return more directly to form as concept: **Tracie Morris**. In her intricately scaffolded work, "Boating Douzetuor," a double sestina, and also a musical composition (according to the title) for 12 musicians. Immediately upon entering the work we find our gates to hold but we need multiple hands and arms to hold them. Morris's entryway implies the multi-vocal, that sound might come from multiple mouths in order to fully render the work. In doing this, Morris calls us to the possibility of the performance as we experience the written word. It's a thrilling prospect—one encounters one thing and is led toward imagining an extension of that thing in simultaneity.

In bringing the musical composition together with the sestina Morris subverts conventional form as much as she inhabits it. But why? Here's one possibility: "Undertows: palavers, patois. New sounds shoulder / People…" The layering like a bringing together of received language and the invented language of escape to produce subversive speech toward a previously unimagined material world.

Dawn Lundy Martin

SECTION SIX

Claudia Rankine

from PLOT

Submerged deeper than appetite

she bit into a freakish anatomy. the head plastic of filiation. a fetus dream.
once severed. reattached. the baby femur not fork-tender through flesh. the
baby face now anchored.

What Liv would make would be called familial. not foreign. forsaken. She knew this. tried to force the scene. focus the world. in the dream. Snapping, the crisp rub of thumb to index. she was in rehearsal with everyone. loving the feel of cartilage. ponderous of damaged leaves. then only she. singing internally. only she revealed. humming. undressing a lullaby: *bitterly, bitterly, sinkholes to underground streams. . . .*

In the dream waist deep. retrieving a fossilized pattern forming in attempt to prevent whispers. or poisoned regrets. reaching into reams and reams. to needle-seam a cord in the stream. as if a wish born out of rah-rah's rude protrusion to follow the rest was sporded. split. and now hard pressed to enter the birth.

In the dream the reassembled desire to conceive wraps the tearing placenta to a walled uterus. urge formed complicit. First portraying then praying to a womb ill-fitting. she grows fat.

The drive in utero is friction-filled, arbiter of the cut-out infant. and mainstreamed. Why birth the other. to watch the seam rip. to roughly conjoin the lacerating generations? Lineage means to step here on the likelihood of involution. then hard not to notice the depth of rot at the fleshy roots. To this outbreak of doubt. she crosses her legs. the weight of one thing on the next. constructed rectitude. the heavy. heavy. devotion of no.

Ersatz

outside of this insular traffic a woman in pink underlining the alias gender. who is she really? call her. could you. would you. call her. Mommy?

The hope under which Liv stood.

her craven face. it clamored. The trumpeter announced it. She stood more steady then. marveling at her stammering. hammering heart. collecting a so-invisible breath. feeling extreme. commencing. deeper than feeling was.

She wanted what he had been told she'd want. what she was. expecting. Then the expecting was also a remembering. remembering to want. She was filling her mouth up with his—

yet it was not. it was not. the sound of sucking on the edge of sleep. not soft brush of cheek. not the heat of the hand along the neck.

There is a depiction. picture, someone else's boy gorgeously scaled down. and crying out. and she not hearing. not having. not bearing Ersatz—

She was filling her mouth up with his name. yet it was not. it was not.

Liv forever approaching the boy like toddler to toy. the mothering more forged than known. the coo-coo rising air bubbles to meet colostrum. yellow. to blue. to milk. not having to learn. knowing by herself. Come closer—

in front the glare. pools in straining veins making Liv nervy. malachite half-moons on each lobe listening inward. the hormonal trash heap howling back.

There is dust from a field nail. the wind lifts. carries it into available light: not monochromatic. not flattened though isolating. solicitous. soliciting. Come closer—

Once Liv thought pregnancy would purify. You Ersatz effacing. her pace of
guilt. her site of murmur.

Then of course. of course. when do we not coincide elsewhere with the
avoided path? a sharp turn toward the womb-shaped void? now

Liv is feeling in vitro. duped. a dumbness of chimes. no
smiles for every child so careful. so careful.

Ersatz

infant. bloomed muscle of the uterine wall. you still pink in the center.
resembling the saliva-slick pit of the olive. resembling tight petals of rose.
assembling

Ersatz

This. his name was said. Afterward its expression wearing the ornate of
torment. untouched by discretion. natural light or (so rumored

(and it. once roused. caused ill-ease as if kissed full on the mouth.

Herself assaulting the changing conditions, Liv added desire's stranglehold.
envisaged its peculiarly pitched ache otherwise alien to her wildly
incredulous hopes: Ersatz

Ersatz

aware of your welt-rising strokes. your accretion of theme. Liv was stirring (no. breathing the dream. She was preventing a trust from forming. still the bony attachment was gaining its tissue like a wattle-and-daub weave.

Ersatz

arrival is keyhole-shaped. it allows one in the assembled warren of rooms. to open the game box even as the other leans against the exposed from her freestanding. exaggerated perspective.

She is on her way in the corridor unable to enter this room and if she prays to be released from you. as one would pray to be released from tinnitus or welt. boy ridge of flesh raised by a blow.

imagine in your uncurl of spinal arch. her eye your eye. an apparition hushed to distortion. her heart unclosed. yet warped by dullness and pure feeling. her lips but a crease recrossing time. needing a softer tone.

Imagine the prayer itself

Ersatz

unswallowed. swollen within her lips. so grieved:

Ersatz,

Here. Here. I am here

inadequately and feeling   cause of not feeling
more, but stopped. For I   you, what your bold
face will show me of me.   . I have lived, Ersatz,
the confusion in my hea   fusion. Could it keep
you? Could it make tho   ious lines, thickening
encroachings?

Oh, Ersatz, my own, bi   l, what is trapped with
it already owns. I coul   ard you, be your first
protection; but I could   s yet unformed, though
named and craved.

Ersatz,

I am here. And here in not analogous to hope.

See past the birth into these eyes of yours, into what increasingly overstates
resemblance, a semblance one might wish to tuck under, into the sweat of
the armpit, into its wiry odor of exhaustion, remembering the self and any
reflection thereof is never a thing to cradle.

Ersatz,

were I coward enough to have you, child, coward enough to take my pain
and form it into a pulsing, coming round the corner any odd day, of course,
of course, I would believe you the intruder, had intruded.

Provoked, Ersatz, the best I could be would be shivering illness, mucus rising, the loud rush, the sob.

I am made uncomfortable and more so, no warmer, no closer to the everyone you are. Already the orphan, suffocating and overlapping a trillion faces—

are you utterly anywhere. have we, have we arrived anywhere.

Ersatz,

has the rudimentary ear curled open. are you here?

THE EXTENDED ROOT

What comes through the bloodstream to be flushed reduces him to human
even as he does not breathe, even as his lids lower to this thick beginning,
one-third of an inch below the upper surface of her swirling pit. The place
he fills fills with viscid fuel and yet, somehow, does not drown him in the
basement membrane of her own convoluted, veined, capillary network,
her own ocean of wear. Nourished, coaxed forward in the presence of her
whole presence, consequence of her consequences, he is blister of cell, grain
named embryo, a climbing substance perceived, absorbing such intimacy as
she can offer.

    Erstaz   of freehand sketchiness   of hollow form

    anonymous   delineation of bone

    of moody hue dipped in fetal city   oh so neatly laid

    within Liv   estranged interlacing   that she is

Are such seasoned movements truly without desire? Is her organized breath
simply indirection as his face forms in his eggplant-purple landscape, the
likeness of no other? There now is the peculiar sound of blood flowing,
a soft, pulpy *whoosh*, aquatic, the spreading heart-shaped mouth opening
into its initialed script. Darkly stained, untidy eyebrows, a mole, blemish-
shaped. In the mind's eye never abandoned are the supposed markings on
the boy. What is seen before his profile splinters is a face that looks and is
certainly startled.

                    How not to smile out loud?

Erland

how not to? when in utero a fetus heartbeat bounces off. scanned vibrations of this newer soul making a self whole.

how not to? as the chilled gel brings to the screen inked in. black and white. glimpsed. scrutinized. joy.

Erland

considers this ersatz image. abracadabra and like. so like. so liked.

by him whose blush tinges with alleluias. so close to life. his dried lips licked repeatedly.

He's breathing within. but breathless in the red of the ribbon-cutting. a sunrise.

ticking giddy goodness extracting arrival. here. here is a slip of fate from a touch that felt right all over.

Erland

in the volumetric space that is him and spilling to become sun-drenched. impossibly tender.

turning to Liv, love, stands in her way in tinted glasses wanting slowly to be

received by her who feels survival. its pencil movements.

even as she moves through the still traffic debating.

assuaging doubt.

What do you mean, are we sure?
Just because we are pregnant doesn't mean we have to have it.
What would we be waiting for?
I don't know . . . to be sure?
Liv, are you saying you don't want to have this child?
No . . . no, I am not saying anything. I mean I am just saying we
    could still think about this a little. We still have time.
Time for what? This is what I am not understanding . . .
Time to understand how completely, completely changed our
    lives will be.
Well . . . sure it's scary and things will change, but we will have
    our lives plus the baby. Others have done it. How are we so
    different?
Look, if I can't talk to you about this, who am I to talk to?
I'm sorry I'm happy. I think it will be great. I don't know what
    else to say.

COHERENCE IN CONSEQUENCE

Imagine them in black, the morning heat losing within this day that floats. And always there is the being, and the not-seeing on their way to—

The days they approach and their sharpest aches will wrap experience until knowledge is translucent, the frost on which they find themselves slipping. Never mind the loose mindless grip of their forms reflected in the eye-watering hues of the surface, these two will survive in their capacity to meet, to hold the other beneath the plummeting, in the depths below each step full of avoidance. What they create will be held up, will resume: the appetite is bigger than joy. indestructible. for never was it independent from who they are. who will be.

Were we ever to arrive at knowing the other as the same pulsing compassion would break the most orthodox heart.

Deborah Richards

In the dark times
Will there also be singing?
Yes, there will also be singing.
About the dark times.
—Bertolt Brecht

Of course when we arrived he could see what had happened—or rather the evidence of what might have been—on the ground, a black man. Bloody and dead. Where should he be but someplace else? Another route another time another life then.

This is what I have heard about the clutter of lives. It scares me when I look. Soon it will be dark and darkness happens and we will die. It's not a wonder that those who imagine terrible pain and suffering search it out.

I've never seen the men chewing bitter greens spitting them out to chew again. I heard it makes the mind race and thoughts detonate and explode like the popping of firecrackers. Nothing happens from nothing and lives are full of temporariness. Those are the corners where the brothers crow.

Chorus:

Bop bop bop bop
Bop bop bop bop

I don't say
girls cannot feel their
limits
some hold their hearts aloft bloody
bleeding muscle mass
some harden everything inside
out
some are dying to live
many holding on
some stuck like tar
like me

chorus:

just hold me
sister
before you go

I don't say
girls cannot
follow through on Plan A
still a struggle of course
or make do with B
but

let's find the studio
do the work
speak with love
my darling

chorus:

just hold me
sister
before I go

Repeat and fade:
Oh oh oh oh

from READING ALOUD: AN INTIMATE PERFORMANCE (2015)

> *A weaving or web... [forced] to separate as well as being ready to bind others together*
> —Jacques Derrida "Differance"

Dear reader:

I am interested in the product of poetry—that is, both the materiality of the page and the live performance. Before the United States of America, I had dallied in London in the funky spaces, stage lights and lip gloss, so I was guilty of show and tell. Though pleasant and exhilarating experiences I was uncertain.

I write from the accumulation, from the ordinary to the strange, the minute morsel to the gaping maw, from rearrangement to a binding together. But my live performances were safe—I rarely played up the tangents, stuttering starts or false endings.

So, here is a closet drama—a performance written to read privately—and this is a play reading that shifts the background a little an inch or two foreground. To be truly Homeric would require a larger space.

This poem/essay does not answer the question on the best way to read a polyvocal performance text, but asks you instead to engage with it as a grab bag.

This project appeared in *Mixed Blood 2* a journal edited by C. S. Giscombe in 2007. Though now it is easier to make performance from anywhere. I return to the page and I imagine connections to the performances of others including Richard Pryor, Janet Jackson, Dennis Brown, Romare Bearden and Derek Walcott.

I want to be brave.

Yours,

Poet/compiler

Note: <Bold titles> that follow come from Sir Anthony Caro's sculptural work, *The Last Judgement*

Stir Crazy (1980)

The Return of Odysseus (Homage to Pintoric-chio and Benin), 1977 Collage on masonite
112 x 1142 cm Mary and Leigh Block Fund
for Acquisition, 1977.127
Romare Bearden (1911-1988)

The basic plot of mistaken identity
sends the two heroes to a brutal penitentiary
somewhere south. Richard Pryor's presence
and Sydney Poitier's direction means race
is inescapable. Though when I wrote this
in 2007 I thought otherwise. Pryor, as
Harry Monroe, is castigated for his willing
participation in the prison rodeo, though this
is the only overt criticism of him in the film.

However, earlier in the movie, Monroe (and
we) are made aware of his lack of street cred,
as he assumes the mantle of toughness in the
holding cell. He sets his jaw and jerks and
struts in front of us. We don't assume that the
other African American men have the same
issue with performance, as it's as easy as the
clothes they wear.

What is extraordinary, and funny for the
purposes of this film, is Monroe's character's
blatant failure to make a Woody Woodpecker
a crowing cockerel.

A black man without the enamel of toughness
is funny. Equally, a black woman with a star-
shaped nipple ring needs an apron and a good
rubdown.

Don't get me wrong. When I speak of Monroe,
I reflect on my own distance from the streets
of Peckham where, in fact, I was an indoor
girl who read. My brother was different and
would rather be out of doors.

Richard Pryor's stage material enacted
what was engaging because we were suitors
looking for an easy bed and 3 squares. He fed
us the lines and we lapped it up. Don't forget
we, too, could kick the beggar to the kerb for
all our goodness and mercy. Pryor's truth is
the loom that stands between us. He shows us
the back of the "stuff" as well as the front of it.

<The Last Trump>	What fools we are for letting people die before us.
The Homeric style knows only foreground, only a uniformly illuminated, uniformly objective present... the story of [Odysseus'] wound becomes an independent and exclusive present.	A scar is a reminder of youthful incident the product of the fall from a step, the freebase flame, the gore from a wild boar. Its evidence is hard to dispute—you/it/they left a mark. Scratching makes it itch
Erich Auerbach "Odysseus' Scar"	

What about the Half:
The half, the half, the half that's never been told
What is hidden from the wise and good
It shall reveal to babe and suckling
The half, the half, the half that's never been told

<The Furies>

In Janet Jackson's case the exposure is a tear in the fabric, as she steps outside the frame momentarily before she is stitched up. You can lay it open and you can pull it apart but you can't tear down the house.

O.K. she put on her glad rags to strut and gyrate against the Timberlake and then in publicity move bigger than the NFL she is bare-breasted. The beast is released from its cage, but it's pushed back and the standards are locked into place. She could say, what have you done for me lately and could claim, of course, to take control in the rhythm nation but now it's history.

The artist breaks apart and puts together.

<Confessional>

My brother, Anthony, had old chicken pox scars on his nose. It made his face distinctive without being distracting. The scars are experience, like the scars on his heart as he fell down to die on the hottest day of that year.

We could not put him together.

Here I Come
Here I come with love and not hatred
surely goodness and mercy
shall follow I all the days of I life
envy no one no wish to be with no evil man
for there'll come the day
when you'll be whipped by the father's hand

\<The Last Trump\>	*\<Tribunal\>*
Supplemental: • Auerbach, Erich "Odysseus' Scar" Essay taken from Auerbach, Erich *Mimesis: The Representation of Reality in Western Literature,* trans. Willard R. Trask. Princeton, 1953. • Caro, Anthony *The Last Judgement* 1995-1999 Sculpture: Stoneware, wood, steel, brass, bronze, concrete and plaster. From Collection Würth, Kunzelsau, Germany. • Homer. *The Illustrated Odyssey* trans. E.V. Rieu The Rainbird Publishing Group: 1980 *Film Source:* • *Stir Crazy* (1980) Dir. Sidney Poitier Columbia Pictures *Music Source:* • Selected Dennis Brown lyrics	Break a vase, and the love that reassembles the fragments is stronger than that love which took its symmetry for granted when it was whole.... It is such a love that reassembles our African and Asiatic fragments, the cracked heirlooms whose restoration shows its white scars.
	Derek Walcott's Nobel Lecture: "The Antilles: Fragments of Epic Memory" given December 7, 1992

Metta Sáma

50 Shades of White. No. 1: The Holy Bib

50 Shades of White: No. 2: I think, there

50 Shades of White: No. 3: Entitlement

50 Shades of White: No. 4: RAID!

50 Shades of White: No. 5: Build the   uild the Man. Build the
    Image. Build the Man. Build the

50 Shades of White: No. 6: For Go   reated man. White man.
    White man. White Man

50 Shades of White: No. 7. There are only two kinds of people in the world. Victors.
    And ~~losers~~ slaves.

50 Shades of White: No. 8: Stratify & Ratify

50 Shades of White: No. 9: Colonize the land

50 Shades of White: No. 10: Colonize the language

50 Shades of White: No. 11: Colonize the mind

50 Shades of White: No. 12: Catholicism

50 Shades of White: No. 13: Moravianism

50 Shades of White: No. 14: Protestantism

50 Shades of White: No. 15: Anglicanism

50 Shades of White: No. 16: Puritanism

50 Shades of White: No. 17: Evangelicalism

50 Shades of White: No. 18: Pentacostalism

50 Shades of White: No. 19: Missionary-ism

50 Shades of White: No. 20 : A flag is a flag is a flag is a flag

50 Shades of White: No. 21: A Thing is only A Thing when we say it is A Thing

50 Shades of White: No. 22: We are going to do us (& you & you & you)

50 Shades of White: No. 23: What's ~~yours is~~ mine

50 Shades of White: No. 24: Serfdom

50 Shades of White: No. 25: Money talks

50 Shades of White: No. 26: Slavery

50 Shades of White: No. 27: Materialism

50 Shades of White: No. 28: The Marco Polos

50 Shades of White: No. 29: "Discoveries" of already occupied lands

50 Shades of White: No. 30: Literary & philosophical isms

50 Shades of White: No. 31: Ralph Waldo Emerson

50 Shades of White: No. 32: Transcendentalism

50 Shades of White: No. 33: Henry David Thoreau

50 Shades of White: No. 34: Individualism

50 Shades of White: No. 34: *The Last of the Mohicans*

50 Shades of White: No. 35: *Jane Eyre*

50 Shades of White: No. 36: Joseph Conrad

50 Shades of White: No. 37: Mark Twain

50 Shades of White: No. 38: *Gone with the Wind*

50 Shades of White: No. 39: Ian Flemming

50 Shades of White: No. 40: Things are better now aka Focus on the good aka Stop harping on the past

50 Shades of White: No. 41: Melting Pot aka the Mosaic aka the Quilt aka the Salad Bowl of Hegemony

50 Shades of White: No. 42: *Eat, Pray, Love*, etc

50 Shades of White: No. 43: Urban Outfitters, etc

50 Shades of White: No. 44: Imitation is the sincerest form of flattery

50 Shades of White: No. 45: Rachel Doležal aka Clarence Thomas aka Bobby Jindal aka Marco Rubio

50 Shades of White: No. 46: #WhiteGirlsDoItBetter

50 Shades of White: No. 47: #NotAllWhitePeople

50 Shades of White: No. 48: #AllLivesMatter

50 Shades of White: No. 49: The Lone Wolf Narrative

50 Shades of White: No. 50: The Unbearable Whiteness of Being

#WHYWECAN'THAVENICETHINGS

I am terribly aggrieved about Atticus Finch being outed as a racist. I'd rather remember the
good he did. Team Atticus!

Saying that The Khaleesi is an imperialist and a racist is anti-feminist & anti-historical.
Team Khaleesi!

I don't know how to talk about rape. . . I'm gonna go watch *The Cosby Show* to clear
my head

I don't know how to talk about rape. . . R. Kelly's *Black Panties* is my jawn!

I'm not transphobic! I thought Hillary Swank played a hot guy!

I'm not transphobic! I loved *Hedwig and the Angry Inch*!

I'm not racist! I thought those Asian guys were the best thing about that *White Castle* movie!

How can I be anti-woman?! I'm married to one for god's sake!

Am I a racist just because I don't care that my favorite press only publishes white writers?

Do we have to talk about transgender people? Can't we just watch *TransParent*?

Ok so Woody Allen is a rapist just because his "daughter" said he was? Getouttahere

I'm not a rapist but yeah, I think, you know, sex is like better when women are you know,
loose, and well, alcohol helps

Isn't it normal to only want to hang out with people who look like you?

No I don't think it's weird that all but one summer film stars all white casts. That doesn't make
me a racist. But it makes you one for pointing it out

I don't want to talk about race. . . it just bums me out

Why gay people always gotta be up in somebody's face with that gay shit!

Saying a woman is a cunt isn't the same as hating women. I mean let's face it. Some women are
cunts! #I'mJustSaying

But. . . don't you think that saying "I looked into a sea of whiteness" when in fact you were
looking at a room of white people can be construed as racist? I mean, it's a double
standard, like reverse discrimination. #I'mJustSayin

How can it be rape if she like changed her mind after she took her panties off? I mean, she did
get him riled up. She's like a cock tease or. . . something. #I'mJustSayin

Wait. . . Wait. . . What's transphobic about wanting to know if it's still there? I mean we have a
right to know. . . #I'mJustSayin'

Instead of POC complaining about presses that don't publish them they should start their own

presses... But that would be racist too...I just don't know. I don't have any answers. . .

What's race go to do with it?

This isn't about race!

The Race Card is staging a comeback, I see!

It's racist to say that someone is Whitesplaining

It's racist to say Whitefolks

I still don't understand why it's racist for white people to say nigger

That's so gay!

It's too much work to remember all these gender pronouns

I can tell he used to be a she

If she don't want all that attention she shouldn't dress like that

She was asking for it

Black people need to get over slavery

Why do Indians get to have reservations? That's not fair. #I'mJustSayin

Why is everybody so damn sensitive?

So he called her a whore . . . Maybe she *is* a whore. . . #I'mJustSayin

Ugh! All this race talk. I need to move to another planet

Rape is bigger than the individual so we're really doing harm talking about individual rapists

#IJS race is an institutional problem so we need to attack that and not people

She needs to just get over it

#IJS the fact that she can't get over it makes me think she knows she's guilty.

What good is it to keep talking about it?

#IJS just because he didn't hit it right doesn't mean he raped her

It's like beating a dead horse

(Did someone say beat a dead horse? That's animal cruelty!)

Be kind to nature and you'll inevitably be kind to humans

They killed Cecil! This is a sign of the apocalypse!

#JeSuisCecil

We're all the same

#LionsLivesMatter

We're all equal

I'm colorblind

I don't see color! Hey, can you pass me that green marker?

#IJS I don't see what's wrong with a team being called Redskins

Stop talking about it & maybe it'll go away

Race only exists because black people can't stop talking about it

I wish women would get over this feminism thing

Get over it already!

Why bring up a rape that happened ten years ago?

Why can't we all just get along?

Kumbaya my lord Kumbaya

#IJS They must hate white people. They're always talking shit about us

#IJS secretly Black people want us dead

I need a vacation from POC. They're just so negative. #IJS

How can she like have a white lover and be like so obviously racist? #IJS

They bring it on themselves #IJS

We're not the problem! If you just stop talking about IT let IT go away then we can all just
    get along

It's not that I don't want to talk about IT, I don't know how to talk about IT, & when I try to

    talk about IT, you make me feel bad. # It'sYourFault

Genius matters more than women

Ok so he used her as a punching bag so what we got *Kind of Blue* right? #IJS

Man Hahahaha did you see that? He knocked the shit outta her!

Fuck that if she slapped me she'd a been drug by the hair too

It's only fair to the other female athletes that they did what they did to Caster Semenya

Boys will be boys

White folks ain't never gone change

Just let it alone

I would say something about the misogyny but hey, it's rap! #IJS

I don't talk about race when I teach Amiri; it's limiting to his art

It's okay to have just one representative of race, right, because my syllabus is full and I really

      don't want to spend a lot of time on race

Does Chaz Bono have a penis?

Just because I don't talk about race doesn't mean I don't feel things!

I don't even bother talking to women about stuff like rape I mean they so emotional about stuff

I'm cool with you being gay and all but I don't need you talking to me about that shit cool?

He called that nigga a fag! Hahahahaha Punk ass nigga! Pussy ass nigga!

It's not homophobic to say That's gay. . . I mean it's just what people say when something is

      like you know gay!

Black people don't own the copyright on nigga. If I wanna say nigga I'll say nigga. Nigga nigga

      nigga nigga nigga

You can't say anything anymore! People are just t

Kara Walker

SEARCH FOR IDEAS SUPPORTING THE BLACK MAN AS A WORK OF MODERN ART / CONTEMPORARY PAINTING. A TEXT WORK DEATH WITHOUT END: AN APPRECIATION OF THE CREATIVE SPIRIT OF LYNCH MOBS-,

CUT OUT A girls Clitoris
to Make her think better
CARVE OUT HER LABIA TO
CONTROL DESIRE. ME AND
MY RUSTY RAZORBLADE RULES
CLEAN PUSSY, BLACK CUNT,
GOOD WIFE, RESPECTFUL OF HUSBAND
SODOMITE ON THE DOWN-LOW

BOYS WILL BE BOYS, ELECTRIC IMPULSES TO THE NIPPLES, FLAYED SKIN AT BACK, BEACH BALL, SKINNED AND LICKED CLEAN. SAND MIXED WITH SEMEN. SEA SALT IN WOUNDS. SCAR TISSUE LOVELY. LIGHTER FLUID, MATCH. SKIN BUBBLES & BOILS. HOT BODIES WRITHING IN LUST. ROPES SINGE, MUSCLE SINEW TAUT THEN SLACK. LIPS CURLED, EYES BUGGIN', TEETH SINK TO NEW DEPTHS. BONE SUCKING

Consider for a minute the delicious
Crime & RAPED 14 year old Iraqi
girl, Family murdered by U.S. Soldiers
a Simple matter of need. Gang
Rape is always about need.
military Code of honor. Don't Tell, Don't
Ask. The incomprehensible last word
of an invisible child.

She enables White Privelege with her nappy hair and penchant for taking His side of the Arguement. She has "Identity Issues", She has no regard for the Persistant Plight of Negros. She Modifies guilt by her Soothing Presence. No one will understand her Untimely death

Rich Poor kids. Money congeals into Little pustules of Privilege and Blame. Torn Jean Moaning over Starving Rwandan fate. Eurotrash craving for the Free life; A Black Chick, Leather Jacket, Country home and Motor Scooter - All Borrowed on no credit

Copy of a Copy of a Copy of a thing
That Loved, Once to call on ladies
AND wear smart Suits in Juke Joints

The same is the Same is
the Same Black Blood Coursing
through her veins. Dumb and
Inert. Juts his chin defiantly
and woos a new girl

Dons a Black Mask from Savage Africa And Swings from a Vine as if to Say "I can fuck an Ape as good as any man" Struts his lank haired Stuff on Stage Calling his Honey Brown Sugar. Boy, you will never be a god like me.

Just take a deep Breath hold it in, Open up your eyes and peer Through the sight. hold Steady And Work through it. follow through is key. Take aim At your target And blow him a Kiss.

Trying to Draw A Black Man
WITHOUT The Specifics of
Nationality or Price. To look
at him is to commit the
Crime of Policing.
Floodlights Revel in the
fantastic Construction.

Open mouths ready to drink your cum. These young sluts never knew what hit 'em! Look at 'em run! Entering Playland for paint ball fun! the Insurgency is under Control.

Kara Walker

URBAN RELOCATION PROGRAM

SPRAWL

Dirty Children

I AM MORE you than youShit Stained Pants ever feared. I look into your Piss Yellow eyes and KNOW I OWN YOU.

Body and Soul. I Never asked to be born. I Know I am a maniac, man, and when I'm shitfaced this whole fucking world better look out.

Afterword 6

I was in PhD school when I first read **Claudia Rankine's** *Plot*. I read the poems over and over but there were sections of language that eluded me, the book forever opening each time I read it, a little more, revealing its logics to me in the eros of the strip tease. In this case, the strip tease of a kind of loss. *Plot* is brutal in a linguistic way—how it occupies language in seemingly disjunctive manners, the use of "Ersatz," for example, as a proper noun but one that cannot escape its denotative meaning: "an imitation," "an inferior substitute." It can be blunt force as in the piece titled "The Dream Play": "Where's the baby, he asks. / I haven't got it, she says." Or it can inhabit theoretical gestures: "Where we ever to arrive at knowing the other as the same pulsing compassion would break the most orthodox heart." How to traverse these linguistically divergent landscapes?

Plot grapples with the body (re)formed or (de)formed by pregnancy as much as it attends to the question of narrative, suggesting in an oblique way that the birth urge is not our own. What I love about Rankine's layering of multiple registers of speech is that fearlessness with which these utterances break the rules about what a poem is. Linguistically, *Plot*, refuses to be confined. It is this playfulness in speech that we might find an anchor for Rankine's later hybrid works, *Don't Let Me Be Lonely: An American Lyric* and *Citizen: An American Lyric*. The excerpt included here foregrounds an unsettledness, a way to speak without foreclosing the subject who speaks. And, this is one performance that radicalizes language outside of the already known.

Deborah Richards performance "written to read privately" is part play, part theory, part private utterance, part Homeric homage, and exists somewhere in an indeterminate in-between—not hybrid as much as "grab bag" within an "elusive present." Formally speaking, Richards does with form what Rankine does with language. Richards dissociates us from any expected approach to what it means to tell a story, or to enter the discursive world of meaning making.

Meaning, of course, is readily available to us in objects and in the familiar use of words. If someone says, "cot," we imagine that thing in our minds. We know what cot is for. But, we live in a present moment where the meaning of actions and the question of "truth" are both contested. What does it mean that professional athletes choose not to salute the U.S. flag? Which media outlet is reporting without evident political bias? Is sexual harassment real or are people simply exaggerating normal interactions? Those of us who have one answer to these questions cannot communicate with those who have other answers. One reason writers like Rankine and Richards are so important is that they create alternate, non-dichotomous languages, syntaxes, and story rules that force us to ask alternate questions about meaning. First, we have to learn new rules, new sense making, and new narrative structures, and in Richards' case, a whole other rationale for the written project and what can be done on the page.

"Bop bop bop," sings Richards' chorus, reminding us that we're inside of a shadow world. **Metta Sama** in "A Very Abbreviated History of Whiteness" and "#WhyWeCan'tHave-NiceThings" tears up the technological moment's linguistic shorthand as a way to critique how white privilege and power haunts. Whiteness is a solid thing, a standard, or is it? That's one thing that Sama gets us to think about in her anaphora that begins each line, "50 Shades of White," a play on the power play of the BDSM enacted in the popular erotic novel, *50 Shades of Grey*. In Sama's work, however, what unfolds is a way of looking at whiteness and white privileges that exposes rather than teases; it lays bare the underpinnings of what glues our society together and makes it so we continue to be on opposite sides of a giant gulf. What is real? What is ersatz? How do religion and literature support this breach in reality? These are the questions that Sama's persistent utterance address.

In "#WhyWeCan'tHaveNiceThings" Sama uses what appears to be borrowed language from social media updates and posts to bring into focus in catastrophic, reduced, internet speak. She traces the hashtag #I'mJustSaying (and others) revealing a strange logic that the hashtag itself allows for—a kind of speech that holds up patriarchal and race privilege. The accumulation of these voices is what holds the work in a stark cultural mirror. And, it is this mirror that the work, also, seeks to shatter. The anxiety of this kind of speech is laid bare as well—the fear, the insecurity, so much so, that what Sama does is produce a sorrow. Not an empathy, but a sorrow that whatever has been on the other side of politically correct protocol is a bursting into oblivion.

The question as to whether we must remember or how we must remember in order to enter a new future brings us to **Kara Walker's** provocative work, particularly the postcards we've collected here. Walker's is a wild imagination, especially insofar as it is able to access the brutal violence that the west has forced onto black women. If there is a more pronounced articulation of how that violence enters the present consciousness I do not know it. Walker does not flinch. Instead, she refuses to turn away from the insouciant disregard of Black female humanity. That disregard is, and has always been, enacted as sexual violence. Walker reminds us of this, and when she does it, it's almost as if she has a special access into the mind of the oppressor. A channeling. A fragmentation of self. A coercion into the unsecured realm. These postcards, handwritten variously, break all the rules. They break all the rules because they understand something that we often cannot bear, the weight of it too heavy for our tiny, soul-like lives to carry.

This is a book of Black women's writing, but we include Walker here because her work interacts with the tension between the image and language. In the case of these postcards, the written rendering is an image, and what it renders is the ghosts of shadows, hauntings so painful to experience that our most peripheral vision becomes blocked, blind. If this is a book about the future, and it is, then these old presences need to be exposed, breaking the rules of decorum—Black or otherwise, in order to do so.

Dawn Lundy Martin

SECTION SEVEN

Renee Gladman

from MORELIA

[nearing the end of a journey]

The problem of "in what city, what district" is a minor one. Just look at the sky today. It's covered in lace. Also, I've noticed something about the wallpaper in this room, which, at long last, is not on some anonymous floor of a hotel but rather is in a sunny room of a townhouse in the secret city, where I have stashed myself. I want the scratches and bruises I've incurred to fall back into my skin before I complete my original task, which was really just to go somewhere and read, to escape Mr. Otis and to read. The wallpaper repeats the map of a place, and I'm lucky in that it's somewhere I've already been. It starts with Sespia, the story tells me, the story that is not yet written. The sky has a look about it that says, "yee," like recycled toilet paper, like it's really tuned into the times. I think my happiness is climate controlled, and that's why I'm still undressed. Even though the room is artificially tempered, it's a climate all the same. I'm torn between the artificial indoors and the real out, as both are approximately equal in temperature. Staying in will allow me to be myself, but going outdoors might lead to answers. I go out. I hesitate. I don't go, but soon I will. I have to make some decisions first: how will I introduce myself should I come upon a person, and, more crucial, how will I not get overwhelmed by all the numbers I'll see? I will want to go after every one of them, every house and store sign, which only will take me farther from the specific numbers I need to locate. I have to remember that mine are different from the others. I have two sets of three, in this order: 8-7-4 and 9-7-6.

The first is attached to a place and the second to a person. I dress in linen and cotton to indicate that I'm free; I'm a person in the world. I gather my things—bag and gun— and as I near the door I see it: the book. Then I think something that does and does not belong: somehow in this life we have managed to fashion only an inside and an outside with nothing in between, and it's because we can't always pick the one or the other that we get lost and weary. I look at the book again and wonder if it could be our remedy, if I should go into *it* instead of out this door. Yet, having dressed so concisely for moving freely about the city, could I now, all of a sudden, switch to a burrowing-in persona, because that's what you need to "enter" a book. To get "in" you need to dig and get skinny and lose your voice; but you don't need to go outside, which is just the repetition of everything. The clock says go.

You go, but going is like staying where you are, just with your eyes facing downward and your body still. I went. I came back. It was reading. Yet, it wasn't so much reading that I wanted to do. Or, reading first, then something further, like walking. Could syntax become a city? It could, but I'd have to forget myself. I wanted to, but I couldn't due to the numbers and the undecipherable sentence and Sespia. Onward, I thought, standing on the transom of the door, the verge of the street. So, there *is* only in and out. The news was discouraging. Yet I had to move. But, at least I could stay fat and scream all I wanted, which now I was doing, but into the palm of my hand. Beneath the noise was the sentence.

Why was that first word so familiar? Was it the same "Bze" I came across in a medieval text on architecture I studied some summers ago in the soft city? A "Bze," which was a mechanism for counting time, something that would only ever be seen in the lower regions of a castle. To see a "Bze" you'd have to be a servant or a member of clergy—if my memories are intact. And didn't someone once grab the "Bze" from the wall and run across a field, soon to be gunned down, soon to spark a war?

The world had grown quiet. I felt my real journey could now begin. I could now head out into this city, which I had changed by first treating it as a book. I wasn't walking in the book anymore but I wasn't not-walking in it either. That is another thing that happens when one has read: the world changes. I stood on a street that flickered, in a mind flickering between scenes of attack and scenes of leisure, in a street that was both a dense street of traffic and one nested in a suburb. I preferred the urban one but felt I would be safer in the other. How did you walk as if you were in both? The sentence would lead me to Sespia if I allowed it to, if I let myself occupy the space farther along its length, where I'd discovered that address: 874, stiasadern. But, I couldn't shake the strangeness of making the leap from "Bze" to 874, stiasadern, without reconciling that middle ground. It didn't seem possible that if one went directly from "Bze" to 874, stiasadern, that this would be the same experience as starting at "Bze," moving through a series of stations (still opaque but eventually readable?) and then arriving at 874, stiasadern. I was re-drawing the map, and I didn't want to do that, because it would no longer be the map of Sespia. I would always be somewhere else. Yet, this was a problem particular to the sentence. There was another problem that was the problem of city space, of physical environments. And I was only staring from the window.

KAHLIL JOSEPH

I began the day in a moment of thinking that the most important thing I would ever write would be the thing I needed to write right then, and this was strange because I wasn't yet sure what it was I wanted to say though I was full of the urgency to say it. It would be the most important thing I'd ever written about my living, about what I saw and what I understood in that seeing, through all the adjacent objects, and what words I would give to that experience and who I would call out to to say "this is what, this is how." But the thing I was writing wouldn't be the thing I needed to say until something transformed in me, turned on or closed down, in the way the experience I wanted to write about became the thing that needed to be written. It was a sudden slowing down, and this happened despite the rain outside. It was raining, I'd had to walk through the rain. And when I arrived I didn't come to the experience immediately. I moved slowly through the exhibition. You never know what's going to happen to you and you don't always know you're carrying something with you that may have accumulated in your walk or over the day or over the past five years and it would be impossible to know the size of the thing once you realized you were holding it: it's massive, larger than the building you're standing in, it's minute but feels like fire in your hands. You don't know, you're touring a show at a museum. And I was trying to stand outside of the writing of this writing so that I could feel what was coming, so I could connect the rain to the feeling that something important was happening and, in the moment of it happening, I wasn't happy. I was uncomfortable; a car had nearly run me over. It had rained as I was walking; my blond leather boots were wet, and this wasn't how I wanted to capture the experience. I wanted to begin already inside the thing I was holding, which was separate from the weight you may or may not have been carrying when you entered that room but most probably were carrying because at the very least someone had almost hit you and you had to throw your body to save your body and this was something that darkened the space inside you, or rather blasted the space with a hard terrifying light, so bright and noisy that you went a little dead to withstand it. I couldn't name all the times I went a little dead and was certain that there were many times of my going dead without my even knowing it, because all day small things happened and sometimes they were just about being in the wrong place at the wrong time but sometimes they were about someone saying no to you because you were black or rather because you weren't white and maybe this was on your mind because of the city you were in when the car nearly struck you, when you were walking in the rain outside, when you entered that museum. But when I enter a museum something quiets in me and this has everything to do with architecture, so, though I might have been carrying something that weighed on me and was massively miniscule, I was in a kind of structure that talked to me as soon as I'd entered it, so entering was like, "Hey Renee, what do you think," and the question would trail off because it was as if the space was open to whatever I might say. "I think…" I'm sure I began to answer somewhere in me where I wasn't a little dead and let the ellipses hum. You were always answering what you thought in how you moved across the floor, in how your blood pounded in your body, as you moved your hand toward something you'd never touch, inscribing labyrinths in the air, and somehow it's the not-touching that leads to your sublimation. It was strange how I'd been standing in place for a while, just gazing at these images, a composition of figures I could never have imagined, and something was being undone in me, but for a long time I didn't know it. Maybe I was pretending to take in the show, going through the motions of gazing without yet gazing. But gazing somewhere where what I saw was exactly what I needed to see to unload the thing I was carrying, which, in this case, I knew I was carrying, because of the car that had nearly hit me and how this filled me with rage. I had been standing in the dark gallery where Kahlil Joseph's Wild Cat was playing on three screens brought together in a triangular form, where the triangle hung between the ceiling and floor, and beneath the triangle, on the floor, in its own triangular shape, was laid out a mound of dirt. The screens were like a triangle tipped over, lying on its side, so that when you were standing there at the threshold of the room you looked at what would be the bottom of that tipped over structure; and extending from each side of that rectangular shape, which formed the floor (knocked over) or the back of the triangle, was another rectangular screen, these two met at a V on the opposite side of the room. This was Kahlil Joseph's presentation of his film Wild Cat, but the screens were translucent, so none of the images landed. There were three channels and three screens but the screens were like the surface of water so this was a different kind of viewing than I was used to. Each image seemed to fall into the one behind it. I had been standing in the back of the gallery, at the V, when I noticed I wasn't breathing or I was breathing but so slowly, with so much distance between breaths, that this breathing was like making a tunnel in the space. I was standing at the back of the room and at the end of the tunnel when I finally saw what I was seeing (the tunnel had formed as a consequence of my seeing but I didn't know this yet: you've walked a mile out across a field but because of what you're carrying you think you're still sitting on that bench but you can't sublimate until you realize you aren't there anymore). I didn't know how to begin describing what these images were because I didn't know how to compose what I'd seen rather than merely list what was there. How do I account for the sound accompanying the images on the screen, a music that was like tones being shot out of something, let loose in an airless room, a sound that gathers and slows down but refuses closure: it pushes you, farther into the tunnel of your experience. I'm saying "tunnel" but what I mean is something wall-less, a *containing* that doesn't enclose yet forms around you anyway; a feeling that becomes a place or an awareness of the mind changing, something clearing out but what's vacated putting a kind of pressure on you, pulling you long and back. I hadn't seen what I was seeing before and I didn't want to know whether it was real; I didn't want to know the story behind these figures: black men in cowboy hats, riding horses and bucking on bulls, black people in the stands watching these events of the men, black women in dresses that seemed centuries old, moving their bodies like birds, two black youths riding a tractor or dune buggy, one of the youths in a fancy white dress; the girl in the dress later walking through the rodeo, everything dusty, dusk everywhere. I couldn't put names to what I was seeing. I didn't understand the time of these figures. Some of the faces were old or tired, staring into the camera, or looking out the front door; in one of the shots, there was a television, but mostly this was a landscape without technology. Their clothes were important; fabric was time and time seemed to dislocate these people. And I was in time but as experienced through a tunnel where something still bounces off your body and you realize you're being consoled. "I am being consoled," I felt in my body and was stunned and sat for a long time in the wake of those words. These figures, their shadow-states, their floating in and out of each other was taking care of something that had never been touched, and the day where it was raining and a car nearly ran me over began to recede, being replaced by a deep unknown. I didn't want to know who these people were; I was beyond asking if they were real. Yet, in trying to say what was most important to my living about what I was seeing, I needed to get at the other presences in the room or in those projected images or in me or in the space between me and those things, in something becoming disclosed, something clearly outside of language, because I had been writing for fourteen hundred words and I still hadn't come close to this reckoning. It wasn't the fact of seeing these scenes, shot in black-and-white, shot out of time and beyond time, slower than time and breath; it wasn't the story of these people riding bulls, living some rural, impoverished life—these were not what had opened me into a tunnel; my body some form of perception. It seemed to have something to do with the making of the film itself, taking blackness and wringing all whiteness from it,

whiteness as a way of seeing, another thing I carried, and
in the slowness, in the silence, a pattern discloses as if,
just in that moment, it has emerged out of the earth, as
yet written or comprehended, without value, judgment,
category: not denied because not graspable

Tonya Foster

> be low be lack be ridge and grudge
> be longing be sotted be ramble and hold
> be come and go; be rim and ram the ball into the basket.
> be ram-in-the-bush important
> be stung be ache be ring
> be reft and reach over
> be attitudes of bee sting
> be head nigger in changes of the light night's brigade
> be moan and own ow!
> below beehives, the haves' harvest
> s/he be   tired

Look back at them;
see if they are looking back
at you and yours.

To know is to be a spoon in a kitchen drawer, wearing expertise.
To know is to be a spoon, bent   burnt, crystalline skeins, shining held hollow.

To know is to believe.
To know is to be made infinitive—grammar and psychology.
To know is to be? This is a math of blood, a math of bodies, a (map of the math of bodies).

To know is to be conqueror, to be light, infiltrating, descent.
To know is to be boundary, bounded—city/lover s/he'll leave.

To know is to become partial, to partition vegetables and fruit—
              To partition the s/he s/he might have become from the s/he s/he is,
              To partition the s/he seeing from the s/he that's seen, made up/over.

To know is to parse you from what you thought you were—my nigga is…
To know is to parse you from what you're told you are—this nigga that…

To know is to be inhabited—this cell of radiant waiting.

What s/he know 'bout
silence? How it settles in
a throat like *s/wallow?*

> How it settles like
> swallowing water or seeds
> they say might take root.

> How it settles like
> feet into the dailyness
> of their own falling.

What she know 'bout
be coming to mind at times
s/he thinks she don't think:

how her throat tightens like a branch on which cataclysmic swallows roost.

How her throat tightens tracks, through slow syllables, memory's algebra:

geometry of a park pool—a boy presses her twelve-year-old head—
geometry of an air-filled-melon—beneath water with deft hands

she struggles against. Someone she can't remember sees her thin arms as
she struggles against his hands, their struggle breaking the water's skin.

As if to make plain the difference between a thought and a need,
as if to map the shifting climates between words and bare knuckles,

As if to show her knowing wasn't needing, he says he was playing,
    his young voice filled already like a snow globe with the coming winters.

As if to show her the winters between words and his budding fists, he laughs.
    His young voice fills all her thoughts of water, wades in each new syllable.

Yesterday swarms in
the m/arrow of (y)our thoughts (,/.) as
        s/he lies t/here (,) sleepless

        yesterday swarms in.
To eat or not to? Then what?
She clears her throat.

IN TONGUES

(for Auntie Jeanette)

1.
Because you haven't spoken
in so long, the tongue stumbles and stutters,
sticks to the roof and floor as if the mouth were just
a house in which it could stagger like a body unto itself.

You once loved a man so tall
sometimes you stood on a chair to kiss him.

2.
What to say when one says,
"You're sooo musical," takes your stuttering for scatting,
takes your stagger for strutting,
takes your try and tried again for willful/playful deviation?

It makes you wanna not holla
silence to miss perception's face.

3.
It ain't even morning or early,
though the sun-up says "day," and you been
staggering lange Zeit gegen a certain
breathless stillness that we can't but call death.

Though stillness suggests a possibility
of less than dead, of move, of still be.

4.
How that one calling your tryin'
music, calling you sayin' entertaining, thinks
there's no then that we, (who den dat we?), remember/
trace in our permutations of say?

What mastadonic presumptions precede and
follow each word, each be, each bitter being?

5.
These yawns into which we enter as into a harbor—
Come. Go. Don't. says the vocal oceans which usher
each us, so unlike any ship steered or steering into.
This is a habit of place and placing a body.

Which choruses of limbs and wanting, of limp
linger in each syllabic foot tapping its chronic (c)odes?

Tonya Foster

NEW ORLEANS BIBLIOGRAPHY

In language   In landscape   Inscape   In language   In landscape   Inscape In

Only after taking *in* my mother landscape (along with the voices of that place)—

a girl who looks like her father is born for luck, alcohol, Algiers, alligator, Amazing Grace, Amelia, Angola, Atchafalaya, Aunt Noni, Aunt Sister, Azerine, back a town, bayou, because her daddy died or left, because the first-born baby died, beignets, bitch, Butsie, café au lait, Calliope projects, Canal St., Cardella, cast iron, catching coconuts, catching sense , cayenne, Clio St., cockroaches, "comb them kitchens," Congo Square, cornbread, courtyard, cousins, CPT, crawfish, creole, dark, darker, dark-skinned, daughters, dead-end, Desire projects, desire unmet is desire multiplied, dirty rice, Dorothy, Elysian Fields, Erato, etouffe, Euterpe, Ezekiel, Father John's, file, first-born, first-born done died, fleur de lys, flood, "for true?" front porch, Galvez, Gerttown, "gimme some," girl, "girl, gimme got shot," "git up in here," "God don't like ugly," good hair, gran'ma, grandpa, grandpa done lost his mind, grief, grief grown rooted and wild, grief like dirt, hard-headed, hard-hearted, her mouth don't know no Sunday, high yellow, holy ghost, hoodoo, "how sweet the sound," "how ya'll doin'?" "how ya mama and 'nem?" I, I, I, "I ain't playin' wit chou no," jacks, jambalaya, jazz, jumpback, jumprope, Katie, kickback, kick your ass, kitchens, kitchens on your neck, knick-knacks, kool-aid, lagniappe, lakefront, left, levee, leveraging, light-skinned, lighter than a paper bag, Louis, St. Louis, Louis XIV, Ma Belle, ma dere, magnolias, make groceries, Martin Luther King Blvd., Melpomene projects, memory, mental ward, Mississippi, Mississippi bridge, Mississippi river, Miss Myrtle, Miss Tit, Moreal, morning, mosquitoes, mourning, mudbugs, muffeletta, nappy-headed, neckbone, neutral ground, nutria rats, "nobody likes a bone but a dog," NOPD, not luck enough to keep a body strong, okra gumbo, out front of town, oysters, pecans, pickled pigs' lips, piss po', po' boys, porch monkeys, potholes, quadroons, quarter, quiet, rain, rain through the living room windows, red beans, red bone, Rev. Profit, rice, river, river, river, roux, rue, Saints, sadity, sassafras, Satchmo, screendoor, semen, seventh ward, snowballs, "speak the word to me," spit on the broom to stay out of jail, St. Charles Ave., Stronger Hope Baptist Church, superdome, swamp, tambourine, Tchopitoulas, tender-headed, tender-hearted, tender-roni, Terpsichore, thought, "throw me somethin' Mister," Tippitina's, "trouble don't last always," uppity, vagina, Virginia, voodoo, wade in the water, water, wishes go the way of sweepstakes, "where y'at?" "where you from?" woman, wrought iron, "yo maw, yo paw, yo greasy, greasy gran'ma," "you ain't nothin'," "you thought like Aunt Hannah who thought catshit was banana," Xavier, Zataran's, Zulu, zydeco, Amen

—was speech possible. Only after taking in my mother landscape was speech possible.

Julie Patton

TIMES SQUARED

Indicative of one of *the waves*
Our interests merged over time…

My mom *picked up on* my fascination with pen & ink—writing or *semblance* of it, sort of short
hand movement, digression and rest (sPeace, sPace).

She sailed in the night of such… Rhythms, pregnant migrations, squalls

She never let go of her "hand" & neither did I.
She would say "You have a nice *hand*"
A complement for anyone on the receiving end of this notion of hand
How handy she was with everything!
Shorthand for sweeping trash into corner, tacking fabric onto disobediant furniture, swooping
hair away from her face.
"Black Jackie Kennedy" someone called her. Or scald'd. For her "wide set eyes"
And *fine brown frame*. Shorthand.

Got her jobs in places where peers delight'd in handing her the *negro pencil* which dated
    the *flesh colored crayon*. And made love to paper in Spanish if you let it.
Picasso. Rudiment.
Her grocery lists were pepper'd with Gregg's Shorthand. Which also hit me in the face.
High school. *Look like nerves we were graded on*. My typing score never exceeded 28
I hunt and finger peck to this day. And write like a drunken boat. Incoherent
Waves I fail'd to decipher the very next day.

Beautiful hand writing. Poetic deaths. As long as one was *copying*

DNA. We never discussed what was obvious. Her love for dancing
Across sheets. Figures. Bifurcating. Rings. Eyes. Sob—little boats
Upturned and sailing swoopslip
Letters hinting at *mother tongue mother hand mother dishes ink land rag nib serif*
Shortchanged for *the nerve of…*
Mom, I burned my bridges with Gregg soon after high school. That is, all but
but and *and*

Connector points. Preoccupied with each other's sense of line—walking
bass—and paper teeth cool masked language. My mother acknowledged

As I was saying the conversation with Virgie inking
eyes never broke off staying the better art of a letter deepening
(illegible) hand mumbles scats scales scats elision
love imprecise as pigment cursive
mambo of blur
black like song
gaps just saying (000...) *I am*
in each of these pieces one way or
mother
009
slant speech speed
vertigo down the ax
us black lines drought
all that can be seen
of nation I's
       'ndia
       'talia
       'done ease ya paper
state of "tooth" and Soho deckle edge
back in the dat
cut off
paper strip

ease
tension

my word!
scribble scrabble

ready for closeup

SKETCHES BY VIRGIE EZELLE PATTON

Julie Patton

IN PROGRESS

IN PROGRESS...

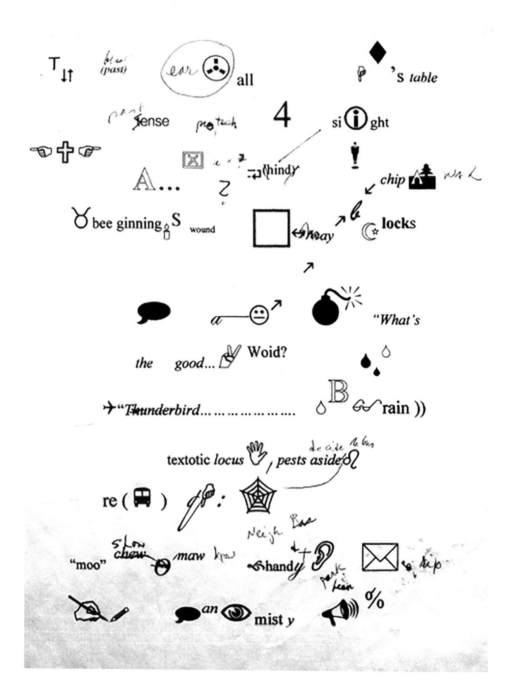

Akilah Oliver

THE PUTTERER'S NOTEBOOK

Unforgivable violence
something dropped   Un   touch/ inhabit a queered more plural
I'm here, sickness face. Theresa Hotel, that collapse a trace
Shinning, a prince Castro, all of us fatigued, this century   I as in

When is the "tipping point"

New York I've been been back many times sacred heart been back been back Many times
Eluding best time then, conquered, then hairdressers   remembering smell Burnt alterity
I'll never leave you no matter what   when I saw you your sad
I architecture shook, house a dangerous weave, house a dagger a dagger a minimal yes
yes, it mimic

Why when I say "outside of history" I mean anything I mean to reconstitute an Other

Why when I say "belated beloved" I infer a politic, I reference a street sign on the bad side of town So when I say "strangers fnd me sexy" I am not an absent erotic seeking refusal

So when I say "we haven't talked for a minute" I mean code for "strawberry letter twenty-two" or hello Richard goodbye Boulder

If when I steal "you can't fall down in this town" I have discovered human bones in the landfill

If when I say "and all the little denunciations" I've solved a puzzle

Therefore when I say "now that I'm done with being dead" I have declared an alternative self

Furthermore when I say "a red flatbed truck just drifted past my window" I am documenting how pleasure

not entirely arbitrary

of

of common corruptions of lovability

loving

lovingly lovely

I attempt history making

Which begs the question: what is history?

And then to add, the vocabularies that come in sleep. Or to sit to stare. To stare

Earlier and am thinking

People commonly think of me as two

That is the job then, to sit and contrive. The making of figment

As if lateral lines and neo-nationalism were essentials, the world
tipped around an image of you I create on the train

collecting ruins.   This is an epistemology of forget, or then
curiously I am a system of relations, later

Devotion.   Los Angeles,   treacherous, a surface recedes
A narrative of whoever collects shorelines

a disassociation between forms   You, my ongoing query
what do you dream, we who are at opposite ends
Of   a myth of lineage, requiring negotiation
All these abstractions in my teeth, I could tell you stories, you skiver

For example: I am seduced, or, I offer me as a proposal
We don't recognize ourselves as vulnerable, landing here in the airport, I hide at a newsstand
for hours, waiting for the terror to fade

My raw sexuality watches horses sleep in Jersey I attempt I, to
de-gender violence, to know God. I remember your body asleep in aspersions
you told me about a childhood in Minnesota and I thought of the movies.

And I thought of how tough it is to learn to read
knowing ultimately I would betray you. And I thought of death, again, as a way
to look through funny mirrors.

Or the tightrope and the angelic failure to catch you. But
even now, when it's all sad and done
I miss the momentary
frail vision, the chaotic bodies in hip black   shimmering down
Bedford, like apparitions, like liars. I had expected to find allies there

Akilah Oliver

Then I command the stage again, as embodied activism this time a gone time from a before
then if so therefore without pretense nothing or used, this phrase, this constituent, this color
lily I've ever seen before, a calculated blue

thinking
I had created metaphor when I said "I can't see" they thought I meant I can't see them thinking again them thinking again to dream a portal through which to bow before walls, a little mystery. Stare

Then
determining
one is lonely in sleep, thus remedies. or then, fences. then questions for the Prime Minister
What we expect, a paradigm of fall
My kitten scratched

not as in love with [   ] as previous, though suspiciously like folly, this insistence on

In love with, not only this, but how we block mirrors, stage ourselves in reference to not, one
another, or declarative subjects
Situational emphasis, shadows, evacuated narrator: no closure, just this

I was considered a last resort I was considering going there, over by the Lost Boys, but I didn't know how to speak of a genocide that wears my face, a calm, & then temple, anyone please, we used to pray like desperados then silence as charade to lay upon

Akilah Oliver

I as navigator fail her petrochemical beauty on both sides of the threshold a light, a city, an artifice in relation to other species failing always as if waiting were choice or desire, a badge to wear, to dress up in, to spit out again I, a result of my own resistance

This inadequate gesture, to perform our lives for the grand old miscreant, History

As in, what happens to a community, when centers of culture dissipate? Penny Lane is in my head. J is in India, I'm dreaming next to S. S is dreaming inside water, F is on an airplane, T is figuring it out today, how to blow this town's curse, V's getting nervous, I'm telling you stories Stories more lush than when I was undead. [the best way to leave] to drive out without goodbye

Akilah Oliver

This body, a public adornment to speak of in relation to scale

in the charlatan's clothes I collect epigraphs to mark this form as
urgent sinking, replicable & twisting like nightmares seeking solitude
nostalgic in postcolonial light I am not seeking

ungrounded for so many refused seasons a
bargaining chip between us

This body

Who we are when we are not love has always caused us shame. Not love I scarred narrative
I gave away a plot a plot I as spectatorial gaze posit a stripped subject, a migratory Other to
eroticize my loneliness
There are few precautions we can take to protect our hearts
those overdetermined biographies from where I construct an enemy of my broken fingers that
rehearse "forget" "retraction" "messianic""thinking""punitive""I love"

As soon named as soon strangeness of living

———————   ———————

In other words, leave me alone motherfuckas cause I'm in a position of trust and responsibility then besides, I can't afford to be off my ass. And then to sea. The underlying violence of Love sticking its pubescent head out

It's Sunday. What happened to Saturday. Is the vague discovery of a 'missing' Saturday a real thing if there will just be a next Saturday?

Was I ever something to believe in?

In which pocket did I leave that "I"?

Is "I" ever a thing to miss, a personage to mourn, if the "I" still lives in the physical body and is capable of re/articulation? If it desires mirrors? History? Or and then narrative sensibility If the mirror breaks one can buy another. Consume then recreate then resume an/other I. History I curse thee, to not be borne in mid-twentieth century garb, a French feminist theorist laboring over 'new ideas' to bounce the vernacular mind.

I could stay here, become fervent in the way I hold the coffee cup, one broken finger stuck straight. Lisa is in Queens growing fat with baby cats in masquerade underfoot.

I don't see her this time or ever really but drunk
I remember one night with Jesus on the upper west side, trying on extensions. It is in part that desire to be fully engaged, performing against mirrors. Pretty pretenders crowding the

how much time is enough time? all i think i feel i've stolen from someone who's already said it before. as if the mind were a doubt. this is the thing: i'm trying to understand how much i loved him [her] [them], and how badly i expressed me. then something would be,

                              salved

silly

California, vomitus paradise. to sleep i must resolve to kick someone's ass. in the dream all this terrain is familiar to me, not sane, doused in incorrect light, suspended

don't know what i did before one o'clock, heartless bastards

Up here, airless but tight, flying, not like a bird, rather, entrapment airborne, ulterior contradictions, air below clouded, cushioned, a scenery that has seen itself but likes to

Irritated at signs of time, streaking. over brokerages. It's Boston, bellows the clouded mirage. I have no emotional comment

Departure, conditional to love, and too, a result of. The heavens, big enough after all Not open, but a different kind of density, sidewalks made bigger, less pedestrian

CHAPTER 6

The line, non-continuous remainder

Waking and walking those streets post drag world, two rationed cities situated in soviet anti-revivalism

'schwarze' appears to be a declaration but I knew I couldn't trust him when he pretended he didn't know that word plus in Boulder once, that lousy apartment building on Canyon and 22nd, he sold me fake meth. a broken light bulb is a sad conductor

foreign then faint

mediocre I first learned on normandie avenue when walking past barbershops those men & beards and what they do when men gather with electric razors and scissors sit in high chairs,

the world a postcard of old black men sitting on folding chairs in front of Brooklyn brownstone with the caption 'my Brooklyn, 4th annual photo + essay contest exhibition'

but looking now I can see they are not so old, just captured by a lens that condenses a body to a dissipation, to a relic, to a mail slot

(this tone must have something to do with the not so alive, i.e. dead father)

I this now,
if this is not how one spells 'leprechaun' then it doesn't exist as an idea or curatorial curiosity

I had a breakfast nook when I didn't pay for anything

Keeping the steady pace seems to be the key, not to look down at the cracks but rather memorize their proximity to the leg's, stride, the motion, so as to not tip (and pour me out)

On the way to the beans and rice, red would be better today rather than pinto, I think I hear a bell-bottom pants leg flapping in a mothership, but that would be the los angeles coliseum hosting history in '72 or so,
the humidity here , but not a here that would indicate there, that place, now pestering the mind like hunger

Shhh, stop that racket, derrida's whispering about the politics of friendship & that French accent is making it two times hard to hear already, like the 'hissing of summer lawns', fanon in his masks

I want the radio on again to discover the new music and it be perhaps sexy, the butt slapping braying on a video screen, wouldn't it be nice

There was a song about a teapot, won't you tip me over and pour me out, & now I see how young you were then,
fun is the password

Daddy's here in a silver buick leSabre and its time for the beach, goodbye mother, so sorry you're not happy but could we have pork n beans next Friday and hug

The beginning notes, an entry into a dream that is a faille like texture, one that does not need to hesitate at the entry into the messiah's denouement

False documentary declarations, like "when time moved forward", as if time were able to do things like that, as if it were an action rather than a calculation, a marker, a decision and counter, a mathematical construction

It was if they had switched themselves, physically, and I had not moved though I had, and by many narrative accounts tragically so
remembering one unmentionable which I told once to my 'best friend', now hoping she's forgotten that intimacy

Such as such intimacies present as the declaration of a perimeter.

Simone White

having had no proper family name I made do
with Stingray never loved a man so-called
for more than a generation black and white
suffer nameless conditions
instigated by the father's line of nobody
murmurs to the baby "goodnight nobody"
there is no longer any way to count
beneath the highways of the Eastern Seaboard
above the Mason Dixon line
underlie so many crossings

what to me the arched wing of a black Stingray
who think weeping over her vicious mouth
somnolent practice of stuck terror, of the wave
is stingray the atomic principle of giantism
make my whole mouth move around the fire
make the fire everywhere or cold
on this street Stingray where a man thinking his boat
beauty knowing moneys or leather, white leather
feeling however the killing power of the great sea monster
her haunch whip a think acquired as a gorgeous capital

wait and sting why Odysseus
always in trouble with the one-eyed
what caused His love of lake demons
(her gauze whimple
under blacklit stars)
His very early anticipation
of the right guitar sound
its fullness, no
re-union of the ocean and the desert
just reflect on the history of the house

57 rays die in Chicago
for want of so lush a malapropism
I wait a long time outside the ocean
and your body sometimes nothing of images
dead brown and such like luminous captivity of the dead
repeated back to our obsessional contemporary
says back a weird lie
when inside me a bit of god comes out your mouth
as the command to feel you what
kind creature will you take me from being to what

her mallow glamor warns
warmed in glowering ripple light
this liquid this death to you
lady come under this death it is ablaze
in its blue white perfection hold your hand like a cup
water light will pour you into the whole day
the deafening memory of your tenth year
occurring in the space between sunup and sundown
on a plot the size of an hibiscus flower
you, miss

Simone White

The Bicentennial was yesterday
write queer and muggy apparently evening
every minute the Declaration must be signed
firework on the barge child mind
to which no Superfund has yet gently repaired
get me a Stingray the color of slate
a little girl switchblade the horizon of which is an arc
gutter oil slick Delaware that horizon
is New Jersey a plot (her shore)
farms send blueberries and war

In this form it is impossible to be together
it is being nothing at all then cast in this court trick
vulvar form o clamped then
between together and nothing
forms of sand coarse pink edible
no seams along which to break
a black flag waves in hot wind
form of formless a craft, a craft appears
materialized hot gas
raucous to suspend life outside of life

Simone White

shadows beyond wishing
and male news emplotted to hover
no wools or porcelain anywhere in sight
of the flat class
Stingray
vanities pool
heteronomous in the tight
grate
withdraw from earth
one fractal
initially

retreat then
the slick thing quavered she said
of sediment rustling abashed
contemplation of stones rushing together
under the fresh
lake not the elementary bite of capital
give that is a wound
and she, raw, bloodless
could you bleed housed gowned
fucked in a prehistoric manner
still sea monster

Simone White

the very source
or the veil
complete silence, silent
inhalation or stopped time
time, being unmet
totally unregulated
slack and unreturned
threshing
the dna then
she becomes another one

M. NourbeSe Philip

THE DECLENSION OF HISTORY IN THE KEY OF IF

A person who has no past, only a future, is person with little reality. Octavio Paz
The awareness of one's origins is like an anchor line plunged into the deep, keeping one within a certain range. Without it historical intuition is virtually impossible. Czeslaw Milosz

The yearning to transcend the insubstantialities of memory and return to a full knowledge of the past (and an unspoiled sense of the future) is an impossible one, but can be a rich source of imaginative insights. Liz Heron

It's important to know your past if you're fighting for your future. Bill Cranmer

History is dream from which I'm trying to awaken. James Joyce
Remember the future;imagine the past. Carlos Fuentes
For most people who assert the Africanness of themselves or of things, there is a standing tragedy. The psycho-physiology of knowledge would confirm the built-in handicap for nay human group who cannot work in their indigenous language form. The standing tragedy of all Blacks and Africans wherever they may be is that their tongues have been pulled out and they must speak strange tongues. Colloquium Proceedings on Black Civilization and Education.

The colonized man who writes for his people ought to use the past with the intentionof opening the future, as an invitation to action and a basis for hope. Frantz Fanon

I am no more than three or four years old. I have accompanied my mother to the library in the largest town on a tiny Caribbean island. It is my very first time at a library and I am excited. I look, no I stare up and up and up—from my very tiny perspective the stacks that appear to go on forever . A sense of wonder fills me—-so many, many books! and I want them all.

I have always loved books. Will always love them and have recreated—to some degree—those stacks in my study. Books have been my life, not to mention lifeline to the past. And to the future. The written word the umbilical cord keeping me connected, sometimes unwillingly, to a matrix of some sort.

THE PAST INDICATIVE

Tense is a change in the form of a verb to express time.
There are three principle tenses, **Past, Present** and **Future.**
The **Past Tense** show that an action is past as, They heard our cries but did not respond.
The **Indicative Mood** makes a direct assertion: as, The white man bought the black woman.

It is a typical Fall day in Wales, the weather changeable, shifting from overcast to bright sunshine and back again. I am standing in a farmer's field after some two hours of walking. Ahead of me is a stile; the map I am following directs me to "Cross next stile in over-hanging hawthorn and continue similarly." To my right is another stile leading to a path through a double row of trees. Like the moment of looking up at the books in the library at age three, the epiphany of the moment will remain with me . Always. I know this place! Have known it for a very long time, although I have never seen it before. I can place various characters from literature in the landscape. There! walking down that path is Tess of the d'Urbervilles. And over there stands Jude Fawley from **Jude the Obscure**. And why, there is Mr. Darcy in conversation with Heathcliff. And isn't that Jane Eyre hiding behind that tree over there? I could put them all in the landscape. But not myself. I am never in these scenes. I do not belong. Not here in this landscape. Although my knowledge of the landscape has been laid down so deeply through the process of a colonial education. In the sudden ache of recognition I know again that which I have never known. I know it through the imagination. Through books. Such is the power of the past—the colonial past in which I am absent. Such is the contradiction, that these books which speak to me across the years constitute the way in which I am held fast to a certain past. And the presence of my absence.

As I stand in the farmer's field there is a greater and even more painful revelation: I cannot place myself in my own landscape—the Caribbean. If you live your imaginative life through books, as I have done, never seeing yourself or your kind represented in your own environment at a formative age, can do irreparable harm. The history of writing by writers from the Caribbean is a relatively short one. While the works of many Caribbean writers are now part of school curricula, these works did not constitute a part of a colonial education. West Indian or Caribbean history was not taught in schools until the sixties. Until then our history was British history. Indeed we were told that we didn't have a history. We were loyal subjects of the empire—descendants of nameless, placeless slaves. Britons, however, in the words of the song, we sang as primary school children, could "never never never… be slaves."

Our landscapes, our place, our "belongingness" were never represented to us in fiction or poetry. More than this, however, our landscape, the very land, has been so permeated with the peculiar, tragic history of enslavement of African people, that positioning ourselves in that landscape is always fraught with tension that arises from the problematic relationship that exists between the African in the New World and the land. Despite its beauty, the land was, after all, the source of the exploitation of African people in the Caribbean. The peerless beauty of these islands, epitomised and promoted by tourist brochures as the unholy trinity of sun, sea and sex, has resulted in the Caribbean being seen primarily as a vacation paradise. Writers like George Lamming, Merle Hodge, Paule Marshall, Derek Walcott, and Kamau Braithwaite have, through their writing, helped to shape the Caribbean as a place and space where people, like people the world over, live the human struggle that is love. It is a space, the Caribbean basin, of massive interruptions, some more fatal than others, where European powers—the French, the English, the Portuguese, the Dutch, the Spanish, even the Latvians, contested each other's strength even as they destroyed the First Nations peoples and their way of life. A space where African life was so cheapened that it was more economically feasible to work the enslaved African to death and replace him or her with a fresh import.

Standing in that farmer's field, I face my past framed by a beautiful hawthorn bush. A past determined by how my kith and kin, long gone now, were brought to the New World. I try to escape my past yet find and feel my self held fast—

—all roads and words lead back to that point in time that deter/mined me

—seemingly forever

"Oh sinner man where you gonna run to/ oh sinner man where you gonna run to/ oh sinner man where you gonna run to..." [1]

If not the past?

—the words worry History. Absent a memory.

Hold we to the centre of remembrance

  that forgets the never that severs

    word from source

    and never forgets the witness... [2]

With a startling clarity I realize that I write to put myself in place—some place. On the cusp of the millennium, I write so that my daughter, my children, those that come after me will not have to feel the anguish. That is being english. That is, being not english. The anguish of being and feeling utterly placeless.

My past is burdensome. Its accumulated weight a drag on the trajectory that is the energy of a life. I long to be liberated from it so that I can turn my attention to things that really matter—the weather, love and romance, manners, fashion. To anything but this moment in time that is a reification, indeed a transmogrification, of a past. Determined a long time ago, appearing frozen yet defying the solid in such a state to reverberate seemingly forever. It clings this past

a skin

—as tightly as—

an odour refusing to leave

---

1 "Oh Sinner Man," An African American spiritual.

2 *She Tries Her Tongue; Her Silence Softly Breaks*

Simultaneously, however, I feel the absence of the past - the burden of the absence. I am haunted by a presence. And an absence. Of the past. Did it really happen? The past? My past. "It was such a long time ago." "It really wasn't that bad." "You should put it behind you." "It's best to move on."

What is the 'it' that keeps me pinned like some moth to a display board. What is the 'it' that draws me a moth to the flame? Of the past. That casts such a long and winged shadow over the future

The **Infinitive Mood** makes no assertion, but merely names the action: as, **To talk** of liberating the past from the future, or the future from the past is **to suggest** that the future, present and past are all discrete spaces, separated one from the other.

Linked only by the individual who leaves a past behind as she moves through the present into the future. Our language and metaphors suggest that the past is back there somewhere, behind us for the most part, and often securely vaulted. Access is controlled and only possible through traditional means. Like the study of History which becomes, in turn, the repository of the past. While the future becomes the domain of science fiction.

The past, present and future are, however, in dynamic relationship invigorating or bleeding into each other as the case may be. Past, present and future, the three dimensions of time, are, indeed, the rhythm of time. Each individual and, perhaps, each culture plays that rhythm in their own unique way.

The **Subjunctive Mood** expresses a condition or supposition: as, **If you wish** to engage with the past in any way, then you must engage with history.

To engage with history is to confront memory. In *Between Memory and History*[3], Pierre Nora writes that "Memory and history, far from being synonymous, appear now to be in fundamental opposition… At the heart of history is a critical discourse that is antithetical to spontaneous memory. History is perpetually suspicious of memory, and its true mission is to suppress and destroy it." Memory, I suggest, is to be found in the interstices, the silences, the half-said, the stories that are passed on, the markers of absence.

The **Interrogative Pronoun** is one which is used in asking questions: as, What did, in fact, really happen?

We enter the past, through the doorway of history.

---

3   Nora, Pierre. "Between Memory and History." *Representations*, No. 26. Spring, 1989, pp 7-24.

We begin with the words of the historian, Hugh Thomas. In the introduction to his work, *The Slave Trade* he writes: "The slave trade was, of course, an iniquity."[4] Fowler's *Modern English Usage*[5] explains the use of "of course" as an "adjunct to a statement of fact" with three examples: the polite, the disdainful and the showing-off. Giving the author the benefit of the doubt, we could say that his use falls within polite usage: the slave trade was an iniquity so well known that the writer doesn't really need to mention it. The reader—this reader—senses, however, that Thomas's acknowledgment of the iniquitous nature of the trade is more lip service to contemporary social mores, than any genuine belief in the reprehensible nature of the trade. Surely the egregiously iniquitous nature of this particular "trade" precludes its "of courseness." How can there be an iniquity which is "of course"? Thomas confirms this reader's worst suspicions when he subverts his own argument and in his next sentence urges historians to "recall Hugh Trevor-Roper's warning (that) 'every age has its own social context, its own climate, and takes it for granted… To neglect it… is worse than wrong: it is vulgar.'" The conclusion must then surely be that the kidnapping, forcible removal, brutalization, terrorising, and murderous exploitation of Africans by Europeans does not constitute "iniquity", of-course or otherwise, since those acts should be judged within the context of their own time. It would be "vulgar" based on Thomas's own logic for us to make any such judgments.

What is the 'it' that draws me, a moth, to the flame? Of the past.

What did, in fact, really happen?

---

4   Thomas, Hugh. *The Slave Trade*, Papermac, 1997.
5   Fowler, Henry Watson. *Modern English Usage*. Oxford: Oxford U.P., 1926.

THE PAST IMPERFECT

The **Passive Voice** is that form of a verb in which the subject denotes the person or thing acted upon: as, Africans **were captured** by Europeans and Arabs.

History bleaches the genocide white, leaving only a corpse, its bodily fluids removed. The horror, however, remains in the memories. Of the survivors.

"International morality," "economic history," "the history of popular movements," "Jewish history," "the history of the British monarchy," identifying "villains in this matter": these are all reasons Thomas identifies why someone might be interested in the slave trade. The "study of this **commerce**," he writes "can offer something to almost everyone." (My emphasis) That the so-called slave trade might be of interest to the descendants of those Africans who survived the infamous Middle Passage appears not to concern Thomas. That this "commerce," which is but a euphemism for genocide, could be investigated as the source of scourge of racism that currently plagues the world has escaped him.

For those of us who have been written out of history as agents, who appear always to be acted upon, more often than not fatally, who appear to be the flotsam and jetsam of history, memory provides us the key to another understanding of these events. By imagining the past through our memory and memories, we are able to integrate those cataclysmic events that brought us to the so-called New World. In so doing we are able to remember the future and live with presence in the present.

CONJUGATION

Conjugation of a verb is its proper arrangement in all its voices, moods, tenses, numbers, and persons.

A **Defective Verb** is one which lacks one or more of the chief parts: as, It **ought** not to have happened.

One of the fundamental issues facing anyone dealing with what is euphemistically called the "slave trade" is the language of the discourse. How does one begin to describe its horror with the language tools at one's disposal. To talk of this event in the language of the perpetrator, as many of us are forced to, having no other language **but** the language of the perpetrator, is to do ourselves a further injury. Given the vital role language plays in structuring our perception of the world as we know it, it is not surprising that Europeans like Thomas structure their analysis in the way he does.

"We dissect nature along lines laid down by our native languages. The categories and types we isolate from the world of phenomena we do not find there... on the contrary, the world is presented in a kaleidoscopic flux of impression which has to be organized by our minds—and this means largely the linguistic systems in our minds."[6]

All phenomena are, in fact, analysed through this process: they say trade. i say murder. they say commerce. i say genocide. they say profit. i say love. they count numbers. i say one. they say history. i say memory. of a mother. lost. looking for her motherless child. a father too. brothers, sisters, a family. a language. a culture. a world. lost in the plethora of facts. and history is no help at all in finding them. they say tragedy. i fall silent. because sometimes silence pays the greatest respect to a crime for which there is no name.

The **Future Perfect Tense** shows that an action will be completed at a certain future time: as, **I shall have named** what happened to me.

In an attempt to convey the enormity of the crime, some use the word "holocaust," already attached to **the** crime of the twentieth century, the attempted genocide by the Nazis of Jewish people along with the Romany, Slavs and other non-Aryans. In its harshly onomatopoeic qualities holocaust conveys something of the slash and burn practices of the European towards Africans. But it is a word fully occupied by the twentieth century horror perpetrated by the Nazis. And it is an English word. We need our own words. Rooted in an African matrix. To describe what, indeed, did happen to us.

The Maafa—Swahili word meaning disaster or terrible experience.

---

6   Whorf, Benjamin Lee. *Language, Thought and Reality*, New York, The Technology Press and John Wiley and Sons, 1956.

Not knowing the language leaves me unsure as to all the resonances of the word itself. And since words like people are more than the sum of their parts, this diminishes the reverberation of Maafa for me. Makes it thinner, less resonant. At the same time, the silence surrounding the word parallels, recreates and represents the not-known, the darkness, the silence that surrounds the event itself. And it is a beginning. A response from the imperfect future answering a call from the imperfect past. Call and response: the ancestors' language; the fundamental language of Africa; the particular language of Africa which resonates around the world, since we humans are, indeed, the response to the call of and to life.

An **Auxiliary Verb** is one which assists other verbs in forming their voice, mood, or tense: as,

The Maafa could not have happened without the assistance of Africans who cooperated with Europeans and, indeed, Africans themselves practised a form of slavery, albeit different in scale and consequence from that of chattel slavery instituted by the European powers in the "New World". These are the two most frequent arguments used by scholars and others in their attempt to deflect responsibility for the Maafa from Europeans and Arabs. In other words, Africans themselves are to be blamed for the Maafa. There is no denying the fact that Africans were involved in the trans-Atlantic slave trade and those whom History ambushed found themselves caught in the nexus of competing forces: one of those was the unquenchable demand for African labour by Europeans as their societies moved relentlessly towards industrialization; another was the insatiable demand for domestic slaves by Arab societies (the Arab slave trade predated and outlived the transatlantic trade); yet another were the more indigenous ethnic demands and needs of African societies themselves.

What is significant about the fact that Africans themselves did practise a form of slavery is the profound discrepancy in the respective legacies. While there are great inequities in African societies, slavery appears not to have created a permanent underclass and caste of people marked by their history of slavery. Compare that with Europe and the Americas where the descendants of Africans brought to the West as a result of the Maafa continue to be discriminated against in all walks of life. Indeed, European and Western cultures have devised a pernicious form of anti-Black racism that continues to plague the lives of those descended from the Maafa.

The **Interrogative Pronoun** is one which is used in asking questions:as, **What** is the 'it' that draws me a moth to the flame? Of the past?

What, in fact, did really happen?

PLUPERFECT PROGRESSIVE

Transitive Verbs express action passing from an agent to an object: as, The English man **purchased** one hundred African slaves.

"The purchase or capture of some fifty million human beings month in and month out for a period of four centuries was perhaps the greatest crime against humanity ever perpetrated by Christendom, not least because those responsible for the most part saw no moral evil in treating men, women and children as merchandise..."[7]

An "of-course iniquity."
"It was a truly wonderful sight to see them all standing there, for some were fairly white and well-formed, some were as yellow as mulattoes, and some were as black as Ethiopians... But who would have been so hard of heart as not to feel Pity for them in their distress!... There were those who sang lamentations, and although we did not understand the words, the melodies told of their great sorrow ..."[8]

A flame drawing me, a moth, to its fiery centre—
... it is no less than four months since traders took five hundred from Cape Verde to New Spain in one boat, and one hundred and twenty died in one night because they packed them like pigs or even worse, all below decks, where their very breath and excrement (which are sufficient to pollute any atmosphere and destroy them all) killed them.[9]

What did, in fact, happen?
    Fifty million. Four hundred years. Some say six hundred million including those who never made it. And made the Atlantic or the Sahara their resting place. Or even died before they reached the coast. The enormity of it all is too much. For me. To grasp. I want to deal in specificities.

As a child of the Maafa, a descendant of Africans who were kidnapped and forcibly removed from Africa, I am able to name the perpetrator of those actions. I can be general and say Europeans. I can become more specific and identify the French, the Spanish, the Dutch and the English. I could even include the African—we know the kingdom of Dahomey was deeply involved in the slave trade. All these nations and peoples were a part of a trade, which was "of course, an iniquity." But—

---

7   Muller, Frederick. *The Shameful Trade.*
8   de Azurra, Gomes Eannes. *Cronicade Descobrimento e Conquista de Guine*, 1414-1470.
9   Fray Tomas Mercado. *Suma de Tratos y Contratos*, Seville, 1581.

INDEFINITE PRESENT

The **Present Tense** shows that an action is going on at the present time: as, Darkness **descends** at this point and the impulse to assign feature and specificity to individuals is stymied.

Even things themselves recede into oblivion—what was the name of the ship or ships that first brought my ancestors to this part of the world? It is a simple request: I want to know the name of the ship that brought my ancestors—
I want to know the name of the ship—
the name of the ship
the name
the ship
Was it the **Jesus**, or the **Dolphin**; the **Sea Flower** or the **Charming Betsey**; the **Dreadnought** perhaps? Was it a sloop, a ship or a brig? The **Africa**, the **Spry** or the **Cleopatra**?
—the ship! that brought my ancestors

—a word resonant with history. And memory. Ancestor. Literally the one who went before. Helping to create a history. A memory. A word conjuring the resonance of tradition. Having so little bearing or relationship to the poor huddled creatures manacled in the holds of ships. Death ships. Riding at anchor. The white wings of death fluttering from their masts in the balmy tropical breezes. Who was the ancestor who first set foot on soil this side of the Atlantic. Borne forcibly on the North East Trades, washing up like some unwilling spore on the crest of the tidal wave of history?

INDICATIVE MOOD

The indicative is used in asking questions:

Was it a child—absent a mother and father? Boy or girl?
A full bodied youth or a young girl perhaps. Maybe she was a grown woman trapped, leaving behind her children—her man. They would most certainly not have been elderly. The hungry maw that swallowed them whole had no use for the wisdoms of elders. Old age was possibly the only protection against capture. If youthful, he or she would not have been entirely ignorant, since, as happens in all traditional societies, they would already have received some training for their predetermined roles in life. Husband. Wife. Mother. Father. They would have lacked, however, the wisdoms that come with age. Their second, scalding birth into the cauldron of New World would more than compensate for this lack. It would be an initiation the likes of which had never before been seen. Pushing back the folds of unremembering, I bear down in my effort to rebirth myself and imagine the past so that I may remember the future.

Who was the unnamed captain of the unnamed ship? Who owned it? Who stocked it? Who were the sailors? Did they have wives? Children? Could all the perfumes of Arabia ever sweeten the stench of murder and death?

CLASSIFICATION

An **Adjective** is a word which qualifies or limits a noun: as, A **little** girl from Africa was taken away from her **loving** mother.

I am on a train. A British train. On my way to a three week residence at a residential library in the United Kingdom. A woman with braids and two children—a boy and a girl —board the train. I learn later that they're from Kenya, having only arrived in London the previous evening; they are on their way to a university where the mother is doing a post-doctorate. The little girl sits opposite me. She has a gravely beautiful face—a face you see on carvings. A high, smooth and domed forehead—it gleams a deep mahogany colour. It reminds me of the bronzes of Benin. There is about her a gravitas that is startling in one so young and yet is only seen in one so young—a combination of innocence and wisdom that is seldom possible in an older person. She appears older than her ten years, with a dignity and weighted seriousness way beyond her years. Looking down, I see that her feet are some two inches above the floor. Such a startling and vulnerable contrast to her serious face. Her brother is younger, more active—a handful—he appears less focused, less perceptive. She and I talk. She asks me what I do. I tell her I write. She looks at the book on jazz that I'm reading and asks if I write about music. I say no. I ask her what is her mother tongue. She tells me Kalenjin. She gazes solemnly at me as I make notes.

Was that ancestor of mine—that child of the whirlwind, hurricane and volcano who was spat out in the New World—a young girl like her, whose feet barely touched the floor when she sat?

Who perhaps spoke. Then forgot. Kalenjin.

Something did happen. A little girl of grave and serious mien, whose feet when she sat barely touched the floor, forgot Kalenjin.

Forgot her mother with braids. Her father. Her naughty brother. One little girl was ambushed by History. Taken up in the whirlwind, consumed by the "of-course iniquity" of the slave trade. We can call her Kalenjin, daughter of the Maafa.

Parsing Model I

Sometimes I feel like a motherless child

Sometimes- adverb modifying the verb 'feel'.

> **I-** personal pronoun, neuter gender, singular.
> number, first person, nominative case to verb 'feel'.
>
> **feel-** verb.
> **like-** prepositional adverb modifying the verb 'feel'

a-	distinguishing adjective limiting the noun 'child'.
motherless-	adjective qualifying the noun 'child'.
child-	noun

A **Noun** is the name of anything: as **Modupe, Abena, Africa, thing, chattel**.

On February 22, 1992, Pope Paul II stood the shores of the infamous Goree Island from which millions of Africans bid goodbye to Africa. He asked forgiveness of his God for the sins of his forefathers and his church.

"I came to pay homage to all victims, the unknown victims; it is not known how many, nor who they were... For a whole period of the African continent's history black men, women and children were brought to this narrow stretch of land, separate from their families to be sold as merchandise. They came from all countries of Africa, and , as they were sailed off to another world, in their chains, their last view of their native Africa was the basalt rock of Goree. This island, it could be said, remains engraved in the memory and on the hearts of the entire black diaspora... How can one forget the enormous sufferings inflicted, in flagrant disregard of the most elementary human rights, on the people deported from the African continent? How can one forget the human lives reduced to nothingness by slavery? It is appropriate that this sin of humanity against fellow human beings, of humanity against God, should be confessed in all truth and humility... From this sanctuary of black suffering we beg heaven's forgiveness." [10]

February 1992 represented the first and only time a head of state in an official capacity broke the long silence about the atrocity of the Maafa. To date there has been no compensation, no reparations and no apologies, and while the Pope has asked Heaven's forgiveness, the Catholic Church has never apologised to Africans for the four hundred years of the Maafa which it sanctioned.

---

10   *Catholic International*, 15-30 April, 1992.

IMPERFECT PRESENT

The **Simple Subject** is either a noun, or a word or phrase equivalent to a noun, in the nominative case: as, **The body** remembers.

When thinking of cataclysmic events around the enslavement of Africans in the New World, there exist very few material markers. The victims themselves are long since dead. Possessing little or nothing in life, not even their own bodies, there was little or nothing to leave. How then does memory function in the virtual absence of any tangible markers? The body becomes increasingly implicated in the materializing of memory. Body becomes. The source of all memory.

Why did you need to come to England? A harmless enough question on the surface. Why, indeed, did I need to come to England? This is my third week at a residency at a library in Wales started by Sir William Gladstone, a former prime minister of the United Kingdom. It is a young historian who asks the question. **After** I had already explained for the umpteenth time that I was there to write and do research. "But why did you **need** to come to England?" he asks again. My reply has an edge to it: "I didn't need to come to England." I reply. He doesn't pursue it any further. Outwardly I am calm, but I feel a flurry of questions pressing in on me; I want to fly on him, tear him limb from limb. Why did I need to come to England, indeed! I want to ask him why his kind felt the need to go to Africa. Or the Caribbean. Or the Americas. Did they feel the need like me to see what it was all about? Were they fleeing their god-awful weather? Were they going in search of their history? Or memory? Had anyone ever asked them why they needed to go to any of those places? Why did you and your kind need to leave England? When you answer that, then maybe, just maybe, you'll understand why I needed to come to England.

The Direct Object is either a noun, or a word or phrase equivalent to a noun in the objective case: as, I am looking for my **history**, my **place**—my **mother**.

I come in search of Gladstone. Although I did not yet know it. A man whose name I vaguely remember, linked in the recesses of my memory with the likes of Stanley and Livingstone. I am sure I have seen his ghost flitting around this Victorian pile at nights sometimes.

Completion of the Predicate

It comes as a surprise, yet I am not surprised when I realize that we are kin after all. Gladstone, and I. Blood kin. The trail was easy enough to pursue after a fellow guest tells me at dinner that Sir William Gladstone himself, three times Prime Minister of England, was in support of slavery and that his father, John Gladstone was a slave owner. John Gladstone grew wealthy off his West Indian plantations. He also had a reputation for not treating his slaves well, although he himself never visited any of his plantations in the West Indies. John

Gladstone used his wealth to help his son, William Gladstone, get started in life and to become successful in politics. One can draw a direct line from Sir William Gladstone's wealth to his father's involvement in the Maafa. The former's wealth allows him to leave a bequest to start a library at which I, a descendant of the Maafa, am resident for three weeks. Gladstone and I, blood kin of the worst kind. Linked, related by a legacy of bloody exploitation—his people of my people. And a memory

The **Predicate** consists of a finite verb: as, The Black body **remembers**.

The Colon Health Routine

There are two types of constipation, the flyer tells me: Constipation proper and hidden constipation, and 99% of people in Great Britain suffer from the second type. I wonder what the percentages are for Canada. The U.S.A? Africa? Maybe this explains the British personality— stiff upper lip and all that. The average person, the flyer says, has up to 10-12 pounds weight of waste matter stuck to the inner walls of the colon! Toxins pass easily into the blood stream from putrefying deposits in the colon, contributing to many illnesses and lowering the overall efficiency of the body. Helping the body to cleanse retained waste out of the colon cleans the blood stream and the whole body becomes cleaner and more balanced.

This would be funnier if I hadn't paid too much for a course of Dr. X's Colon Cleansing Pills which the flyer assures me will remove all the caked shit inside me. But it's the caked shit inside my head I need to remove and there are no pills for that. Only a single memory. Standing in for five hundred years of history.

I have come to this place—ostensibly to do research on memory and history, but really to confront the memory of my missing history and the history of my absent memory.

There is a certain symmetry and balance, I suppose, to cleansing my insides while I cleanse my mind. The parallels grow stronger on realization that here on this sceptred isle, filled with the sepsis of History, I am indeed in the belly of the whale. Here where the layers of History are encrusted and caked centuries deep, there is an overwhelming need for a cleansing of the nation's colon.

There is more to this than meets the eye: The gut contains within it the enteric nervous system, a complex and sophisticated system of circuits and synapses that function like the brain. Is this, perhaps, why Eliot observed that he wrote from the gut and not the heart? In cleaning my gut I am improving an entire system of perception and response.

Dr. X's flyer tells me that the trick to this cleansing is to maintain the friendly bacteria within the bowel. These helpful guys go by names like Rhamnosus and Bifidus which propels them straight into the world of science fiction.

Wanted! one small history. Last seen lurking in the bowels of History.

Why, I'll just send my knights Rhamnosus and Bifidus to find it.

FUTURE PERFECT

The Imperative Mood expresses a command, desire or entreaty: as, **Go** directly to jail and **do not pass** Go!

During my time at the library two major political events took place: one was the decision by the House of Lords that Augusto Pinochet, former dictator of Chile, was not entitled to claim immunity for crimes he allegedly committed during his presidency of Chile. The other was the release of the report by the Truth and Reconciliation Commission (TRC) of South Africa on the events that took place during the apartheid regime.

Both these events are deeply implicated in issues of memory and history. However, as an Afrosporic African, a descendant of the Maafa, South Africa was of peculiar interest to me. It was the closest thing to slavery of African people that existed in the modern world. The racial exploitation and oppression of Africans by Europeans that we read about in text books, the "of-course iniquity" of the slave trade was very much alive and present in South Africa. It wasn't past and it wasn't **in** the past either. We knew that African people had to carry passes. We knew they couldn't live where whites lived. Our television screens brought us images of white soldiers and police shooting African children and tear-gassing unarmed demonstrators. It was the shameful secret of Europe writ large for all to see.

The rogue regime of South Africa was genocidal in its practices towards African people. This was a regime that actively promoted the development of biological weapons targeting African people. A regime that carried out a war against African children, a regime that thought nothing of firing on unarmed school children. This was an unabashedly white-supremacist regime that hung on for as long as it could, while it destroyed the lives of Africans, or caused them to flee the all-consuming maw of its racist machine, blown hither and thither like so much chaff before the wind.

The assumption behind the TRC was that there would be amnesty in exchange for telling the truth; there would be "understanding but not vengeance"; "reparations but not retaliation"; and "ubuntu but no victimisation." [11] Knowing the "truth" would clear the way for and, therefore, become a bridge to reconciliation. Victim and perpetrator would be treated impartially, which would result in the liberation of the future from past acts through the revelation of the truth. Reconciliation would follow and the country could move on to another stage of development.

Speaking the "truth" without fear of punishment would also assist in filling in the gaps, silences and spaces in the memory of the traumatized. These are ideals, which may not have been accomplished but South Africa did avoid a bloody civil race war. As importantly, there is a record, albeit incomplete, but a record in the voices of the victims of the acts committed against them and how they survived and resisted. The value of being able to name and face one's perpetrator cannot be underestimated. Are some crimes, however, such an outrage to

---

11 Report of the Truth and Reconciliation Commission, November 1998.

civil society, so contemptuous of the victims' humanity, that to allow the perpetrators to avoid accountability only buys a false peace and puts off yet again the final reckoning.

The desire and need to bring the architects and perpetrators of injustice and crimes against humanity such as apartheid to justice have less to do with retaliation and vengeance and all to do with justice. Until justice is served, until the perpetrators are held accountable, there can be no truth or reconciliation. It was this desire for justice and accountability that brought the former victims of General Pinochet out on to the street in response to the verdict of the Law Lords. To cry, to ululate. To give vent to the very human need for justice. Simone Weil writes that hunger presupposes the existence of bread. So too does the hunger for justice—a righteous justice—presuppose the existence of that justice. And justice is not satisfied with mere naming. Or truth commissions. Justice demands more and its demands are both legal and extra legal. There is an aesthetic and poetics to justice; it demands the precision and elegance of a geometric theorem. Indeed of Poetry.

Australia, Ireland and, most recently, Canada have all followed the TRC model to address long standing historical wounds. The other model for reckoning with History, the Nuremberg trial, appears to have more to do with bringing the perpetrators to justice and less to do with truth and reconciliation

There has never been a TRC on the human and civil rights abuses of African Americans in the US. How might that have affected the present climate where even getting people to accept the racial bias in the killing of Black people appears a Sisyphean task? There has never been a reckoning of any sort in the former European colonies for the crimes committed against African descended peoples. Liberation wars have been fought as in Zimbabwe, legislation changed, as in the case of the US coming out of the Civil Rights movement, restitution has been paid by the formerly enslaved for lost property, as in the case of Haiti (an egregious example of injustice if there ever was one), but no apologies have been forthcoming and no reparations paid. Most recently, several of the tiny Caribbean nations have instituted a legal claim for reparations against their former colonial rulers.

Disguised Compounds: Many words, really compounds, do not appear to be such. In others the component parts are difficult to recognize.

Since the beginning of the four hundred year abomination and scourge that was the "of-course iniquity" of the slave trade, the truth commissions have taken the shape and form of texts written by European historians who have given chapter and verse about the mechanics of the Maafa. From their perspectives. And how those texts proliferate. But what of the truth of it, that in its Biblical sense is supposed to set you free? To liberate you from the past and the future into a more fulfilling present.

Mood (Latin modus) is a change in the form of a verb to show the manner in which an assertion is made.

It is a typical Autumn afternoon in north Wales. Somewhat overcast, a bit chilly. I am on an archaeological walk through a small village. We enter the park to view the ruins of an old castle. The guide talks to us about the history of the site, then invites us to follow her up to the ruins that have been specially opened for us. "First," she says, "we will enter through King Leopold's Gate." Once again the past ambushes me. Roughly and with no apologies. I hurry to ask her why the entrance was called King Leopold's Gate. She doesn't know much: she believes he came to visit. Being Queen Victoria's uncle there was nothing surprising about that. But I had not expected that deep in Welsh countryside I would have to confront one of the most brutal European rulers of Africa, King Leopold, who created the Belgian Congo and imposed a rule of astonishing—even by European standards—atrocity to obtain rubber. Rubber collection involved looting villages, attacking African men, seizing their wives and holding them hostage. Once rubber was obtained, the women were then sold back to their families. The system of accounting involved cutting off ears, hands and other kinds of mutilation. In one six month period in the Momboyo river region more than 6,000 people—including children—were either killed or mutilated by having their right hands cut off.

Here in the bucolic Welsh countryside the stench of blood is fresh. The past has reached out and touched me. And among these twenty or so people, I am the only one even aware of this man's history. We all troop through King Leo's gate to see the ruins of the castle. What ho! and Tally Ho! Their history. My memory.

The **Superlative Degree** of an adjective denotes that one of more than two things, or sets of things, possesses a certain quality in a greater degree than all the others: as, Africa is the **richest** continent and contains the **poorest** people.

Europe's contact with Africa has always exacted a great price from Africa and Africans. Indeed it was not that long ago—1864 to be exact—that predictions were being made about the extinction of Africans: "Africa will be shared between England and France... Under European rule, the Africans will dig the ditches and water the deserts. It will be hard work, and the Africans themselves will probably become extinct."[12] More recently during the early AIDS crisis there was similar discussion about the populations of Africa being decimated and the suggestion that South Asians would prove to be an ideal group to replace the population.

At the dawn of the new millennium, this daughter of the Maafa, looked behind her and saw a history strewn with the bodies of her people brought to the New World. Those who carried out these crimes have walked free into History. Richly compensated for their lost property—their black ivory, their pieces of the Indies. Rewarded for their genocide. The example of South Africa, the rainbow nation, presents the same picture of the European walking free after his concerted attempt, in the words of Conrad's Kurtz, to "exterminate all the brutes."

---

12 Lindqvist, Sven. Exterminate All the Brutes, Granta, 1998.

EXTENSIONS OF TIME AND PLACE

Africans in the New World have been locked into the present ever since they were brought here. They constitute the only group brought to the New World against their will, their past literally lost to them. There was no information, if such information was even kept, that would allow them or their descendants to reconnect with kinsfolk in Africa. More than that, the European actively promoted and promulgated the view that the African had no history or culture.

For the European the "New World" represented a tabula rasa; she or he would leave behind all the ills of the Old World. There (or here) they would find their utopias free from control of king or pope. And a future rampant with possibility. This is the powerful mythology of the "New World" that **all** peoples since the Pilgrim Fathers, **with the exception of Africans**, willingly subscribe to—that life will be better in the U.S.A. Better for most people, that is, fleeing something worse. But not for the African. S/he could not live out that dream of unlimited possibility. And of progress. Sealed off from their past, being told they had no past, and cut off from the future, they were, and far too many still are, condemned to a present in which they live out the modern version of being hewers of wood and drawers of water. Some twenty years after writing this essay, in the closing days of the administration of the first African American President of the U.S., the wanton disregard for Black life has given rise to the movement, Black Lives Matter. Black lives have always mattered: these lives generated unbelievable wealth for European powers; they were the raw material that fuelled the speculative financing of the 18th century that we still live with today and which almost brought the world's financial systems to a disastrous end in the early 2000s. You could, for instance, live in Liverpool, purchase an African in Lagos or Accra, have him or her shipped to Jamaica or somewhere in the "New World" and sold, and eventually receive payment through a complex system of promissory notes. Black lives have **always** mattered but for the wrong reasons. It is macabrely ironic that today we utter these words as a challenge to those who insist on devaluing Black life and lives.

Sub-atomic particles which have once been in contact and then separated display a continuing connection. A "change in one is associated with an immediate change in the other. The distance is arbitrary. They could be stationed at opposite sides of the universe."[13] This image becomes a startling metaphorical ideal for the interaction of African peoples who have been physically and figuratively isolated from each other and our histories. The image of sub-atomic particles plays itself out in subtle ways: the impact of the U.S. Black Power movement on South African freedom fighters like Steve Biko was central to the latter's development of his Black Consciousness movement. In turn, African Americans took up the struggle for their brothers and sisters in South Africa, as did Black folk around the worlds. Reggae music which African Jamaicans created would return to Africa to inspire musicians like the South African Lucky Dube, while jazz musicians like Abdullah Ibrahim would bring their African inflected jazz back to the West; Randy Weston would infuse his music with the rhythms of the Gnawa of Morocco, who themselves are the descendants of sub-Saharan Africans enslaved through the Arab slave trade.

---

13   Dorsey, Larry, Prayer is Good Medicine

There was and is a history and a memory that connect me, a descendant of the Maafa, to an African living in Soweto. Just as it connects me to an African living in Brixton, Watts or New York, Port-of-Spain or Kingston.

The image of the sub-atomic particles also have bearing on the relationship between the past, present and future. Any change in one of these rhythmic time frames will affect the others. In other words, making a change in our present will, indeed, affect our past and our future. A change to our past will immediately affect our future, which begs the question of how or even whether we can even change our past. I'm suggesting that the work of imagining the past, the work of poets and writers and artists in general is a way of changing or bringing detail to that past, which in turn will affect our future.

African peoples have an enormous potential for forgiveness. Such forgiveness, and the healing generated by it, can only come with an acknowledgment—a public acknowledgement of the history of the crimes carried out by Europeans and Arabs against African people. It can only come when there is an acknowledgement that the pain of the African is the same—no less no more—as the pain of the European. It can only come with full reparations, which does not only mean monetary reparations. Indeed, there is no sum large enough to compensate for the losses and tragedies endured by Africans. If we understand what was broken and fractured by the trade, then reparations would naturally address those areas such as language, culture, genealogical records and so on. Forgiveness can only come with a genuine seeking of forgiveness by Europeans. It can only come with apologies. For the sin. That was the "of-course iniquity" of the slave trade. The Maafa. While these are not forthcoming, the past and future will remain locked in a macabre dance with each other—the dance of death.

There comes a time in the individual life when the past becomes almost as important as the future. I continue, therefore, to imagine the past: I have the general outline and pattern of the event. Too many details are still missing, however, including accountability. In revisiting this essay, written at the dawn of the millennium, I have become keenly aware that my book-length poem **Zong!** was an attempt on my part to imagine that past—to shatter the archival noise with the silenced sounds of those on board that fated ship. I remember the future in the gravely sweet face of Kalenjin. Her feet, when she sits, barely touch the floor.
"Are you writing about music," she asks.
"Yes," I answer, "the music of justice. And I write for you."

Syntax of Grief
What will I take? With me. Back to the future of Africa?
Exactly what I came into the present past with.
One body.

The **Parenthesis** is used to enclose an explanatory phrase or sentence: as,

(where west remains

west

and east becomes

the never in meet

are you the I

in am

or the sleeping enemy

within)

Afterword 7

Rene Gladman's excerpts from "Morelia" and "Kahlil Joseph," offer compelling examples of the transformational energies of attentive, innovative writing. In "Morelia," Gladman explores the words "in" and "out," playing amidst narrative ideas of place, setting and mood. The word "in" is a flexible adverb, used to refer to a city, "I studied some summers ago in the soft city, and at other times, a narrower location," as when "in a sunny room of a townhouse in the secret city." Most consistently, though, "in" is "in" a book, "could I now, all of a sudden, switch to a burrowing-in persona, because that's what you need to 'enter' a book."

At times, the boundaries between "in" and "out" blur, suggesting a grammar of travel, as in "Staying in will allow me to be myself, but going outdoors might lead to answers. I go out. I hesitate. I don't go, but soon I will."

At other times, Gladman's work operates like a telescope: scanning broadly then slowly lighting on a fixed object, concentrating awareness and readerly attention on the minutiae of consciousness, meditations in "Morelia" on inscrutable nouns (Bze, Sespia, stiasdern).

Marvel at Gladman's rich ontological sentences through which glimmers of feeling, being and thinking bloom in text. In a few poetic strokes, Gladman evoke atmosphere and period: "I want the scratches and bruises I've incurred to fall back into my skin before I complete my original task, which was really just to go somewhere and read, to escape Mr. Otis and to read." This reader can't escape the sense that this sentence could have been written in a 19th century slave narrative, in back to the future move, calamity hovers then and now, where a Black woman with a book is an instigation, an invitation to interrupt.

The telescoping movement from expansion to contraction is present also in the work of "Kahlil Joseph," based on the images and technique of the noted Black filmmaker, whose meditative dreamscapes seem to inform Gladman's methodology in this section.

A paired reading of "Morelia" and "Kahlil Joseph" with Octavia Butler's "Mortal Words" could be launched from Gladman's sentence: "It starts with Sespia, the story tells me, the story is not yet written." Compare that sentence with this Octavia Butler's "She said nobody could change the past, so I could only write truth about the future."

Start a discussion with the idea that a story you write then might happen, and that a story that is not written yet, is waiting for you to tell it. Gladman's writing charts what might happen if you slow story telling down into its phenomenological detail, in order to witness in attentive surprise and recognition, a story about the future as it happens.

Tonya Foster's "New Orleans Bibliography" may be one of few abecedarian poems that's also a GPS (geographic positioning) device. It spans several domains and makes it look deceptively easy: the alphabet, the landscape of New Orleans, language and social memory and personal memoir.

These poems re-create a hyper-local specificity, words from an ecological or environmental niche in the space of language. The abecedarian aspect of "New Orleans Bibliography" fascinates because each word brings its own vector of affect and particularity, the way a phrase like "Elysian Fields" is positioned next to "Erato," "Etouffee," "Euterpe," "Ezekiel," words that originate from very different etymological sources and yet in some sense, concentrate and represent the creolized/hybridized splendidly threaded through New Orleans, the Gulf region, and Louisiana. Greece lives in New Orleans, and Greek proper nouns wander the quarters yet showing their roots in some other tongue. The landscape gives birth to nouns, coming out of the mother tongue. As if the poet comes to her language only after taking in a mother landscape along with the voices of that place, a girl who, like her father, "is born for luck."

Who're the parents of this language? Where do we learn our tongue? The tongue comes both from the people around us who teach us to speak, and the landscape that teaches us to speak and to use words, with particular connotations.

In the poem "In Tongues," it's back to a woman, Auntie Jeannette, you know, who "stutters" and "staggers" and "struts," who is the progenitor of the language in the poem. Again, we are to consider the question, who transmits and how is language transmitted to us. We learn it without even knowing that we're learning it.

Foster's poem "In/Somniloquies" records and retains the slightly hypnogogic qualities of insomnia. Without sleep, the mind is a hive of busy self-talk; the poems record the resulting pressure in lyric and haiku forms. Poems trace wakefulness in language that's particular to place, Harlem, and family, complex seismic peaks and valleys in the language wallpaper we grow up hearing.

These poems comprise an ecology of words and place, situated in a particular time flowing from a mother tongue flourishing and flushed in New Orleans and stuttering in Aunt Jeannette, post Katrina. This selection from her collection, *A Swarm of Bees*, works to restore the root system of an existential Black New Orleans.

Akilah Oliver (1961-2011), performance artist, poet, teacher, mother called *The Putterer's Notebook* an anti-memoir, a memoir written by "backing into memory as disjuncture."

Notional, playful, yet somber Oliver is very concerned to name the "evacuated narrator," and to subject history to her discerning metaphysics of trauma, of grief with an unending trail—aporia. In examining "history" and "History" Oliver reveal its ribs, the skeleton that holds story and memory upright when the "evacuated narrator" would like to fall down. In these excerpts from *The Notebook,* the reader receives a glossary:

"Why when I say 'outside of history' I mean anything I mean to reconstitute an Other." Therefore when I say "now that I'm done being dead," I have declared an alternative self.

But "time moves forward," or out, even moving forward, has to be spit out, even if time is experienced as fragment., and seen from the perimeter. Oliver's poems are "echoes" and "texts" connoting a "galaxy of signifiers," where the "I" and the body's solidity is not to be taken for granted, but to be re-perceived, and retrieved, again and again.
In which pocket did I leave that "I"?

Is "I" ever a thing to miss, a personage to mourn, if the "I" still lives in the physical body and is capable of re/articulation? If it desires mirrors? History? Or and then narrative sensibility. If the mirror breaks one can buy another. Consume then recreate then resume an/other "I." History, I curse thee, to not be borne in mid-twentieth century garb, a French feminist theorist laboring over 'new ideas' to bounce the vernacular mind.

Julie Patton, poet, visual and performance artist contributes "Time Squared," a poetic libretto based on the life of Virgie Ezelle Patton (1928-2015), Cleveland-based painter and artist, the mother of Patton and her five siblings. Of course, Virgie Patton is heroic, in the ways familiar to Black women, making art in between hours, in minutes scavenged from days dense with child rearing, work outside and inside the home. It is not hard for me to think of Shiva, her dozen arms cajoling the impossible from the predictable and squaring, even cubing, "time."

Here Julie Patton enters Trickster-ish, Janus, double-handed and double-jointed, pairing image and texts composed of her mother's correspondences (letters) and newly composed images, collage, correspondence theories and chimera.

Simone White's ten-section, ten-line poem, "Sting Ray," bears rereading, and in each iteration yields insights into formal innovation, wide ranging vocabularies, biography and pathos. In one reading, it is possible to find motion in line choices, and unmarked breaks as lines shuttle forth and back and front to back without commas, a pluralist sampler:

> having had no proper family name I made do
> with Stingray never loved a man so-called
> for more than a generation black and white
> suffer nameless conditions
> instigated by the father's line of nobody
> murmurs to the baby "goodnight nobody"
> a collision of texts.

In another reading, "Sting Ray" becomes a tale, hinging a "before" and an "after," occurring roughly half way through the ten poem sequence, and chronologically denoted as the day before the Bicentennial.

> The Bicentennial was yesterday.
> write queer and muggy apparently evening
> every minute the Declaration must be signed

Later, the poem marks the place of rupture:

> when inside me a bit of god comes out your mouth
> as the command to feel you what
> kind creature will you take me from being to what

This poem weaves—its lines are weft and warp—and locates memory's persistence, slipping between and through the present, a flickering bruise.

M. NourbeSe Philip's essay takes us on a voyage through language by way of grammar and history and memory by way of History, through landscape and literature. A literary memoir, "Declension in the Key of If," describes a love affair with a language that does not love back fully in return, a language in which there will always be exile, and will never quite be home. English is a place, a topology; landscapes here are storied, relationships are mapped, Philip suggests. And for Philip, English, in its volumes parsed in its marked and unmarked aspects, contains subtle arrangements of tense and mood that conceal power, voiced resistance and voiceless acquiescence.

Philip focuses on the Maafa—the Great Disaster of the slave trade, the holocaust of lives lost in the Transatlantic Middle Passage and its long afterlife. "Declension" in linguistics means inflection (changing the form of a word) of nouns, pronouns, adjectives, and articles to indicate number, case (nominative or subjective, genitive or possessive, etc.), and/or gender. This essay wades through the limp and half-hearted apologies offered in the wake of the castastrophe of colonial exploitation, the outright denials, the stubbornness and refusal of reparations that leave scars in our language and hemorrhages in the contemporary.

Of the future, Philip hypothesizes: "The image of the sub-atomic particles also have bearing on the relationship between the past, present and future. In other words, making a change in the present will, indeed, affect our past and our future." "Declension" is its remarkable demonstration of time's mutability, intertext threaded through new texts, prerequisite to a transformed future.

Erica Hunt

AN ELDER HOMAGE

Lucille Clifton, Sonia Sanchez

Good evening. I'm Robert Polito, Director of the New School writing program, and it's my immense pleasure tonight to welcome you to this special evening of readings and conversation with Lucille Clifton, Sonia Sanchez and Eisa Davis. This evening is jointly sponsored by Cave Canem and the New School, and I want to thank everyone at Cave Canem, especially Carolyn Micklem, Sarah Micklem, Cornelius Eady, and Toi Derricotte.

This evening is planned as the first in an ongoing series of evenings with Cave Canem, and everyone at the New School is honored by the collaboration. Originating in 1996 as a vision of a retreat to support African-American poets, Cave Canem is a vital catalyst in the American poetry renaissance with a steadily expanding program of summer workshops, regional workshops, public readings and now public programs along the lines of this evening's convocation of two remarkable writers.

Lucille Clifton is a distinguished poet and teacher. She's the author of many books of poetry including *Next: New Poems; Good Woman: Poems and a Memoir 1969–1980; An Ordinary Woman; Generation: A Memoir; Quilting Poems: 1987 To 1990; The Book Of Light;* and *The Terrible Stories.* She's the recipient of many honors including a 1999 Lila Wallace Readers Digest Writers Award and on two occasions she was nominated for the Pulitzer Prize in Poetry. She won the 2000 National Book Award for her latest collection, *Boats: Blessing the Boats, New and Selected Poems 1988–2000.*

Sonia Sanchez is an essayist, poet, teacher and activist. Her many books include *Homecoming; We A BaddDDD People; Love Poems; Sound Investment And Other Stories; Homegirls and Hand Grenades; Wounded In The House Of A Friend; Does Your House Have Lions?; Like The Singing Coming Off The Drums;* and *Shake Loose My Skin.* Her many honors include an American Book Award, a Pew Fellowship in the Arts, the Langston Hughes Award for Poetry, finalist for the National Book Critics Circle Award and, on this stage just last spring, she was awarded the Robert Frost Medal by the Poetry Society of America.

The moderator this evening is Eisa Davis. She is a poet, performer and playwright; her play "Paper Armor" will be read at the Langston Hughes Centenary Conference at Yale in February.

So please join me now in welcoming Lucille, Sonia, and Eisa.

[Applause]

DAVIS: Well, I wanted to welcome everyone and thank you all for coming. We know that Toi Derricotte could not make it tonight and we want to send our blessings to her and to her family. I know she'll feel every wonderful word that these two pillars will speak tonight and this is the—

SANCHEZ: Did you get that we're pillars?

DAVIS: Pillars of literature.

SANCHEZ: We got it, we're gonna mess with you; right, you're our student, so we can mess with you.

DAVIS: You can, that's right, and this is Cave Canem, so we're going to do this all the right way. And I think some of you here know what that means. So this is the vanguard, the Cave Canem people out there to keep it all live and keep the love flowing.

SANCHEZ: Tell them to raise their hands, the Cave Canem people.

DAVIS: Cave Canem people, could you raise your hands by Sonia's request? [applause] So we're gonna have a reading tonight: first Lucille Clifton will read, and then Sonia Sanchez will read, and then we'll have a conversation here, followed by a Q&A in which you will be able to ask some questions from the audience. Afterwards there'll be an opportunity to purchase some books and have them signed.

SANCHEZ: Is this the 10-minute reading?

DAVIS: Yes, and I think what I wanted to say before we begin is that our work tonight is listening and that our play tonight is also listening and that this conversation series was inaugurated because Cave Canem members and faculty believed, particularly after the deaths of Barbara Christian, Gwendolyn Brooks, and Dudley Randall, that our ancestors while living needed to tell their stories one more time for those who hadn't heard them. And so as part of that cause, I wanted to preface what we do tonight by saying just a few words about my grandmother.

She spent most of her life in Birmingham, Alabama, which is where Sonia was born, and she raised me and she served us breakfast, she packed us lunch, she made us wash the dishes after dinner, she had four kids, and she taught elementary school for over 30 years, and she was involved with the fight and the struggle for the Scottsboro boys, and she was an activist when she met my grandfather. She wanted to continue, but he wanted her to stay home and be safe. And she did and she did that exceedingly well, and I think that these women tell her story. Both of you who have raised children and taught and who write poetry and teach activism— you've written it all down for us, all of us, and so tonight we thank you for telling these stories. Never bitter, never sweet, always steady, embracing, clear as water, your work nourishes us and knocks us against the rocks sometimes with its power. We thank you for teaching us not only in classrooms and in your books but in how you walk, how you cook, how you wear your hair and for your bravery, which is as relentless as music. We are training ourselves to fill your shoes, so tonight we ask you to show us the compass and the river. And our pens will cast shadows by your moons.

SANCHEZ: Beautiful . . . [applause] Lucille and I just want to correct one thing. How we used to cook! [laughter]

CLIFTON: How we used to walk.

DAVIS: So now if you'd like to begin your reading . . .

CLIFTON: I would like to take a risk and read some poems—ending with some poems—written after September 11th. And it is a risk and they may not be very good poems and I'm going to read them anyway. [Laughter and applause]

First, I'd like to acknowledge our sister and friend Toi Derricotte who is modeling once again for us what it means to be human, who understood that, when her mother died, her place was with her family and there in the space her mother lived in. And I congratulate her, and know that she is here with us, know that we are there with her. This is a poem about my sister. I had a sister who was a prostitute, and she was a very good prostitute. My mother used to be a little embarrassed that we would visit my sister (for a while she lived in a brothel), but as she would say when other people would ask, "Why do they come and see you?"—she would say, "We're family," and that made sense. I want to say that in the poem I mention someone and that what you should know is that his name was not Richard.

HERE RESTS

my sister Josephine
born July in '29
and dead these 15 years
who carried a book on every stroll.

when daddy was dying
she left the streets
and moved back home
to tend him.

her pimp came too
her Diamond Dick
and they would take turns
reading

a bible aloud through the house.
when you poem this
and you will she would say
remember the book of Job.

happy birthday and hope
to you Josephine
one of the easts
most wanted.

may heaven be filled
with literate men
may they bed
you with respect.

[Applause]

This next poem—somebody said it didn't sound like me, but it is me, and it is written for Nkosi Johnson. Do you know who Nkosi Johnson was? Born February 4, 1989, dead June 1, 2001, [he was] a young child on the African continent who died of AIDS and who was a great spokesperson for AIDS, the scourge that is terrorizing that part of the world.

STOP

what you are doing
stop
what you are not doing
stop
what you are seeing
stop
what you are not seeing
stop
what you are hearing
stop
what you are not hearing
stop
what you are believing
stop
what you are not believing

in the green hills
of Hemingway
Nkosi has died
again
and again
and again

stop

[Applause]

One of the things that I really believe is that we are all capable of great good and great evil. In America's culture we like to think that for some reason we can tell the bad people. Not only, I guess, because they wear bad people t-shirts or something, but we think we are the good people and they are the bad people, without realizing that we are all capable of great good and great evil. Knowing that allows us to work toward the good if we can, and this is a poem—now I read this poem somewhere and somebody thought I was talking about their child—I assure you I am not. I don't write about other people's children. I've got enough babies to write about my own and also I have a new granddaughter. I'm very proud of her. Every mother looks down at her child and thinks "this is the one." I did it lots of times. But anyway this is called "The Baby."

THE BABY

perhaps he'll be an artist
the way his fingers
feel my hand
how his eyes follow colors
in the room
until they settle themselves at white
and while he has not laughed
perhaps a scholar then
lifting our name
in universities across the world.

I suppose I am dreaming
as any mother would
I know this
he is mine own
I can teach him to smile
my love will bunker him through
though who can know

what fate decrees
Gunther
I will call him Gunther
no Adolf
yes
Adolf

[Audience laughter]

I've never heard anybody laugh about that before. I don't know what it means—you'll all have to tell me after. I think it's an old poem, but I don't think it's appeared in a book. Long ago, you may remember the name Rodney King, and he's had many escapades but long ago, one of the officers who beat Rodney King was a man called Officer Powell and one of the things I also try to do is understand the other. I tried to understand, if I can, why this person behaved in this way and this is a poem called "Powell." It is written in the voice of that person. It has an epigram, what I overheard a black man saying to a white man: "I am your worst nightmare." This is Powell speaking.

POWELL

I am your worst nightmare.

This is that dream I wake from crying
then clutch my sleeping wife
and rock her until I fall again
onto a battlefield
here they surround me
nations of darkness
speaking a language
I can not understand
and something about my life
they know and hate and I
hate them for knowing it so well
my son—I think about my son
my golden daughter
and as they surround me
nearer, nearer I reach to pick up anything
a tool, a stick, a weapon
and something begins to die
this is that dream

[Applause]

Thank you. This is something that was written in Squaw Valley. In reading the guidebook, the lodge guidebook, there was a story about John Freemont and Kit Carson, who discovered Lake Tahoe in 1844. So the title is from the lodge guidebook.

IN 1844 EXPLORERS JOHN FREEMONT AND KIT CARSON DISCOVERED LAKE TAHOE

in 1841 Washo children danced like otters
in the lake
their mothers rinsed red beads

in 1842 Washo warriors began to dream
dried bones and hollow reeds
they woke clutching their shields

in 1843 Washo elders began to speak
of grasses hunched in fear
and heard thunder sticks over the mountain

in 1844 Freemont and Carson . . .

These are some poems that wanted to be written, and I was available. [laughter] It isn't that funny.

TUESDAY NINE ELEVEN '01

thunder and lightning
and our world is another place
no day will ever be the same
no blood untouched
they know this storm
in other wheres
Israel, Ireland, Palestine
but God has blessed America
we sing
and God has blessed America
to learn

that no one is exempt
th
al
a
a
a

[Applause]

TWELVE ʻ01

This is not the time, I think
to note the terrorist inside
who threw the brick into the mosque
this is not the time to note
the ones who cursed God's other name
the ones who threatened they would fill
the streets with Arab children's blood and
this is not the time, I think
to ask who is allowed to be American
America, all of us gathered under one flag
praying together, safely
under the single love
of the many named god

THURSDAY NINE THIRTEEN ʼ01

The firemen
ascend
in a blaze of courage
rising, like jacobs ladder
into the mouth
of history
reaching through hell
in order to find heaven
or what ever the river jordan is called
in their heroic house.

FRIDAY NINE FOURTEEN '01

Some of us know
we have never felt safe
all of us
Americans
weeping as some
have wept before
Is it treason to remember?
What have we done
to deserve such villainy?
Nothing
we reassure ourselves
Nothing.

[Applause]

SATURDAY NINE FIFTEEN '01

I know a man
who perished for his faith
others called him infidel
chased him down
and beat him like a dog
after he died
the world was filled
with miracles
people forgot he was a Jew
and loved him
who can know what is intended?
who can understand the gods?

As I said, I have a new little granddaughter. She was born one week before the tragedies and one year and a week after my second daughter died.

SUNDAY MORNING NINE SIXTEEN '01
for Bailey

The Saint Mary's River flows
as if nothing has happened

I watch it with my coffee
afraid and sad, as are we all
so many ones to hate
and I, cursed with long memory
cursed with a desire
to understand
have never been good at hating
now this new granddaughter
born into a violent world
as if nothing has happened
and I am consumed with love
for all of it
the everydayness of bravery
of hate, of fear, of tragedy
of death and birth and hope
true as this river
and especially, with love
Bailey Frederica Clifton Goin
for you

And finally:

MONDAY SUNDOWN NINE SEVENTEEN '01

Roshashana which is the Jewish New Year.

I bear witness to no thing more human than hate,
I bear witness
to no thing more human than love
apples and honey
apples and honey
what is not lost
is paradise

[Applause]

SANCHEZ: Thank you very much. It is so good being here, most especially because we have so many people that we know, in this place called New York City. I think we all kept a journal, every day. I'm not going to read it because I think, at some point, I want to talk—maybe—about where we are in this place called New York City and where we've got to be. Because at some point we mourn, and at the same time we've got to live. We've got to understand also at some point that we can't give up the things that we need to be human and those things are, indeed, our rights, our civil liberties.

[Applause]

And I hope we don't give it up willingly. Okay.

I call on living and ago ancestors, Toni Cade Bambara, Vincent Harding, Barbara Deming, Angela Davis, Elizabeth Catlett, Maurice Bishop, Nat Turner, Maya Angelou, Shirley Graham, W.E.B. Du Bois, Mister Micheaux, Gandhi, Gwendolyn Brooks, Amiri Baraka, Diop, Dorothy Day, June Jordan, Ida Wells Barnett, Ella Baker, Chris Hani, Oliver Tambo, Chavez, Odetta, Bernice Reagon, C.L.R. James, Fannie Lou Hamer, Victoria Grey, Sitting Bull, Sister Lebrón, Paul Robeson, Geronimo, Jose Martí, David Walker, Margaret Walker, Alice Walker, Walter Rodney, Nkrumah, Sojourner Truth, William Wells Brown, Sterling Brown, John Brown, Dada and Mama Sisulu, Mandela Nelson and Winnie, Martin Luther King, Audre Lorde, Ngugi Wa Thiong'o, Viola Plummer, Ruby Doris, Frantz Fanon, Robert Moses, Queen Mother Moore, Septima Clarke, Bobby Sands, Patrick Hill, Toni Morrison, Malcolm, Chinua Achebe, James Baldwin, Pam Africa, Ramona Africa, Lucille Clifton.

This is the letter I wrote to Chinua Achebe on his 70th birthday:

> Dear Chinua, it is today. Not yesterday. Hoy ha llegado. Today has arrived. Sometimes I have gotten lost in this journey called today, where nothing moved, when I gathered up the country's hysteria, when I looked at the world's delirium, when I saw Africa try to disagree with its blood. But I always remembered your voice, feasting on rain and laughter across telephone wires as you talked, your voice a prayer in exile, pushing past the débris of human sacrifice.
>
> This new century appeared, my brother, a fragile bird caught in its past wing flow. This new century arrived and we saw death, beboppic death, peeling our skins down to the minerals in our blood plasma. And I asked you question after question, distracted by the scandal of whores accessorizing our flesh with newly minted bullets. Where are we on this food chain of life to be eaten so easily, century after century, decade after decade? Are these meditations of insane saints from a take-out menu, imperializing our taste buds till we sweat, crouched junkies, vomiting into the ears of our unborn fetuses? Are we like Okonkwo fated to end hanging from a morning sky of death? Are we always frightened of being our father's son? Our father's daughter? I had a dream last night where tongues, leotarded tongues, pirouetted buildings like hummingbirds and wagons with children's legs circled the campfires of our founding fathers. But I awoke breathing an avalanche of air, remembering that James Arthur

Baldwin had called Okonkwo, Father, had said, "That man is my father. I don't know how he got over here but he did."

How to recognize our fathers, even when they behave opportunistically, even when their hands hold up, as you said, "The colonial belief that the ruler doesn't have to be responsible to his people."

This is the right time for comedy, I think. I miss the wandering spirit, the blue black gusts, out-of-control humor of Richard Pryor, prioritizing the hunchbacked pain of a people, catching our afflictions as we ascend in throbbing laughter at ourselves, opening up our hearts to the possibility of butterflies.

A coon show crouches over the land though, and we get lost in this greenhouse contagion of money belts growing out of armpits, mumbo jumbo sambos dancing in tune to what I yam, I yam, a fat hand getting fatter, getting fatter, getting fatter. What I yam, I yam . . .

Everything trembles in early morning dawn. The day almost freezes in little patches of purple, and I wonder if this day will burn down the blue from the sky? How many dawns can hold a people? I return to your genius, my brother. I ask you to tell me about the genesis of your book *Things Fall Apart*. I want an easy way of explaining this. I am part American, in thought, you know. What is the continent's chi? What is Okonkwo's chi? What is America's chi? I ask. Is it good or bad? And your Igbo teeth smile. "Yes, it is this, Sonia, but it is also that. So that you know life is not simple. The Igbo are anxious not to put it all on your chi. The cards were stacked against Okonkwo. I mean, his father was not successful, so Okonkwo had this fear in him that he was actually his father's son and that was what scared him. That is why he was fighting so relentlessly to kill that possibility of his father resurfacing in him. Whether you call it genes or fate, Okonkwo knew he was this man's son and he wanted to be as different from his father as he could be. So he exaggerated everything. He heard the loud sounds: bravery, success, wis- dom, strength, but not compassion. He failed to hear the subtle admonition of his culture, which is that it's wonderful to be brave. But remember also that the coward outlives the brave man. This legacy of colonial rule is not something we can just shake off one morning, Sonia, and say now it's over. There are many things we must unlearn and learn how to be free."

—Amen Amen Awoman Awoman. When one day our children's children ask, "What did you do?" When they rise like the Guatemalan poet René Castillo rose and asked us what we did "when their nations died out / slowly / like a sweet fire / small and alone." When they ask us, "What did you do when the poor suffered, when tenderness and life burnt out of them?" We, the lovers of selves, the lovers of people, the lovers of justice will turn and say, "We resisted. We resisted the ego. We resisted the gossip, the rumor in ourselves. We resisted the greed, the people imperialist in ourselves. We resisted the exaggeration, the hatred of selves and others. We resisted the quick killings and quick retaliations of others. We resisted war, we resisted war, we resisted war. Can you do it? Can you resist? Can you say it? Can you resist? Can you remember? Can you resist? Resist, resist, resist.

Black voters in Florida, can you resist? Can you remember 41 bullets? Can you say 41 bullets? Can you remember, ccccccccccccccccan you ressssssist, even in this death, can you resist??????????????

[Applause]

I'm going to do a striptease in a minute. [Sanchez fixes a problem with her skirt to audience laughter.] I got it, thanks, I'm trying to keep this—I can only wear long skirts and wrap arounds because of this broken foot. Mos Def said, speech is my hammer, bang my world into shape, now let it fall. That's a bad brother.

These are some remarks I gave when I got an honorary degree at a place called Temple University where I taught for 22 years.

[Applause]

President Liacouras, Provost, Deans, trustees, students, parents, guests, fellow participants on this stage.

How can I bind you together, my brothers and sisters?

How can I bind your old wounds so that they stay dormant until newer surgical methods come about?

How can I bind you together, my brothers and sisters, away from Racism. Sexism. Homophobia. Exploitation. Militarism. Extreme
materialism.
Toward unity,
with varying shades of color moving the world in tune to sanity,
love for self and others'
respect for self and others,
ambition without exploitation.

How can I weave you into a rainbow symmetry, letting your

brown, yellow, white and black laughter sprinkle our lives with
non-destructive tints?

How can I bind you Asians. Latinos. Whites. Africans. African-Americans.
Jews. Chicanos. Muslims. Lesbians. Gays. Into a future world away from
the Orwellian image of the future of a boot smashing a human face forever?

How can I bind you to responsibility in a non-responsible world?
How can I bind you to yourselves so that you know the human face will
triumph over the boot forever?

Perhaps through telling you that if we drop our twin seasons of privilege
and inferiority, we will see a world free of myths and social ills.

If we act in the interest of world humanity. If we help improve life for our
sisters and brothers in our country and in the world.

Then we will truly move as human beings

standing upright in a world that is fed by passions of greed and envy and
jealousy and hatred;

You are an important generation to us, my brothers. My sisters. You have
come to us through centuries of man's, woman's inhumanity to man,
woman.

I say, listen to Tolstoy:

there are men who say,
I sit on a man's back, choking him
and making him
carry
me and yet
I assure myself
and others
that I am sorry
for him and wish to lighten his load
by all possible means
except by getting off his back.

You are important to us because the earth can no longer hold
those people who choke or who are choked.

We need you, my brothers and sisters, to learn to build, to lead,
to educate, to respect, to love,
but in a way that your eyes take on different landscapes and
become more human.

For if we lose you to Saturday afternoon murders, extreme
materialism, drugs, alcohol, selfishness
if we lose you to Wars. Pollution. Red, white and blue rhetoric.
Germ warfare.
Then we are finished.

And I, for one, shall not give you up to a life of just three cars, two and a half
children, and four martinis before dinner.

You didn't ask to be born at this point. At this time. But you are here looking
at the 21st century and you must look it squarely in the eye so that there
will be a 22nd century.

Your fate is to be blessed and burdened with knowledge that no other
generation has known or tasted.

You will walk with a technology that stuns the mind;
You will walk with a history of Africans jumping screaming into an ocean
in protest to that obscenity called slavery in the Americas;
You will walk with a history of Native Americans defending their country
against invaders, walking their blue death walk of relocation;
You will walk with a history of Jews and others dying in concen-tration
camps, their children moving in a rain of ash unraveling minds;
You walk with the Japanese in Hiroshima where open flesh was replaced
with commemorative crust;
You will walk with madmen goose-stepping in tune to Guernica; You will
walk with Africans slaughtering two hundred thousand in four months in
Rwanda;
You will walk with the slaughter and rapes in Bosnia, the many massacres
of the spirit and body;
You will walk with New York City startled by the blood in steel and glass
skyscrapers, the morning whispering wings of precocious human birds in
an avalanche of smoke;

You will walk with drugs in suburbia, North Philadelphia, South
Philadelphia, Manhattan, the Bronx, Beverly Hills, Park Avenue.

Yeah, yeah, yeah, yeah. Here s/he is. Step right up, step right up, step right up, right up. A good sale on girls and boys today. Now give me my crack-crack-crack-crack-crack-ing my mind.

We must finally say, I hear your daughter's laughter in the wind, I see your son riding in the morning waves there in our eyes and we never let these intoxicating ideas of race superiority, economic superiority, social superiority, sexual superiority, religious superiority, terrify the earth until it swallows itself whole again.

Your fate today as you begin your walk toward abundance is to say, I remember, I remember. I shall always wear memory on my forehead; I shall never forget the earth. The sea. The people. Love for peace. Justice. And truth. I shall always be arriving, as I am today, a ceremony of thunder waking up the earth
and if you do, if we do, then we know it will get better on this earth.
EBE YIYE.
It'll get better.

So I say to you new graduates on this taffeta day, dropping blue white sapphires,
Inaugurate, across the sound of your words not symbols and serums,
not peepholes and posturing, not lesions and lechery,
Inaugurate a new day, a new way for all Americans and people. Inaugurate like new men and women should, coming out of themselves toward peace and racial, sexual and social justice. So come with yourselves, singing lifeeeee, singing eyessss, sing-ing handsssss.
Alarming the death singers for we have come to celebrate life. Until we become seeing men and women again,
Until we become seeing men and women again, Inaugurate a new way of breathing for the world, a new way of breathing for the world,
and it will get better.
EBE YIYE! EBE YIYE! EBE YIYE!
It'll get better! It'll get better! It'll get better!

[Applause]

DAVIS: I wanted to read one of Toi Derricotte's poems from *Captivity* for her and for her mother. It's called "Christmas Eve: My Mother Dressing."

My mother was not impressed with her beauty;
once a year she put it on like a costume,
plaited her black hair, slick as cornsilk, down past her hips,
in one rope-thick braid, turned it, carefully, hand over hand,
and fixed it at the nape of her neck, stiff and elegant as a crown,
with tortoise pins, like huge insects,
some belonging to her dead mother,
some to my living grandmother.
Sitting on the stool at the mirror,
she applied a peachy foundation that seemed to hold her down,
        to trap her,
as if we never would have noticed what flew among us unless
        it was weighted and bound in its mask.
Vaseline shined her eyebrows,
mascara blackened her lashes until they swept down like feathers;
her eyes deepened until they shone from far away.

Now I remember her hands, her poor hands, which, even then
        were old from scrubbing,
whiter on the inside than they should have been,
and hard, the first joints of her fingers, little fattened pads, the
nails filed to sharp points like old-fashioned ink pens,
        painted a jolly color.

Her hands stood next to her face and wanted to be put away, prayed
for the scrub bucket and brush to make them useful.
And, as I write, I forget the years I watched her
pull hairs like a witch from her chin, magnify
every blotch—as if acid were thrown from the inside.

But once a year my mother
rose in her white silk slip,
not the slave of the house, the woman,
took the ironed dress from the hanger—
allowing me to stand on the bed, so that
my face looked directly into her face,
and hold the garment away from her
as she pulled it down.

[Applause]

DAVIS: So how are you? [laughter]

SANCHEZ: Fine. How are you? We're still alive.

DAVIS: What do you want to talk about?

SANCHEZ: What do you want to talk about? Lucille, we're still alive.

CLIFTON: It was a triumph.

SANCHEZ: We're still warrior women.

CLIFTON: It's a great blessing.

SANCHEZ: And you've got to be warrior people out there. You just can't give in to fear. You know, hey, you've got to be warrior people out there, okay? You can't give in to fear. Isn't that so, you New Yorkers? I'm a New Yorker, you're New York people, okay? C'mon New Yorkers, don't give in to fear, alright? Right, and some of them people down there, it's still funny in Washington, okay? And that's why I love Aaron Magruder. Don't you love that young brother? "Boondocks."

CLIFTON: Oh my, yes, he's from Columbia, Maryland—he's from my town.

SANCHEZ: That's an amazing young brother, and people are writing saying how terrible that he's talking about America in a time of tragedy, right? But you should write, you should call, just call, you know, they really do get on the telephone. Just go, "Hey, hi, I love Boondocks," hang up. [laughter] But do it in the midst of emergencies. We still must have the poets who would tell the truth, the cartoonists who would tell the truth, and people who go to work who will turn around and tell the truth about the country, about the city, about the world, period. I'm not a sentimentalist. You know I don't believe in sentimentality. I look up and say, "Okay, right, I mourn like everyone else mourned that morning as I sat and watched the destruction." The first thing that came to my mind was, "I'm so glad my father's not alive cause he couldn't process this." That's what I thought, you know, "he can't process this, he cannot process this," because it was difficult for us to process—if you understand truly—and then I thought about what we were, about some of the environmentalists, who were against the building of those two buildings . . .

CLIFTON: Yeah, that's right.

SANCHEZ: I thought about all that disservice—my son standing next to me, I was sitting down glued. I said, "You know, I remember we fought against this." And then I said, "I got used to those buildings when I was coming into New York. I used to look on the right side on the train, and look cause once I saw it, I knew I had five minutes to pack up my briefcase.

[Laughter]

You know and you got used to it.

CLIFTON: Yeah, that's what I did today.

SANCHEZ: Yeah, you look for it.

CLIFTON: The thing that I think is interesting, too, is, if you really, really examine yourselves, your lives, when have you not been afraid? When have you not been afraid? Three times, twice?

SANCHEZ: Three, I think. Three times.

CLIFTON: In how many years? 40?

SANCHEZ: In forty years . . . [laughter]

CLIFTON: You're lucky. If it brought you to caring, what a blessing—because we have to care. I don't believe I called it a blessing but when you think about the fact that everybody, when the ship goes down—it doesn't matter if you happen to be brown or black and whatever your father's name. When you go back where you came from, you've got to watch people and then you have to listen to people debate whether profiling in this situation is different from profiling on the highway.

SANCHEZ: Right.

CLIFTON: Surely we know about that, surely we know about this. Surely this is not new on the planet, but we go on, we go on.

SANCHEZ: When black folks wouldn't say it out loud, they said it in the hallways of their homes, in the doorway in the beauty parlors, in the barbershops, but never out loud, you know. Because I'm not a revisionist; when he [Malcolm] said it out loud, I ducked.

[Laughter]

SANCHEZ: Like everybody, I went, "Whoa, don't say that out loud—people are listening, you know what I mean." And he said, "Yeah, yeah they are listening, they should be listening." And the joy of him is that when people, when they begin to change history, they become revisionist. People don't understand that whites, blacks, everybody loved Malcolm. See people, ya'll—some of you young ones—don't realize that [when] you get the history. I remember following him around, and, at every university he went to, the majority of people there were white, and they stood up and clapped and stamped their feet for this man. Some of you older people there know that's true. You know and blacks were cringing at that time, like, "Oh no, don't say that, don't say that, don't say that, don't say that." [laughter]

But it is a terrible thing to realize—that's why I say at some point too—that you can't live in fear. I'm not saying you don't recognize it, but you can't cringe in fear. You know what you gotta say, like one of the things you said in that exquisite poem, "that some of us have lived in this fashion for years" . . . all our lives, whatever. Dick Gregory said once in a speech, he said, "America is now making niggers out of us all." Hear that? He said, "Once upon a time, only blacks were 'the niggers of the world'; now America has made niggers of us all." Like everybody now, you know, because you're expendable. Working-class people are expendable. Maybe even the lower middle class is expendable. You know what I mean—maybe even the middle class. We have to figure that one out, you know, with the machines, whatever. But look at us—on that level, you have to begin to think what that really means.

But I think maybe some of the students want to hear something about Lucille and myself, like when we first met. What I remember is that I first met you at a place called Baltimore when I came to do a reading at Morgan State and you were reading also, and I remember you at that time, meeting you at that time, and then you came down to Margaret Walker's.

CLIFTON: Oh yes, I remember that, and what I remember was everybody was like . . . there were these women writers, and we were all so cool. I mean we were just so very cool.

[Laughter]

SANCHEZ: 1973.

CLIFTON: Yes—big earrings, you know, all of that, and then on the last day—I don't know if you remember this—Sonia had her program and said, "I wanna get autographs." And we were much too cool for that—but then everybody ran and got their programs. We got autographs for all of you.

SANCHEZ: Because it was about history and herstory every place we were. Sometimes I stumble over autographed napkins. You know, once in Chicago, Shirley Graham DuBois, a bunch of people were in Chicago at the same time, performing together. Shirley Graham DuBois, Gwendolyn Brooks, we were all on this one napkin. We all signed our names and I looked at that napkin and thought, "Oh gosh, look at this. I mean look at this," and that's the history. You're right. I mean, if we've got a program here, I'll pass it to everybody to do that—because we need to remember some of those things and those places.

I know one of the things that I always remember; I talked to Miss Margaret, Margaret Walker that is, about the program. She wanted to know how it was, and I remembered everyone reading together, the respect we had for each other, and there were about twenty African-American women in one place in 1973 in Jackson, Mississippi. And it was recorded in either Negro Digest or Black World.

CLIFTON: It was still Negro Digest then.

SANCHEZ: Negro Digest. Get that one—that is worth a whole lot of money if you can find it.

CLIFTON: [laughter] If you can find it!

SANCHEZ: Because it was an amazing, amazing group of people. But 'Lucille' means 'light,' isn't that so?

CLIFTON: Yes.

SANCHEZ: Well, someone asked about some of the similarities—a sister from the Continent told me that 'Sonia' means 'light,' so we are quite related.

CLIFTON: We know this.

SANCHEZ: We know this.

CLIFTON: But I have a photograph still from that conference in Jackson and we're singing. It's me, June Jordan, Audre Lorde and Alice Walker and we're singing, and I bet you can't find that photograph anywhere.

SANCHEZ: No, you can't.

CLIFTON: And we were young. And thin. [laughter] Let's don't go there.

DAVIS: And that was the first time you met? Had you encountered each other's work before then?

CLIFTON: Yes.

DAVIS: What was that story?

CLIFTON: I don't know—wasn't she always there?

SANCHEZ: No, we had read each other's work, and we had taught. The interesting thing about teaching in those early days, we started teaching all the way back, at least I did, in the late 1960s at San Francisco State and what that meant is that we took into the English department all these black folks . . .

CLIFTON: . . . who had not been there.

SANCHEZ: And then we turned around and brought in the other people. I brought in Neruda, I brought in Guillén—they weren't teaching these people. We brought in DuBois. You know America had successfully boycotted Robeson, DuBois, Garvey. And I tell this story—at San Francisco State I was home this day with my Samoyed. I had a Samoyed and I was getting used to it . . . my next door neighbor had brought this big Samoyed and said, "Here, here you need protection," and left this big dog, and I looked at the dog for about two days and kept saying, "If I feed him, maybe he won't eat me up!" [laughter] But there was a knock at the door and I opened the door, and this man said "FBI." And I said, "Yes?" And there was another guy with the landlord, and he turned to the landlord and he said, "Put her out, put her out, put her out." And the landlord said, "She's there teaching," and the FBI agent said, "DuBois, Garvey, Robeson."

I said, "Yes." Now I'll tell you how innocent we were when we first went into teaching Black literature. How naïve. I said, "Yes, I'm teaching Black Literature." [laughter] And this man looked at me like "what kind of fool are you?" You know he said, "You're one of those radicals. Put her out of this place." And the guy [the landlord] said, "Well, she has a lease." He said, "Put her out of this place, put her out of this place." He was livid. And I'm looking at this man and he put his finger in my face again, and the Samoyed leaped for him—"Woof!" [laughter]—and I looked at that dog and I said, "Snow." You know, even I was impressed with Snow. Snow came back and sat down, and I didn't realize that dog would protect in that fashion. They left, and I'm walking down the hallway and I'm petting Snow and I said, "Oh, I've been teaching it wrong." I was teaching literature, thematically. I said, "Sonia, you've got to teach the sociology of the literature, the economics of the literature, the culture of the literature." And I thank that FBI man, wherever he is today, for teaching me how to teach literature. We were taught the other way.

He was angry because we had rescued DuBois. In America nobody taught DuBois. People in America, they didn't teach him; they were scared to teach him because he was on the list. No one taught Robeson—they were too scared to teach Robeson. But you can't teach history without teaching DuBois, Black Reconstruction. You don't know America without reading Black Reconstruction, people.

Years later I was at my father's house. He had a stroke here in this place called New York City, and I went in and he wasn't speaking. I believe if you touch, if you rub the limbs, [you] bring the life back in, so I was rubbing him but I'm also working on my memoirs, so I'm talking out loud. I kept saying to everyone who comes in, "Talk, keep talking, keep talking," so I'm saying "You know, Dad, it's so funny." I said, "You know, I'm there in San Francisco and this FBI man comes and points his finger and says, 'you're teaching DuBois' and he was angry at that." And I'm just talking, and this man, my father, leans forward, opens his eyes, and says, "What you expect, girl, they communist." [Laughter]

CLIFTON: I remember getting a letter from Langston [Hughes], and it came to my father's house, and my father was sitting there. I went by there for something, and my father was sitting there with the letter in his lap looking at me. And he had known this was gonna happen, I'm sure. And he said, "You got a letter from a communist, what you gon do?" Who's a communist? Stalin? But on the other hand, my father—who was not . . . he was an uneducated kind of man, an interesting human—he'd have me write the notes for him; he sent me, I remember, to school with a note, "She do not have to pledge to the flag. When it means to her what it means to a white girl, then she may stand." So I'm thinking, yeah, but, people, I was twelve—you know what I mean. So when I took the note to the teacher, when they started pledging, I jumped up. I mean, it was terrible, it was so embarrassing because you know I didn't know what was going to happen from this, but I got that kind of message from him all the time, all the time.

SANCHEZ: That's a wonderful thing.

CLIFTON: And they were not educated people—that was the good thing, they were, yes thank goodness, for isn't that so, isn't it so, it is my great strength.

SANCHEZ: Good working-class people.

CLIFTON: I'm working class; I work every day.

SANCHEZ: I know but you know what I mean.

CLIFTON: I know the way they use that language.

SANCHEZ: I know the way they use the language—good working-class people but they could have some sense about them.

CLIFTON: The thing in Washington right now with the Anthrax business and the postal workers.

SANCHEZ: . . . working-class people.

CLIFTON: . . . and there was no interest in seeing about the postal workers.

SANCHEZ: That's right.

CLIFTON: The interest was in being sure about the senators and people in the Capitol building. These brothers are taking this mail around and two have died and now suddenly everyone is being administered to.

DAVIS: Sonia, talk about the battles so the young people realize the struggle we were in at San Francisco State. Could you talk about that and that being the origin of Black Studies at the non-historical black colleges so we can know what that was about?

SANCHEZ: You know, Malcolm had died, was killed . . . and Baraka started the Black Arts Repertory Theater. But there were dissenting voices at the BRT. We were the women who were organizing and writing proposals to make sure the projects took place and we were harassed by two of the people from downtown. They came upstairs with guns and said, "You bourgie bitches"—you know what I mean—"You bourgie bitches, come downstairs. We'll teach you about revolution." And we went down, and I'm looking at these people with guns, and I said to myself, "Uh huh, what am I doing here?" And for three hours they harangued us about what America was about and I'm listening and finally I said, "Can we go?" And we went upstairs and packed up my books and left. But we came back the next week and ended up there and it happened again. And they brought us down, and it was always with a gun, and I said to Barbara Hamilton—I can't remember the other sister with whom we were doing all this work in there—I said, "We need to meet outside this building." So we started meeting in these little mini parks to do this work. It was okay for awhile but then chaos . . . Larry Neal was shot, you know, and complete chaos happened there. Baraka went back to Newark, and I just got outta

Dodge and went to see a dear friend in California. And I said, "I'm gonna go to Mexico." And there was a plane strike and planes couldn't fly, so I took a train into Mexico City, which was amazing, like traveling over the pampas. The train kept going around and around until we got to the top. And I was walking down El Paseo de la Reforma, and someone called down from a bus and said, "Hey Sonia Sanchez!" and I kept going and said, "Even in Mexico, you know . . . " [laughter] And I kept walking, you know, and they came running and said, "We've been sending you letters, letters about helping us begin Black Studies." And I said, "Come on." I was hurting so from Malcolm's death, hurting so from the destruction of the Black Arts Repertory Theater. I turned and said, in my New York way, I said, "You call anything black today, it's gonna get destroyed just like that," and kept on walking. And they said "Come on, hang out with us," and I hung out with them. I refused to go [to California] until they came out to New York City. We talked about it, and I said to my father, "I'm gonna go to San Francisco." My father said, "Girl, you don't want to go to San Francisco." I said, "You know, you're right, you're probably right because," I said, "can you imagine making a third-rate movie actor governor of a state?" And Reagan was governor at that time. We went out there and helped to begin this thing called Black Studies. My supervisor from the English Department was a woman by the name of Kay Boyle who was a fantastically political woman, a fine writer, an amazing feminist who had been a writer with Hemingway in Paris. She was chairing the department at the time and that's what we did—we started this thing called Black Studies. And I taught a creative writing class where people wrote about themselves. Can you imagine? And students were told for the first time, "You can write about a black experience: it is not negative, it will not limit you. You will not be limited as such." And they did, and it was just amazing what happened at that particular time and the history classes and sociology classes and all the things that happened out there. It was an amazing time—until a man by the name of Haya Kawa. Haya Kawa came, and Haya Kawa appealed to the Japanese-American community. He said, "I want you to support me and come out against these radicals here at San Francisco State." And one of the people, a representative from the Japanese community, said, "Oh, we didn't know that Mr. Haya Kawa related to being identified as Japanese American . . ." It was an amazing moment for everybody at State; we just rolled on the floor with laughter. But he was calling on that community to help him with these so-called radicals. What was amazing was that for the first time in an English department you were teaching the Langston Hugheses of America. You were teaching by going all the way back, teaching Langston Hughes, Phillis Wheatley, Marcus Garvey, Martin Delaney, and the Harlem Renaissance writers—isn't it amazing? I had to pull everything out. And I'll forever give thanks to a woman, Jean Hutson, who was curator at the Schomburg Library. She supplied me with all the information I needed to teach that Black literature class at San Francisco State University. Because of her I could teach DuBois's *Souls of Black Folk* and Jean Toomer's *Cane.*

We rolled out selections from DuBois's "Of The Coming of John" from *Souls of Black Folk* cause we didn't have the books and then they finally brought the books out. Why? Because there was a market for it. This is America, don't forget, and that same year they brought out

Jean Toomer's *Cane* because we had just xeroxed part of *Cane*, and I took the whole class into the library and there was *Cane* there and I took that book. I would not do it again but I . . . [laughter] I said, "Let them buy another book—whatever."

DAVIS: Lucille, you worked at the Department of Education, right? Were there similar struggles that you went through in terms of curriculum or literature at the time?

CLIFTON: We dealt with children's books at the Department of Education, and we went to schools in three states. This is really a long time ago, and I had to find books that had characters in them that looked like my children, which is why I started writing children's books. Because I wanted to have my children be able to relate to someone like that. American children's literature ought to mirror American children. Now that seems to me quite obvious; however, it didn't seem at that time particularly. I borrowed something from Rudine Sims who said that all children—and I think that all adults as well—need mirrors and windows. Mirrors in which they can see themselves, windows through which they can see the world.

And everybody's children are disadvantaged by not having that. There are some children in our culture who have only seen mirrors—they are disadvantaged. There are some children in our culture who have only seen windows—they are disadvantaged. So it's one of the things I like to do—to provide balance, to provide windows and mirrors—if possible for my own children. I have six children. When they were little, they had me; but what did their schoolmates have, you know? And even now, I teach a class called Unpopular American History. [laughter] I taught it because at Duke I was asking, one time, if people had ever heard—now Duke is, right, big time—

SANCHEZ: Supposedly.

CLIFTON: Yeah, right. I was teaching a class, and people had never heard of Paul Robeson. Well, I thought, "Okay, he's dead, I suppose." But when they said they had never heard of Julian Bond and he's over in D.C. and . . .

SANCHEZ: . . . alive and still kicking . . .

CLIFTON: I said, "We can't have that." So at St. Mary's I'm very fortunate. They let me teach whatever I want to, but the students don't get credit for the class. Isn't that interesting? The history people don't like it, so we talk about it . . .

SANCHEZ: But you get credit for dancing, taking a course in dancing—in spitting, probably, too.

CLIFTON: You don't get credit for learning about the Trail of Tears; they don't know about My Lai; they don't know about the Salem Witch Trials, which was an offense against women and humanness—the youngest child imprisoned in Salem was? Most people guess 12—she was 4, some authorities say 5.

AUDIENCE: Richard Wright, I haven't heard that name used.

SANCHEZ: Well you will, have patience.

CLIFTON: We wasn't finished!

SANCHEZ: You've got to have patience; we're not finished, are you? Just hold tight.

CLIFTON: That's why we're talking about the class, because in that class I do teach about the things that people don't know about. I have a friend who was a Tuskegee Airman, who was a general. He was court-martialled but he got back his brass or whatever that is they call that, when he was in camp one day and the officers' quarters were segregated. There were the officers' quarters and then he would go around in the back where it was like the officers' room for the African-American officers. And the African-American soldiers were not allowed in the movie house. He was riding by that one day and saw them marching in German prisoners of war to the movie house. And he went off—I mean he went off, and I try to teach about that. And I do it because I don't want anybody to be able to say, "Nobody ever told me." I don't want any of them to ever say, "I never heard of that." Now what they do with it is on them but they will have heard that. They would have heard the story, the whole story, because it is important. You only love something that you know wholly, including one's self.

SANCHEZ: And he should've gone off. You know, I think that one of the things when we first started to write—I mean, people always ask me, "Why did you write such angry stuff?" I said, "Because I looked up after I was an educated woman and found out I had not been taught my history."

I was in the Schomburg: I went off, I went off, I started to cry—that's why I love Miss Jean Hutson to this day. I just—you know how you get out of school? I went to Hunter College and waited to get a job teaching in the system here. I answered an ad in the *New York Times.* You know how they have the ad—a thing about someone to write for the company. Write XYZ 465 New York Times. I did and they sent a telegram on a Saturday: "report to work on Monday." I went around the house saying to my father, "See, see, see, you can get a job writing. See, see, see, you can get a job writing." And my father looked at me and said, "Uh huh." The interesting thing was that he was not excited at all. He said, "uh huh," and I said, "see see see," all Saturday and Sunday.

I got ready to go to work on that Monday. I had a blue suit on, a blue hat on, blue shoes, white gloves, and a blue purse.

CLIFTON: Gloves?

SANCHEZ: Oh yes, gloves, yes, and I didn't show up at CP time. They said, "Show up at nine." I was there at eight thirty, before anyone. The receptionist came in at a quarter to nine, opened the door, and I showed her the telegram and she looked at it, and she said, "Yes."

And she got up, but there must have been another entrance there, because other people had come in. They didn't come in the front; they came in side doors or whatever, etc. So about ten minutes to, someone came out and looked and went back. . . a male. In about another two minutes, someone came and looked (again) and went back. A male. And then about five minutes to nine, this guy came out and said, "I'm so sorry the job is taken." And I said, "What do you mean?" I said, "No, I have my telegram there." And he said, "You know, the job is taken." I said, "Oh, I got it." I stood up. I said, "This is discrimination." He just stared at me coldly—coldly, no emotion at all. I said, "I'm going to report you to the Urban League." I laugh about that now, and he said, "uh huh," you know, like "Yeah, you do that."

I went out of there. I took the hat off, you know. I was so mad. I got on the train. I didn't get off at 96th Street where I would have to stay on the number one to go uptown. I ended up at 135th Street and 7th Avenue. I woke up out of this real daze and started walking across 135th Street, and there was this thing that said Schomburg on the side—the old Schomburg—and I was hot, I was mad, I was everything. I said to the guy who was standing outside, "What kind of library is this?" I said, "I just got out of Hunter, I've never seen this library." He said, "Go inside and ask." And the old Schomburg had a long table and the glass door, you know, where Miss Hutson stayed, and I went and knocked on the glass door. I said, "Hi." She said, "Hello." She used to tell this story to my students. I brought my students every semester to the Schomburg for study, and she used to tell this with this very sly smile on her face. And I said, "What kind of library is this? She said, "This is the Schomburg, dear." I said, "What kind of library is this?" She said, "We have books only by and about Black folks." And I said, with my sly self, "There must not be very many books in here." [laughter] And she said, "Dear, why don't you sit down," and she eased me in and she said, "Just a minute," and she brought me three books: *Up from Slavery, Souls of Black Folk,* and *Their Eyes were Watching God,* and put them right there. For some reason *Their Eyes Were Watching God* was the top book, and I start reading. I had trouble initially in terms of the language—you know, the Black English. After I was about a third of the way in, I eased out and there were all these old men scholars sitting there working. They haven't looked up yet, you know, just writing, and I eased out and knocked on the door, and I said, "How could I have been an educated woman and not read this?" and I started to cry. And she said, "That's all right, dear. Go back and just read." I eased in and sat there and started reading some more, and I started to cry and I eased out and knocked on the door. I said, "Well, how can they say we're educated if we don't read this?" And she said, "Yes, dear. Now go back and sit down and read." I eased back. One of them said, "Miss Hutson, would you tell this young woman either she sits still or she has to leave."

And I sat still because I was supposed to be going out to work every day. I didn't. I came to the Schomburg every day. I sat still for two weeks just going in, just reading. Then Miss Hutson did a wonderful thing. She gave me the name of Mr. Michaux. She said, "Go. You need to get some books of your own." She sent me to Mr. Michaux, who had his store diagonally across from the Hotel Teresa. For those who don't know the Hotel Teresa is there at 125th Street, right where the old Chock Full Of Nuts used to be—something else is there now, God knows what. I went to Mr. Michaux. "I don't have any money; I don't have a job yet. I'm supposed to be looking for a job." He gave me books. He said, "Here, you'll give it back."

And then she sent me to—what's the Caribbean bookstore?—Richard Moore. Remember how small it was? You had to go in sideways. And he said, "Girl, have you read . . . ?"—and he did this litany of Caribbean writers I hadn't read, and I didn't know who they were, didn't know they existed. And he pulled that little roller up and went up there and started pulling books. I said, "I don't have any money." He said, "That's all right, you'll give it back."

Miss Hutson did that; therefore, it wasn't by chance that when they started Black Studies, they said, "Who can teach black literature, who knows that?" "Sanchez, she's always talking about those books, those black books." That's how I got to San Francisco State because I was always saying "You should read this; you should read that; you should read that." And that's the strange kind of herstory that we have.

[Applause]

DAVIS: Do you want to talk about some of the mirrors in your life that sort of led you onto the road of poetry?

CLIFTON: My life has been so very different because I—everybody knows I didn't graduate from college—I went to Howard. I got a scholarship from Howard in the 1950s. I went there for a year. Howard in the 1950s was a most interesting place. I had never been away from my father's house, my mother's house. I'd never spent the night anywhere, and we got to DC in the 1950s—you know they had the dome over the station. I first of all, of course, thought this was not outside. I thought it was a building, maybe Howard, and I was there with a couple of friends of mine from Buffalo. They used to have sophomores and juniors come and greet the freshmen at the train, and I remember I had a little friend. I can't remember her name now, and I remember one of the sophomore gentlemen came and said to her (she was awfully cute), "Oh we're so [glad]—you're gonna love it here" And he looked at me and said, "You must be her mother." And I remember thinking to myself—I was still me, right—"As soon as I eat, I'm going home." [laughter] I swear, I have been myself for about 60-something years, but the things that I did learn were that—when I was very young, I've said many times, I learned to distrust authority quite a lot because I learned it a long time ago, I learned in those early years.

I was born in a little town that had very few African-American people, just our family really, and it was mostly Polish. And so I learned to understand Polish and to speak it when I was child, but I knew that people talked about niggers and I didn't know what that was. But what I did know was [that] I wasn't one, and so that led me to believe that anything they said could be suspect because they were saying this and it wasn't true. Maybe these weren't telling the truth and when I discovered that people were not going to teach me, were only going to teach me what they thought I could learn or what they wished me to know, I grew into a nosy kind of curious person. So I wanted to learn about all the rest of it, too, and I still, today, don't know whether I can teach or not. But I've been teaching college 31 years, and I do know I can learn. And I vowed then I was gonna learn a lot about everything I could. So I went to the library and in Buffalo [with] Ishmael Reed—I've known Ishmael. Ishmael and I. I'm not gon tell that story.

SANCHEZ: Don't, don't!

CLIFTON: But I've known Ishmael since we were about fourteen or fifteen, and Ishmael worked at the library, and he would liberate a book from time to time. [laughter]

SANCHEZ: Tsk tsk tsk . . .

CLIFTON: And anyway he used to steer me and some others toward books. And I would find one book, and it would mention something or someone, and I would go find another. I was always a learner and a reader in my life, and my father—I don't think he would call himself a Garveyite but he was a person who had very definite opinions about things, and he would voice them.

My father used to always tell me that I could do anything in the world I wanted to because I was from Dahomey women. I went for that, you know, I believed it. I was a Dahomey woman and so I could just be that and it was a good thing. When I went to Howard at that time in the 1950s—I'm sure it's all different now—but in the 1950s I was not light enough, you know, excepting that I was from New York State and you see they didn't know New York City was nowhere near Buffalo. And so they thought I was acceptable because I was from New York and I didn't even mention upstate on the border.

I was there at a wonderful time because my classmates were . . . do you know Joe Walker, who wrote the *The River Niger*? Joe was my first crush. Oh I thought he was . . . girl!

SANCHEZ: Ooh fine . . .

CLIFTON: I thought he was so smart and Roberta Flack, she was there. Sterling Brown was my teacher. James Lavelle was my teacher. A lot of really remarkable . . .

DAVIS: Toni Morrison was there, too.

CLIFTON: Yeah, Toni. I've known Toni since I was that age—she was there. So many people, so many people who I didn't even realize. I was in the first production of James Baldwin's "The Amen Corner" which was premiered there, and I was in Sterling A. Brown's writing class. Now, here's this big kid from Buffalo who'd never been—I had on jeans all the time, not because I was that casual but I just had some jeans. We were poor people, we was po', you know, and they thought I was so exotic and I had on jeans. Sterling Brown had a group of writers who met, and, now, how he let me be a part of that, I have no clue. But it was Sterling Brown, Owen Dodson, James Baldwin (when he was there), Joe Walker, and me. And I then didn't appreciate it, of course, but later I did; and I have no idea why I was—why he allowed me to be in his presence. That's where I first heard Billie Holiday.

SANCHEZ: That record collection he had, he had an amazing record collection.

CLIFTON: It opened me to a lot of possibilities. And then when I was published—I had no idea you could be published and look like me—I never sent things out. I still rarely do but I did not send that poem to the *New Yorker*. I want you to know that. I've talked about sending stuff to the *New Yorker* a lot. But they asked me for the poem. I had been writing, I had been writing poems with serious intent since I was a girl. I was twelve, eleven. I saw Robert Hayden's name in a book, and I thought Robert Hayden, and I thought, "He's a colored man." And so I sent him some poems (and, oh, Baraka was there at Howard too when I was there and A.B. Spellman— I've known them 40-something years) and Hayden took them to Carolyn Kiser, who was at that time head of the National Endowment for the Arts literature program.

Carolyn took them to the YMHA 92nd street Y, and I won the Discovery Award in that year. I had never heard of the Discovery Award, plus I didn't believe there was a YMHA. Cause I know the YMCA—I mean I'm not a fool, right? At that time I was 30-something years old. I had six children, the oldest was seven, and I had never imagined such a thing. But I had taken great care in my work.

Now I must say this to you. I must say this. People, I think, sometimes are surprised that Sonia and I are such good friends because we don't write alike. Particularly when I was first writing, African-American writers didn't particularly think . . . didn't validate what I did because it did not seem to be political, forgetting what Gwendolyn Brooks said—that when she walked out of her door, it was a political decision.

SANCHEZ: That's right, that's right.

CLIFTON: That's true, but that's all changed.

SANCHEZ: But that's how you get back to the point of how people become friends. It was because in this strange thing that we have out here in this literary world, people will identify you as such. I mean, they put tags on you very easily and there was a tag on her and there was a tag on me. And because we were tagged, I used to always try to contact the people who were tagged—like "Let us hang together" because it means simply, people are seeing something in us that they don't like, that they don't appreciate in a very real sense, and I think that what's important—we looked up at each other and you don't have to. You recognize what I do. I recognize what you do. You recognize what people do—the intent and the content, you know, and the love. The thing about Lucille's work that you constantly see is always, the subtext is always love. The subtext is always love and the subtext is also, "Let me do this well, let me give you the best product I can possibly give you." And that's always been there. That's always been present.

You know, what we've tried to do on this earth, I think, in part, is to say simply, "If you can possibly read other political poets and say they do it well, then we too will do it." Every poem is political—it either maintains the status quo or it talks about change, period—okay?

DAVIS: Bottom line.

SANCHEZ: Always this idea that it's political because you mention a couple of words—that's pure nonsense. But the point is that one of the things that you see, that you saw in Lucille from following her work, is that we taught.

We brought all this work into the classroom—every time someone did a book, we brought it into the classroom so all our students had to read these people, period. Here they were, not being done in the English department or in what they called American literature. I mean, the thing that's so parochial about America is that it's still called the English department—isn't that wild? Think about that! The English department, right?

I started to teach American literature because nobody wanted to teach American literature. Everybody wanted to teach English literature: you give me Shakespeare, give me Blake, you know, and they always were talking about the Irish writers—called them English. Cause a whole lot of English writers weren't writing, so they took over the Irish writers and said, "They're English also." So we were left with African-American writers and American writers also, their work saying, "Look at these people"—and that's what we did. Finally because we introduced into that English department the whole idea of saying, "You've got to deal not only with African-Americans, you've got to deal also with Native Americans, you gotta deal with Chicanos."

I had in my course at San Francisco State two Japanese-American young women and we had come across the thing that said report to the location, the relocation, the concentration camps, internment. I brought in a picture of it and said, "Do you know anything about this?" and they got pissed. They said, "Sonia, I don't know anything about that." I mean, really, like "How dare you!" I said, "Well, go home and ask your parents." They came back in on Tuesday with tears in their eyes. Their parents had told them a story of silence—see what this country has been about?

The great thing about the poets, I love people who say they write poetry. Don't you ever see me stop you, whenever you say it. I look you straight in the eye and say, "Do you really? No, do you really love this thing called poetry? Are you willing to do the work? Are you ready to study? Are you ready when you come study with me?" As they come into the class, I make them do form. They say, "Why are we doing form? You're too hip to do form." I say, "No I'm not." I studied with a woman by the name of Louise Bogan at NYU and we all came in free versers. You know what I mean?

CLIFTON: Cool and modern.

SANCHEZ: Cool and modern words. On so many pieces of paper. She would look at it, you know, in her aristocratic voice and say, "Sonia, do you know why you did the following?" You know, I didn't know why. I just did it. Why should I know?

But she made us study form, she made us understand that all free verse has form, she made us bring it in, bring it in, bring it in. So as we struggled through blank verse and villanelles, you know, and ballads and blues, as we struggled through that course, I chose the Haiku finally as mine. Finally it was the thing I wanted to do because it just seemed to me that if you're all over the page, that haiku brings you right home. Three lines, you know, make you deal with some very real things on this earth. But I guess what I'm saying is at some particular point, I look people in the eye, these young people, and I say "Are you willing to study? Are you willing to learn this craft called poetry? And above all are you willing to love the language?"

CLIFTON: Because what happens, I think, is that people don't want to write poems as much as they want to be a poet.

SANCHEZ: Yeah, there's a difference.

CLIFTON: I want to be a poet; I don't know what's so cool about it.

SANCHEZ: Being a poet, being on stage . . .

CLIFTON: Oh . . .

SANCHEZ: Being on stage, that's what it is.

CLIFTON: Be a poet, big deal. I still have to do the dishes and everything else.

SANCHEZ: You do. One of the young men—he came from, I think, some place in the South—when I was living up in the Bronx came for the weekend for an interview. And he came in and my twins were little, little; and I had just fed them and I was cleaning up. I ran the bath water because that was the one time I had a chance for peace. I just threw 'em both in the bathtub and it just flooded, you know, they would flood the whole bathroom. I told the guy "I gotta clean this up." He said to me, "But you live in such an ordinary way, Sonia." I said, "Yeah I'm an ordinary woman." [laughter] I said, "There's no help here except my aunt who helps me with the children when I'm teaching during the week. She goes home weekends. I'm with the children, I'm feeding them on weekends." You know what I mean—that was real.

CLIFTON: Nobody would watch my kids—I had four in diapers at once. My sister said to me, "I love you and I love the children. I will not watch four in diapers at once."

SANCHEZ: That's hard, four in diapers is hard.

CLIFTON: We didn't have a washing machine and I said many times—this was a while back, of course—but I'm one of the few poets who fusses about this.

SANCHEZ: Yes, we fuss about that a lot. Say it.

CLIFTON: I've been evicted twice, you know—a long time ago, so if you've been evicted once, I am not at all impressed. [laughter] I haven't been evicted anymore though, so everything's cool.

SANCHEZ: A young sister just called me from Boston. She just had a baby, and she was a writer and she was interviewing me over the telephone. She said, "Well, how did you do it, how did you do it?" I said, "How did I do what?" She said, "How did you stay alive and keep writing with babies?" I said, "You do it." I said, "If you ask me how I did it, I can't tell you. You know," I said "but there was many a night after I put everybody to bed, I went crazy during those midnight hours from 12:30 till about 5:30. I was crazy and I walked in my craziness." What is today? It's not day, it's night, oh it's night ho ho ho ho. Should I read a book, why should I read a book? Should I write a book, why should I write a book? Who's gonna read the book, who's gonna care if I write the book? But at 5:30, like clock work, like clock work, cause the kids were gonna get up—snap back to sanity. I could not afford to go insane.

CLIFTON: Indeed.

SANCHEZ: And that's the point that she's saying, and so I would put the children down. I'd run out to the corner, you know, some of you, to the Laundromat to throw my children's clothes in to be washed and then I ran back to make sure they were okay. And I timed it, and I ran back to put them in the dryer, then I ran back to try and make sure they were okay. Then I ran back to get them out of the dryer . . .

CLIFTON: I had a friend one time when I was in Buffalo, and her husband came running to the house, and said, "Lucille, you gotta come and see about her, cause she's gone catatonic." Now they had two children, see. He said, "Come and would you take the children?" I've got six, right! "Come and take the children." And I went over to his house, and she's laying up there on the floor, you know, and I said, "Girl, you have to get up!"

SANCHEZ: That's right.

CLIFTON: "You have to uncatatonic. [audience laughter] I'm not catatonic and I've got much more reason than you do to be miserable and I'm not taking your children." So she just sorta shook herself, got on up, and went on with her life.

SANCHEZ: Didn't have the leisure.

CLIFTON: We didn't have time for that.

SANCHEZ: You didn't have the leisure to go crazy permanently, you know. You know you could do it, you know you know it—don't be looking at me. You women know what I'm talking about, but you know I know and you know we know and we know what happens, you know. Mmmh mmmh, yeah.

DAVIS: Alright. [audience laughter]

SANCHEZ: But you don't stop laughter. She's startin', she's startin', but you don't have any insanity in the poetry. Think on that. Think on that.

CLIFTON: The poetry sustains.

SANCHEZ: The poetry says, "I'm not gon take none of this insane shit—you know what I mean—you know what I mean." Excuse my French. [laughter]

SANCHEZ: "You know if you're gonna come here and do something, you gonna come with some kind of sense of the world, girl. Get your head together before you start writing me." And you say, "Yes, I will. Yes, I will." And you do.

CLIFTON: Because you serve the poems.

SANCHEZ: That's right.

CLIFTON: I'm here to try and help the poem become what it seems to want to be. This is what I do. This is what I am. I can no more not write the poem . . . Now publishing is something else!

SANCHEZ: Yes, it is.

CLIFTON: I had been writing for thirty years before I was published, but that's not the part that matters. What matters [is that] the poem wants to come and I'm here to receive it, try to be faithful to it and remain open to the possibility—and it shows up.

SANCHEZ: And you young writers understand that. That you open yourself up to the universe, you open yourself up to what it is you see. What I'm saying is don't think about "I want to be on a stage someplace" but think about "I want to receive from the universe these words that will not only sustain me but will sustain other people."

Just think what your books do or your writing. Just think what they do for other people. There are people who will write you and say you have no idea how you saved me during my midnight hours. That is something. That's better than anyone writing any review about your book; the idea is those things that come in. I did a book called *Wounded In The House Of A Friend,* and I got this letter—I was in my office at Temple—and this letter came from this young brother who said, "I have read you"—it came from the state of Washington—"forever since I was a little boy." I'm always amazed by that when people tell you. I start looking "aw yeah right, that's a long time there, right." He continued, "I started and then stopped reading that book and I got upset, because you too are now joining that company of people who are damning men." It was written in blue (ink) and then there was a date there, let's say 9/14 and then there was a date 10/14 and it was written in another ink. And he said, "I went into the kitchen"—he's a grad student—"I went into the kitchen to tell my wife that I was going to go on campus and my wife was insane, collapsed. She was insane in the kitchen, talking to herself." And he said, "I know why she was insane, because I was having an affair on that campus and it was an unspoken thing between us and that was why she was going insane." He said, "I went back and read that prose poem." He said, "I want to thank you, Professor Sanchez. I will never ever again make my wife go through that which I put her through." Now that's simple on many levels but it's profound. I went to a place called Washington in that great bookstore—you know that great bookstore in Washington in Seattle . . .

AUDIENCE: Elliott Bay.

SANCHEZ: Elliott Bay, oh I could live [there] for days, you know what I mean. Go there for Elliott Bay—it's an amazing bookstore and there was this line, I was autographing books and this person was at the end and I looked up and I said, "You're the one who wrote me that letter," and he said, "Yes," and I got up and I hugged him. The point, my poetry and the poets that I know who wrote well, is to keep us all human. And that is what we finally have got to understand. That we've got to make you turn around when you're fearful and say, "Don't be afraid. What are you afraid of? What are you afraid of? And why do people want you to be afraid?" You know. Why do people want you to be afraid? And if you can say, "I'm not afraid." We are a nation of people who will not succumb to this fear at all, then that's what we do as poets—make you understand what it is finally to be human and to walk upright.

CLIFTON: The poem, I think, the thing that poetry can do, is speak for those who have not yet found their ability to speak.

SANCHEZ: That's right.

CLIFTON: And to say you are not alone.

SANCHEZ: That's right.

CLIFTON: You are not alone and if that's all it does—that's enough, that's sufficient.

SANCHEZ: Oh yes, it is, yes it is. [clapping]

DAVIS: What we're going to do now is take a few questions. We're going to take a few questions from the audience.

AUDIENCE QUESTION: What relationship does your work have to the theme of regret?

CLIFTON: I am a whole human. I don't think of that as a theme, first of all, but if it is, I'm a whole human. It is human to be angry, it is human to be glad, it is human to be afraid—all of that. I wished to express in all of my humanness. I wish to see myself wholly and to be seen wholly—I wish to see others wholly and to have them see me wholly. What I regret is that I have not been more human—perhaps that's what I regret. But if I do, it is all going to make me what I am. And whatever that is that I am, I try very hard to honor it and to respect it and to know it. What I tell audiences is that it is quite all right. It's interesting (when I say) "I'm just like you" and for people who think of themselves as liberal, that's easy: "I'm just like you are." But it is a little more difficult for them to understand that they are just like me and I know that's true too. I know that's a little more difficult but it's not impossible. We do the difficult every day. I do difficult stuff all the time. Getting up.

AUDIENCE: Regarding school?

CLIFTON: School is not the only place you can study. Sonia's very educated . . .

SANCHEZ: Shhhhh. [laughter] But if you want that degree, get it. Don't let it cloud what you want to do. And then once you get it, put it aside and keep on going. But you can study everything.

CLIFTON: Yeah, learn.

AUDIENCE QUESTON: But as a writer, I have to [go to] the English Department. I don't belong in the English Department, but yet I'm stumped as to where I'm supposed to go. I don't know where to go.

CLIFTON: Go to the books, read them, go to the library. I've never taken creative writing classes. I've never taken them but that doesn't mean I don't know anything about it. There's a lot of stuff I don't have to deal with because I don't have to unlearn it, you know, which is a great blessing. But learn. Learn. Learn. If you wait for people to tell you what they know, that's all you'll know.

DAVIS: There's a question back there. Right there in the front with the black shirt.

AUDIENCE QUESTION: I just wanted to ask you. I'll keep it brief but I just wanted to ask you. Dr. Sanchez, I don't know if you'll remember me, but back at the University of Chicago about two years ago we were doing a reading for a group and your plane was late, it was horrible. I don't know, but we had this auditorium full of people and they were all like, "Where is Mama Sanchez?" We have food waiting, we started eating before she got there. Trying to keep the crowd quiet and she finally came in. And I was organizing, I didn't know that you had come in.

And you were sitting in the front and you were listening to other poets but you were kind of nodding, nodding off. I know you had had a hell of a time at the airport. And they turned the lights out on you and you were so tired.

I just want to let everyone know how real this woman is. She went ahead and took us out to dinner after we got through—we didn't get finished until about 11:30, and she just wanted to go back to the hotel. And we said, "Well, we were going to take you out to dinner," and she said, "Well, I'll go out to dinner." We went to Leona's in Hyde Park, and she was kind of nodding off as she was talking then and telling us about history.

You know that changed me as a writer because I too wanted to be that writer, I wanted to be on stage, I wanted people to read my books, and professors to talk highly about me. But I thought about that moment, us sitting at Leona's and eventually after they kicked us out. I just thought about you sitting with us, 6 young black girls and talking to us and teaching us. I was like, you know, this is what it's all about. I just want to thank you for that evening. We took you to your hotel and we wrote you a letter thanking you, but I just wanted to thank you personally.

SANCHEZ: Thank you. [clapping]

AUDIENCE QUESTION: We spoke earlier about Cave Canem. I just want to take a moment to acknowledge your old heads from the Sonia Sanchez workshop on Countee Cullen . . .

SANCHEZ: Three years.

AUDIENCE: I'm gonna ask the Sonia Sanchez workshop folk who are here to raise your hands. Sonia has been doing it for a very long time, and there's a lot of us who can point back to where we started to learn the craft and thank her. I don't know if you remember, Sonia. National Black Theater on Sunday afternoon. Close your eyes and something was passed around in each of our hands and we were asked to think about what it was and what the image was. It was a grape and we were asked to create the image off of the feel of that grape and that was one of the early exercises that Sonia had in her bag of teaching tricks, so I just wanted to take this opportunity to acknowledge and thank you because an awful lot of where my work is now today is the result of you.

SANCHEZ: Thank you.

CLIFTON: Testify, I love this.

DAVIS: We're going to take just one more question and then that will be it for the evening. There will be a signing again after this, and you'll have an opportunity to buy books if you'd like.

SANCHEZ: Before we take the last question, Lucille and I thank you for coming out on a Wednesday night. [clapping]

CLIFTON: Thank you.

SANCHEZ: Talking about poetry—ooh.

CLIFTON: That's right.

AUDIENCE QUESTION: The war and everything that's going on. What do you think now should be the issue? Should we be more focused? Would this have happened if George Bush hadn't been elected in the first place? There seem to be so many questions.

SANCHEZ: Me? You just continue to do your work and you don't let what I call "that red blue and white patriotism"—you know, the idea that you should put a flag in your hand every time you move even when you go to the bathroom.

I'm not being disrespectful. I'm saying that is not what you are about. As someone said to me, "Do you have a flag in front of your house?" I said, "I understand the flag quite well you know, and I don't have to have that flag in front of my house at all." Do you understand what I'm saying? And the point is that for a moment we're all stunned and we stop.

Because you stop and you have to say, "Well okay, let me reconnoiter here. Let me look and see how I go." You see and you don't come out stupidly. You don't come out making comments that will offend people. People have had losses, okay, you don't offend people's losses. You don't offend the whole point of people mourning—what's that about? But you also don't let a country offend you and make you believe that you're stupid. You know, when people begin to say, "Now I will take away your liberties" because we're at war, and the point of all of us should be now on this earth, peace. We've got to begin to teach this thing called peace finally and it's an opportune time to do it. [clapping]

CLIFTON: Now do you see what I'm saying?

SANCHEZ: Sure.

CLIFTON: One of the things I believe very strongly is that cultures and civilizations are lost in groups, but they are saved one on one and so doing your own work is a good thing. You know they are saved person to person—this is where Michael Jackson has it right. I looked at the man in the mirror. [laughter] I changed his ways. "If you want to make the world a better place, get a get a, what is it—Take a look at yourself and make a change." [laughter, clapping]

SANCHEZ: That was good.

CLIFTON: Yeah, that was good.

SANCHEZ: Thank you.

Wanda Coleman

WHAT SAVES US: AN INTERVIEW WITH WANDA COLEMAN
BY PRISCILLA ANN BROWN

I first became aware of Wanda Coleman and her work on July 16, 2002. One of my friends and I were talking about writers who were "junky" and "pushing the edges" of several genres. I was fascinated to learn of a writer who had been creating for decades and who had received several accolades but who was not, at that point, a staple in the African-American Literature canon. That night I went on-line and visited many of the websites where Coleman's poetry, interviews, and reviews appear. I became intrigued. The following day I made a trip to the University of Virginia and was ecstatic to find that many of her books were in its collection. I have since read all of her published works and am totally convinced that I have found the perfect subject for a book, for a vacancy, indeed, exists in the body of scholarly criticism addressing significant pieces of African-American literature, namely her work. The breadth of the topics she explores (gender, race, urban society, connectedness and disconnectedness, psychological hurting and healing, and love—in all its many facets); her experimentation with forms; the span of her career, particularly her persistence in the face of frequent slights; and her philosophy of what constitutes art and literature—all deserve deeper, scholarly exploration.

As a part of that deeper exploration, I flew from Washington, D.C., to Los Angeles on Halloween night 2002 to interview Wanda Coleman the next day. Because of her gracious hospitality, I actually spent two days with Ms. Coleman, both of which gave me keen insights into her world as a woman, a wife, a mother, and a writer. We spent much of the first day taking "the tour" of Coleman's home city. She showed me the places that are key to her life and to her writing, from Marina del Rey to Hollywood to her childhood home in South Central. After showing me the city through her eyes, Coleman invited me to her house for breakfast the next morning. Over a deliciously deadly feast of real bacon, eggs, toast and leaded coffee, we began to chat. What follows is a series of excerpts from that conversation.

* * * * *

BROWN: Will you talk about the purpose of art? One of the things that you do in your poetry, in your books, in your short stories, even in the columns that you've written is to foreground these very common, very marginalized, invisible people incorporate them into poetry, into short stories, into an art form. Is your work art for art's sake, or art for the sake of social change?

COLEMAN: The Aesthetic Movement? *[Chortles]* Baudelaire and all those guys?

BROWN: Yes, exactly, all the way back to that. But will you talk about the purpose of *your* art? You're definitely about creating artistic forms and artistic expression, but that creativity is often coupled with the marginalized or invisible.

COLEMAN: Well, I'm interested in the world—the world the way I've lived it. One of the things that drove me to read so voraciously when I was a child was the fact that the world as

I observed it didn't exist in literature. And so, therefore, I wanted to put things that I saw in the world into literature. And because I've seen things here [in the world], they're there [in the literature]. They exist. Others must see them. And I started to ask myself, "Why isn't this in literature?" I would go to the library shelves and start with the "A" sections and just go, just start reading, working my way toward "Z." You know, looking to see who else sees what I see.

BROWN: Right, and where is my experience recorded in this literature?

COLEMAN: Or something that corresponds to it vaguely because I realize that for people who have lived in other times, that's their time and this is my time; but there should be things that correspond. You know, looking for clues, not only clues as to what my perceptions are but into how to present these perceptions, and therefore how to write. Since I'm interested originally in that road that we were talking about earlier—that "road less traveled"—I'm not interested in imitating or doing what someone else is already doing. Or looking at the people or the things or the events, necessarily, that everyone is going to grab on to. And so, if everyone who is writing about Hollywood writes only about the actors...

BROWN: And the glitz and the glamour...

COLEMAN: ... and then there are those who have written about the seedy aspects of L.A. also (thinking of Charles Bukowski, Raymond Chandler and Anne Nietzke), then I want to present maybe something that's even outside of those realms. I've never seen the Hollywood I know presented. So, in *Mambo Hips,* especially, *here I am*—I want to show some of the Hollywood I know that people don't want to talk about or SEE that exists.

And I'm interested in the flip side of Hollywood because it carries our images to the world. Because that causes damage too by misrepresenting us. I'm more interested in the inner workings of that, and I try to present some of that in *Mambo Hips.* People who have studied cinema and know something about movies will recognize that those little Zen-like passages are really about images and camera work. Those opening passages are called analects—a lot of people don't like those. One of my dearest friends, she just skips them: "Let me get back to the narrative," you know, "skip that." *[Both laughing]*

BROWN: When I read *Mambo Hips,* I wanted Tamala to experience some measure of success before her demise. And then she never made it. Death came right on the eve of her *making it BIG*—albeit, through channels that were destructive to her.

COLEMAN: That, I guess, is the mystery of Tamala. Because the reader goes away never quite knowing what happens in those final hours. And the conclusion was basically irrelevant. I wanted to show evil at work ... because my interest was in the social forces that worked against Tamala.

I have a clipping from when I was about twelve, buried somewhere in my archives in there *[indicating a hallway].* I found an article about a man who comes home from work one day to find his wife has left him. He was fired from his job earlier that day, got a severance check, cashed it, then lost his wallet. While looking for the wallet, he's bitten by something poisonous and rushes to the doctor. After treatment and examination, the doctor, tells him he has cancer [chuckles] and less than six months to live. So, he goes home, and gets a gun and blows his brains out. Now, what do you do when all your twenty-four hour periods are like that?

I think that it's like that, especially for African Americans. You know, there are formulas that psychologists lay out that say you can have only so many traumatic experiences in your life before it leads to suicide [referring to the last stanza in the poem 'Late Broadcast News' from Bathwater Wine, pp. 231, based on an article culled from her clip archives]. These are White people talking … social scientists assessing what is considered the normal amount of stress to have in one's life and considering how much stress leads to the average (meaning White person's) suicide, without a thought about the amount of stress that attends surviving in a racist society. And I'm thinking to myself, "Really? Well, I would have committed suicide a hundred times over, if that—their absurdly minimal criteria—were the   case."

BROWN: Exactly.

COLEMAN: I would have been gone a long time ago, and I think that most African Americans would have also. So, what is this quality that allows us to refrain from self murder? In other words, traumas and horrific crises have traditionally been a way of life for African Americans. When people talk about the strength of the Black woman, you know, I say, "I'm not a strong Black woman." I don't feel like a strong Black woman. Whatever, in my mind, *does that mean?* Compared to what? So … thinking about what is meant by this strength, the physicality can be obvious, being large in the world, being big; but being strong in terms of endurance, bearing up under the unbearable? Examining that issue too is something I feel compelled to do in my work. In Tamala I am presenting someone who doesn't have that cultural underpinning to protect her, although she could possibly access it through her Black friend, Erlene. But that would require acculturation! Tamala doesn't even have the protection the traditional pedestal offers. Plus, she doesn't have a nurturing mother; she has no one in her universe to buoy her up. She has nothing to tap into to reinforce her or to give her this feeling of centeredness or strength.

BROWN: I often look at the contrast between Tamala and her inability to cope and at Erlene's being more realistic about the world, her understanding more about the world. Erlene's behavior reflects those role models and that sense of *community* that Tamala wants but doesn't have.

COLEMAN: But when you say it's a strength, it's not necessarily a strength. It's a reaction. It's a survival mechanism. And that's the difference. Tamala's allowed entree into a world that Erlene isn't allowed into. So, if you really look at it, you know, as Tamala says at one point, people accept her as a White person. So ostensibly she is, regardless of what's in the gene pool. She's—for all intents and purposes—a White woman.

BROWN: And a beautiful one.

COLEMAN: … and a beautiful one. So here she is—I mean—she's like a Rita Hayworth type. So that is what the expectation would be for success. Society allows certain people, if you can get it together, to have access.

BROWN: That's right, and others don't.

COLEMAN: Whereas others don't. Those who aren't allowed access, those of us who have to get along, don't have those soft expectations. And maybe that's what saves us.

* * * * *

BROWN: I'd like to read this excerpt from a review of *Mercurochrome.* The writer, Charles Allen Wyman, says, "For a number of years many young African American poets have been given a broad pronouncement of frustration and anger, with good reason, of course, the oppressed have a perfect right, even a responsibility to cry 'Freedom'; however, in these days of the new millennia, it is a strange truth that such protest has begun to sound cliche through over use. In a way this descent into cliche shows a degree of social promise, for when people of many races recognize a single race's cry as cliche, it is a sign that that oppression has lessened and that the voices of the oppressed have been significantly heard and given due credence."

COLEMAN: There was a competition, locally. The International Black Writer's Association was putting together one of their early anthologies. They had a diversity in editors. David Ulin, who just edited the *Writing Los Angeles* anthology for the Library of America, myself and two other women whose names escape me at the moment, but I think one was teaching at UCLA at the time. So here we are, a panel of two Blacks and two Whites judging the manuscripts, and when we got to the poetry, virtually all the poems from the African Americans of Slave Origin were saying the same thing in the same way. The rhetoric, the same rhetoric in virtually the same phrases. The experience wasn't coming through the individuals themselves; they were the appropriate things to say, at one point in history, but we've gotten past that now. But people are still there and a lot of us are still expressing ourselves in that way because we've come to be taught that this is what is expected of Black people. This is Black. This is what Black poetry is. That's the influence of those people who have culled out their place and are reproducing themselves in others when they're teaching. Instead of encouraging people to move forward, they're creating replicas.

BROWN: Of themselves?

COLEMAN: That's right. And that, I think, is negative. That goes against the idea of voice.

BROWN: And individuality.

COLEMAN: Because we all may have experienced police brutality, but the specific incident and how it occurred has to be varied—in other words—the Devil is in the details. So my experience with police brutality out here on the West Coast—I'm going to give it my particular flavor. If I do it artistically, I'm going to render it so that when someone comes to my experience of police brutality, even though it has my particular flavor, they will be able to appreciate it, ideally, no matter where they are. And it's probably going to carry more power because of those details that I bothered to be very devilish about. But if I'm just speaking in these phrases...

BROWN: Jargon almost?

COLEMAN: Exactly. Then eventually it becomes meaningless. This so-called *universal language*, this generic rhetoric, where you're saying the right things in the right tones with the right degree of militancy—it's just dreadful art. And unfortunately, we get a lot of that in young or inexperienced writers who are imitating the writers of the Black Arts Movement, what they think is the correct way to write. Rhetorical devices are wonderful and useful—the didactic, the diatribe, the speechifying and preachifying can be truncated and used—but they can be used in a more sophisticated manner. They can enhance the work. They don't have to be the be all and the end all, so that every poem is a rant where you're shaking your fist, and you hate this and you hate that. Because that's deadening, and ultimately no one responds to it—ultimately, it is dismissed. It's not only dismissed as art, but the content is dismissed as having any kind of value, and it doesn't shake anything up and it doesn't change anything. So once you get past a certain point in the time of a social/literary movement there is an opening, and there is a rush, and there is a moment when all that ranting and raving and all this madness has to be expressed—and then we get past that and go on to something greater.

And what I enjoyed is that this reviewer [Charles Allen Wyman] saw that I'm doing several things: I'm letting people know what I read, where my focus is. I'm also making that statement that it's all mine, and I have the literary option to pick and choose and be self-defining at any given moment. I don't have to mouth the going rhetoric. I am tired of being defined by the limitations of others. And that the scope of what I am capable of is beyond the usual narrow definitions of what Blacks/ African Americans (I prefer the term *Blacks* or *Black Folk[s]*) are about. And that the Black experience is infinite—and it has to be—and that it is not, really, as graspable as you want to assume, in your superiority, that you think you can pigeonhole or even contain it.

I mean this is what America has done—it thinks that it can contain and control us, and not even look at its own history to see that *that's* an impossibility. But it has got us here; America has got the tiger by the tail, and the tiger has got big teeth.

BROWN: And the tiger is turning around and taking control. The idea of *a* Black Aesthetic, *a* New Black Aesthetic, and *a* newer Black Aesthetic—that doesn't fit in with the largeness that you or your subject matter represent?

COLEMAN: Again, that is artifice at work; that's someone who wants to control things, who has their own agenda, and who's probably got a book in the works. *[Laughter]* Or—and to be kind—it's also an attempt to validate. Because we live in a culture where "authority" is rewarded.

So, as the gates of academia have opened and allowed us in, we are forced into postures of basically justifying our existence. And we're going to be aggressive in doing so. We're in Rome here, and we're going to have to do what the rest of the Romans are doing. So that means that when we go into academia, we are going to be, likewise, under that pressure to write that book, and we're going to have our conferences, too. And now we're in it, full tilt boogie. So what do we do? We start looking just like any good academic. Where is my area of specialty? I'm going to become an authority on this; I'm going to carve out my little niche here. I am going to create this—which is what the dominant culture academic has been doing all along.

So, now we're IN THAT; so now, we're IN THERE. And, sometimes, it gets ridiculous and niggly. I hate the word *Africana,* for example. But all of a sudden, you know, it's *[Finger snap]* FAD TIME, and all the Black is gone. Whatever happened to Black Studies? Now, it's Africana Studies. And we all know we ain't Africans.

BROWN: And Africans know, "we ain't Africans."

COLEMAN: That's right. And so in our effort to define ourselves, we usually don't have the time or we don't have the budget, so loudness, sometimes, makes up for what we don't have *[Laughter]* in terms of time or budget. And that's when we start to do things like developing the New Aesthetic. So today we all are this, or today we all are that; we're all going to do this dance; and, you know, we're all going to wear this set of clothes now; and we're all going to tilt our hats this way, this week. And it all starts to get ludicrous at this point, I think. *[Laughter]*

BROWN: What younger Black writer is the child in "American Sonnet (95)"?

COLEMAN: Literally, that's my deceased son, Anthony. He died of HIV/ AIDS at the age of 31. He also wrote poetry and wanted to be an actor and dancer. Figuratively, it represents such younger writers as Lisa Teasley, Sesshu Foster, the rock singer Beck—not necessarily a Black child (you know, on my son's death certificate, under race, he was classified as White)—but certain urban entities who have responded to my influence, each in a unique way.

BROWN: When I sat down and reread the sonnets together—the ones from *American Sonnets, Bathwater Wine* and the section in *Mercurochrome*—I felt this oppressive sense of disappointment and weariness and disillusionment at the state of Blacks in America in general but in the arts in particular. Especially at the end.

COLEMAN: You read them right—although I thought I ended delightfully, on a high Shakespearean note. When I wrote the American Sonnets—those two books contain them, *Bathwater Wine* and *Mercurochrome*—I wrote most of the work in those books after my oldest boy was dying. And so the poetry couldn't help but reflect my angst and disappointment, my sense of failure, my sense of *being failed*—directly related to the fact that I have received relatively little reward from my hard years of work as a writer-that accompanied the fact that I didn't have a dime to bury my son. I had to use his social security money to cremate him. I just couldn't help it: it's in the work. That's not the full story, although that is alluded to in the poems "Salvation Wax," "American Sonnet (58)," "At Son's Set My Boys," "Notes On a Departure," and "Amnesia Fugue." The energy is in the poetry. I'm that kind of a writer. Some people call it confessional. Well, the actual confession isn't there, but the energy is there. So those poems came out at a peak moment when I was feeling so—you know, it caused me to reexamine my life. When I felt like I had wasted my life, because my hopes were so high ... So, contrary to what has usually been said to my face—that I'm negative, that I'm this negative individual—I'm totally the opposite. I have always been extremely hopeful, and I had hoped that by that time in my life, that certainly by age fifty, my literary work would support me. Fool that I was—even though I know—even though I'm looking at poor Mr. Guggenheim who blew his brains out because he couldn't make it in the literary world; and, I'm looking at all these other unsuccessful poets, and, you know, the odds were really, *really* against me, but I still had so much genuine belief in my ability as a writer that I thought "Hey" that I was going to get *there,* by then.

BROWN: By then?

COLEMAN: By January 1997, the month my son died. I was going to be *there* at The Moment, on the Money, and I was going to be able to handle The Pain. But I couldn't. I couldn't. I was just maxed out. And even though, in the two years preceding his death, I had made more money than I had made in my entire working life, in a very small period, too small to make a significant difference. The extent to which I had to extend myself—the energy I had to put out was so great and the return I got was so little, *compared to what I imagined.*

After I got the Lenore Marshall Prize, I don't think I got one call to do one reading behind winning that prize—one invitation anywhere to do anything. That spring after the award, I got about twenty manuscripts from people asking for a blurb on the backs of their books, and then the rest of the year, there was nothing. And then I realized that there is this hierarchy now in prizes. There are these big humongous ones like the MacArthur and the Lannan, and I haven't received any of those, for probably the obvious reason, having refused to censor myself or to write to other's expectations. For me, that goes against the very reason I'm a writer. Because then my freedom is being curtailed in the name of the Almighty Dollar. And, I did not start out to be a poet writer for any money. (Although I have written for money as a scriptwriter and magazine editor.) But, ironically enough, if you are going to be anybody in this literary world now, a dollar is attached to that. Even *that* has been co-opted—by the very people who set out to foster it They're crippling it, ironically, with these huge prizes. I don't mean to imply that I wouldn't want to win them. I enjoy being competitive when the competition is fair. But in the literary world, like Hollywood, fairness if often not the reality.

BROWN: So that freedom to create from whatever the artistic imagination finds to play with really is no longer there because you are being herded?

COLEMAN: That's right. Some people, they're flipping to win, and sometimes it's not conscious. I mean, there are decent people out there who—like me—are writing for the love of it, and they still manage to get rewarded, and they get awards. But they're usually not writing caustically about racism.

"Safe" poetry isn't going to change anything in this world for me; it isn't going to change my sociopolitical landscape. It isn't going to make people stop and maybe reexamine a few things, which is what I'm interested in having done. See, I'm not looking for applause when I write. I mean, it's wonderful when you get it. Sometimes I'm looking for the silence that indicates thoughtful reconsideration or stunned realization (what I imagine my reader might experiece, or following a presentation of my work before an audience). In general, I'm looking for appreciation—which is not necessarily the same as applause. And I had to realize that these awards some times represent applause.

BROWN: Talk to me about your brand of feminism. Looking at some of the women you portray, your work seems to show women as victims. The idea of feminine power as I perceive it appears in your works, but your work also contains numerous images of women as victims who don't seem to have much power at all. Yet, here you are, the writer, who is a very powerful person on so many different planes.

COLEMAN: Power is something I've always been interested in, and it's something I want. The catch phrase was "The Power of Self-Determination" in the 1960s. To me that's one of the things that we as African Americans lack. We lack real, meaningful power—that is the power of life and death in our society. Because we're still at the whim of others and the generosity of others; we're still at the whim of the humanity of others. As long as we're at the whim of, we're powerless. Social parity means sometimes they're at our whim. That means it's not a power dynamic until it's among equals. So as long as we're being *given* things in this society, as long as there has to be legislation passed, as long as there have to be laws changed or enacted—as long as those inequalities exist, then we're at the whim of others.

So I want to see the time brought about when there is parity—when there are those of us who have genuine, real power as movers and shakers on the social terrain. The only sanction you have is the quality of the product that you're producing and that you live and die just like everybody else does, governed by whatever market you want to bring your product to. So that we have a truly open society and truly open discourse and exchange of ideas and experiences. And I say this realizing full well that I don't expect to live to see that, but there will be others and we must take steps; we must make sacrifices and we must struggle. To me, that is the goal; that is the ultimate goal that I must move toward—if only in my chosen role as poet and writer. That is what allows me to get past something like losing my older son. Because you know that in a war, there is going to be loss, and not all of us are going to make it.

BROWN: Talk to me please about the significance of family and, particularly, the significance of your father. I hear the voice in your poetry soften whenever the poems are about your father, and the one "From Watching Daddy, I Learn About Men & Stuff" (from *Bathwater Wine*, pp. 38) seems particularly tender.

COLEMAN: Family motivates me. I may cop out on myself, but it is killin' to cop out on them. Whenever I don't feel like working, I think of family, my children, friends of those I love who are deceased and no longer have the privilege of work. That gets me up on my feet, to the typewriter or the monitor. *[Laughter]* Well, I'm working toward really writing extensively about my father. I've been collecting bits and pieces to eventually do an article because I have something to say, representing my father's life in putting forth an agenda, and these poems are precursors to that. I'm thinking about that, and it makes its way into my poems. Meantime, those little poetic moments find themselves to fill that gap between thinking and doing, and I identify with my father's way of being in the world, even though I physically resemble my mother. So sometimes the conflicts and the contradictions that arise out of that also become the stuff of poems. In looking at my decision to be a writer and become who I am and my parents' role in encouraging me and what that meant in terms of sacrifice and what that meant for their lives. Yes, my voice softens when it comes to my father because I see my father in Shakespearean terms. I see his life as being tragic. I see him and his partners as Black men coming along at a point in history where they were not allowed to be the men that they could have been. And our race and our nation were deprived of their magnificence.

And, oh, what a magnificence it could have been! America needs to know what it has *cheated* itself of in terms of my people and our potential and what we could yet give our nation. But it, in its meanness and its cruelty and its stinginess, it has hurt itself. It cannot deny its Black contingency … America cannot damn us without damning itself.

* * * * *

COLEMAN [...] I ended up in [the] Watts Writer's Workshop for a hot minute. When I tell people this, they don't want to really write about it; they always want to pretty it up or write around it or whatever, but I went to about four sessions. And I got really upset because I was the baby of the group and given a hard time. It was right after the riots.

BROWN: The earlier riots?

COLEMAN: The riots of August 1965. So, this was like the first—what the Watts riots did was they extended what Malcolm X had already started. The Watts riots really took the lid off of the Black/White dialogue. These workshop Brothers were feeling their manhood in a way that they had never felt it before. They were very effusive and macho and all that, so they were ripe for just running over anybody, like lil' ol' me coming along, Lil' Miss Mud hen here. I was bearing the brunt of everybody's critical urges. So when they got ready to dump on somebody, guess who? Including the workshop leader who happened to be a White male, one of Budd Schulberg's colleagues. He didn't know how to handle the Brothers. That kind of open Black bravado was new to everyone at that point, so if he was going to give anybody any criticism, it was going to be me. He couldn't say nuthin' to them Brothers! *[Laughter]* You'd better not, because they were feeling the power—Black Power. The Black women in the workshop were older women and they would just kind of sit there. They wouldn't say much. But I was very vocal and would get nasty with them, too. So I just finally said, "Fuck you" in my way in a nasty little letter. (Now, I've gotten famous for my nasty little missives.) And they even had it tacked up on the wall. I was later told that my letter inspired the torching of The House of Respect, the building where the workshop sessions initially took place. In that letter, I told them what they could do, what they could kiss and how they could kiss it—you know—*that* kind of letter.

But I tried to be politically correct in my analysis. *[Cackling]* I told them they were sellouts, and they were this, and they were that and the other thing, and I took myself out of there. But I knew I hadn't learned what I needed to learn, and I knew that if I stayed in that workshop I was not going to learn anything. They were going to keep ragging on me and dumping on me and making me feel miserable, and then hit on me. That was all I was going to get out of that workshop. So I had to go someplace else. I had to start looking across town at places like Beyond Baroque. I had to leave. They forced me to find some other space in which to grow— in the same sense that I got disgusted with the Black Arts Movement for rebuffing me. If I had stayed in that workshop I would have been an echo; I would have written just like them. I would have been Sonia Sanchez West; so in a sense, they did me a favor by rebuffing me. Because that allowed me to find my own path and develop my voice; to decide what poetry was going to be for Wanda Coleman, who she was going to be, once I took that name.

By the way, I kept the name Coleman—it just happened to be coincidence that I married a man named Coleman—one of my father's boxing partners was named Spencer Coleman. I dedicated one of my books to Spencer, not because he's blood kin to me, but because he was my father's partner, and he was the first adult to *see* me.... So I kept the name Coleman because of him, and I dedicated *Heavy Daughter Blues* to Spencer Coleman. After appearing in divorce court, I was informed I had the option of returning to my maiden name, but I looked at Wanda Coleman, sounded it out and said, "That's my name."

* * * * *

BROWN: Talk about—and we're coming to the end of my questions here—talk about your playing with poetic forms.

COLEMAN: I'm continuing the dialogue of form and content. I find it fascinating because I have a visual arts, a graphic arts bent; so the relationship between form and content continually fascinates me and all of its little convolutions. You know, when you break a line where it places the emphasis, the "enjambment" in the poetic line, the juxtaposition. How when you move text around, meaning becomes altered; some how, just by changing the position of something, meaning sometimes leaps out at you. Meaning wells up. That kind of movement in language. I enjoy word games and word play and all the tools—the writerly tools. I like the tools that rhetoric gives you—the figures, the use of figures of speech, breaking rhyme and meter, using rhyme and meter, how it was done in the Enlightenment and the Renaissance, and how the Greeks did it—all of those things. To me, that is pleasurable: that *interests* me, so when I'm focusing on taking on a traditional form—you know the sonnet has many forms: the Petrarchan sonnet, the Spenserian sonnet, the Shakespearian sonnet—here I am coming along and I get an idea *[Finger snap]—the* Jazz sonnet. And, what is that? So here I've taken a traditional form, and I want to say: now, as a Black person … suppose that I were an architect, how would I design a building? How would I make it? As an African American, how would I make it express my ethnicity different from what, maybe, Mr. Frank Lloyd Wright did? How— if I design an automobile—how would my sensibility, how would it differ from a Cadillac as a way of expressing my ethnicity? Or, what Mr. Olds did?

BROWN: Yes. How does the "me-ness" …

COLEMAN: What would that look like? What would that be? So here I am with forms like a sonnet, a traditional form. What would Wanda Coleman's version of that be?

BROWN: Then you start to play.

COLEMAN: That's right: Then I start to play. And then I factor in an abandoned music background. So there's another level of complexity overlaid with my childhood bent for the visual arts and with my love of language. Not to mention the frustrated Emmy winning scriptwriter kicking in. So I have these other arts interacting in one context, coming through me.

BROWN: When I read the "Dream" poems ("Bathwater Wine," "African Sleeping Sickness," "Handdance"), I kept seeing surrealist painting, seeing that connection and wondering, too, what particular paintings you may have seen.

COLEMAN: *The Eye of Silence* by Max Ernst, *The Christ of St. John of The Cross* by Salvador Dali and *Dividing Line* by Kandinsky—I was enthralled by those three paintings in adolescence. Well, you may look at Max Beckmann; you want to look at Klee, at Man Ray, Schwitters, Kandinsky—I was in love with Kandinsky. So you want to especially look at what the Dutch did with light. The visual influences on me—so all these things are moving through me and finding their expression in the language, and I enjoy bringing all these various aspects of my psyche together and maxing them out. Also, my readings. Who were the influences on me? From the absurdists to the surrealists and then the existentialists and the expressionists. German expressionism is one of my favorite periods. I could name one or two African-American artists, now, but that would be dishonest, because I didn't encounter Black artists during my formative years. My father exposed me to the work of Charles White and the handful that gravitated around him, when they were exhibited at the Golden State Life Insurance building's lobby in L.A.'s West Adams district in the early 1950s, but I was too young to appreciate them.

BROWN: We talk in educational terms about "life-long learners" and giving our students the "tools" with which they may become educated "citizens of the world." The thing that I find just wonderfully fascinating and refreshing about you is that you are this broadly educated person, even though you...

COLEMAN: I don't have the sheepskin. *[Laughter]* That has nothing to do with it. We have confused intellect and education. You can have people go all the way through and get their PhDs and be documented, certified by the system as being authorities and PhDs and be as dumb as they come, because that has nothing to do with intellect and intelligence. Intelligence transcends all of that.

BROWN: And the impetus to go and to learn and to see...

COLEMAN: Transcends, and informal education transcends the institutions. Now, we need the institution. That is not to denigrate them but, unfortunately, education has also, largely, succumbed to that Almighty Dollar—as a commodity. And it's not to denigrate the educational process.

BROWN: I understand that. But, I'm glad you said it. *[Both laugh]*

COLEMAN: Essentially, I am in a sense—self-taught, an autodidact. I wanted but was never able to afford to pay for the completion of my formal education. I only had roughly a year and a half of college. Now, I feel that the kind of self-made writer that I have become is disappearing. At one time in our history, we had more of that, at least in America, than we have at this moment. That's a byproduct of the Civil Rights Movement and the push for education—that push for education to make our young people competitive, test scores and all. Yet, for all the focus on education, there doesn't seem to be much room for the intellectual and/or the artist in this country, or acknowledgment of the variety of levels on which intellect expresses itself. Not all genius is rewarded, and when it comes from the Black subculture, it is usually held suspect. Genius often expresses itself in different forms. Sometimes you can't expect people who operate in the visual realm to be articulate when they give their oral exams in English. That's unrealistic and it's unfair. People who think mathematically, or think musically, their brains operate in another way. Forcing intuitive thinkers, or creative thinkers, into linear modes of thought—that's imposing artifice, or an artificial way of learning that may ultimately hurt those who are sensitive. Many educators have developed new techniques to help that kind of learner. But it is way too late for me. As a student, I usually didn't test well for reasons that had nothing to do with the test itself. Usually I was depressed and emotionally overwhelmed about the constant onslaught of belittlement I endured daily because of my hair, my teeth, my weight, my dark skin, my shape—my Blackness. I was the third darkest female in my entire graduating class. I couldn't concentrate on absorbing dates and facts. Once I left the public school system, that onslaught ceased, and I could direct my mind in private study. Then the Watts Riots took place and Black became so-called Beautiful. Otherwise, I was extremely inarticulate when I was coming along. Eventually, forensics or public speaking courses would help that. But to this day, I cannot tell a joke. That's not my thing. That's not my gift, but should I be penalized for it?

BROWN: And society at large is penalized because we miss out on (as you were talking about with your father) that "magnificence" that *is* the person, what they bring to the table because they don't look like what we expect.

COLEMAN: And what we're going to keep ending up with is what we've got now. A society that doesn't take its intellectuals seriously. Here we are (and I said this before); we turn our kids' minds over to people whom we denigrate by denying them security and full-time jobs—substitutes and adjuncts. Yet we give our athletes and those pretty faces in front of the camera gazillions of dollars, and we waste our money and we give our money to these empty vessels. Instead of feeding our educators, our thinkers and our philosophers, the people we're going to turn our kids' minds over to.

Instead of worrying about national health care—although that's a valid issue—we need to be nationalizing education. Everybody should be entitled to a free college education. And go as far as... let water seek its own level. Because, usually, that's what happens anyway. Ultimately, if the person is lucky, if he or she decides, "College is not for me; I'm going to go and work in dad's factory. I'm going back to the farm; I'm going over here, but I have the option—if I want the education—to go and get it." Instead, education is made a commodity too, and now it's as if we've turned everybody into whores. Everybody's whoring; everybody's being whores and pimps these days, even in the educational system. And it's ugly, and we're forcing our professors to be whores.

BROWN: That's right because if you don't publish you perish. So it really doesn't matter—really—what the quality of your teaching is. It's "How many papers have you published?" "How many books have you published?" That's what's being considered when you're being considered for tenure.

COLEMAN: And that is really, really ugly. If the person's real gift is to be a teacher and teach, and not a writer and write...

BROWN: Let him or her teach.

COLEMAN: And give them their reward, based on what they're capable of doing. This is really screwed up here. It needs to be re-evaluated and looked at. So you can get that basketball in the hoop: lovely, lovely. Keep doing that. Don't penalize them for being able to do that. Let them go ahead and do that, but at the same time, reward the person who has that intellect who can be the poet, the writer, or the teacher. Here we are in the new century and the humanities departments are cutting back if not closing down left and right. Funding for the arts and the humanities is closing down left and right.

Why? What mechanism is driving it? Racism. Racism and greed—and the greed is parasitic and profits from the racism that's driving it. You want to know what's happening? That's what's happening, ultimately. The few people who have courage enough to be vocal about that, they are being silenced. They are denied access to the mainstream media.

So the battle lines are being redrawn again. Here we are thirty, even forty years after the Civil Rights Movement, having to cover the same ground, having to re-fight the same battles, and still listening to the same empty rhetoric.

WORKS CITED

Coleman, Wanda. *African Sleeping Sickness: Stories and Poems.* Santa Rosa: Black Sparrow Press, 1990.

—. *American Sonnets.* Milwaukee: Woodland Pattern Book Center and Kenosha, WI: Light and Dust Books, 1994.

—. *Bathwater Wine.* Santa Barbara: Black Sparrow Press, 1998.

—. *Hand Dance.* Santa Rosa: Black Sparrow Press, 1993.

—. *Mambo Hips and Make Believe.* Santa Rosa: Black Sparrow Press, 1999.

—. *Mercurochrome: New Poems.* Santa Rosa: Black Sparrow Press, 2001.

—. *Native in a Strange Land: Trials and Tremors.* Santa Rose: Black Sparrow Press, 1996.

OTHER WORKS

Heavy Daughter Blues: Poems and Stories 1968-1986. Santa Rosa: Black Sparrow Press, 1991.

Imagoes. Santa Barbara: Black Sparrow Press, 1983.

Love-ins with Nietzsche: A Memoir. Fresno, Ca: Wake Up Heavy, 2000.

Mad Dog, Black Lady. Santa Barbara: Black Sparrow Press, 1979.

A War of Eyes and Other Stories: Santa Rosa, Black Sparrow Press, 1988.

Jayne Cortez

CAVE CANEM LEGACY CONVERSATION WITH JAYNE CORTEZ AND SEKOU SUNDIATA, MODERATED BY TRACIE MORRIS.

October 24, 2002, presented at the New School, New York, NY.

All these questions. I don't know what to ask. No. I'm going to get out of the way and let grown people talk. Well, I had one or two questions for each of you and then questions for both you all. You had this like ditty bop in your—the way you read stuff. You have like a chant—

JAYNE CORTEZ: What do you mean by ditty bop?

TRACIE MORRIS: Well, you know, this chant.

CORTEZ: No, I don't know what you mean. Tell me, show me.

MORRIS: Well, I can't do it. I can't do it. But it's not my show.

SEKOU SUNDIATA: Anybody can do.

MORRIS: But the way that you use tone, it's not just that you repeat the words but you sort of do some sort of contrast with the tones.

CORTEZ: Well, why would you call that ditty bop?

MORRIS: Because it sounded like, you know, when you—like when you walk you put like a little lean on it.

CORTEZ: O.K. It sort of has like a hipness to it or something like that?

MORRIS: Yeah. But hip ain't hip enough. You know, I had to go back, I had to find some other word besides hip, because, you know, hip is like in magazines, when they start using that word sometimes it doesn't seem appropriate.

CORTEZ: Well, you know, when we used to use ditty bop, it wasn't the coolest thing to say.

MORRIS: Uh-oh. See? Now I'm showing my age. Well, you have this tone thing. O.K.? Words could change. You have this tone thing and I'm going to ask you what ditty bop used to mean later, but—and I'm just curious about how you work with the idea of repetition and chant and tone in your poems, because each poem has repetition but they don't sound the same.

CORTEZ: Well, I think that the repetition is good as long—if you're using it to make something stronger. In other words, if you're using the repetition and it's going in another direction, it's going to something else, and so you're using it for that reason. Especially you notice a lot years ago with the musicians that I work with, they use a lot of repetition and it does the same thing, it goes back, it goes forward. It's just another way of advancing whatever it is you're doing and making it stronger. If it wasn't going to do that, I wouldn't use it.

MORRIS: O.K. You got this—how do you work your voice with that, though? I mean, you do such interesting things with your voice, but it seems—there's a lot of undertone in there.

CORTEZ: But, you know, Tracie, being a poet—poetry is life to me. Everything is based on experience, wanting to discover and, you know, just your action. And so just from that, that's what it's coming from. So if I pause, if I have a certain tone, if I do it that way, that's the way I feel, that's the way I see it. That's my, you know, that's the way I am.

MORRIS: Well, it's amazing.

CORTEZ: You know, I mean, in other words I don't sit back and say, oh, this should go like this or I should go low here. I mean, it's not like that. It's what you feel at the moment that you do it, so that you never do it the same, you'll never do it the same.

MORRIS: The idea of chant and the different things that that connotes or implies to people in terms of like spirit and stuff, is that something you deliberately put in your poems or is that just how we end up feeling?

CORTEZ: That's the way you end up feeling, that's the way you relate to it based on your own experience, your own chantology, you know. Because if I hear something and I just—I'm just relating to whatever the feeling, whatever I hear or whatever—if it's with music such as on that Taking the Blues Back Home, it's what I'm hearing and what I feel should go there at that moment.

ON THE BLACK POWER AND CIVIL RIGHTS MOVEMENTS, HIP HOP AND RAP

CORTEZ: Well, certainly the time is a little different, but I think that—and you know, during the 60s, I mean, there was a movement, the civil rights movement. The Black Arts Movement came out of the Civil Rights movement and what was happening at that time. And people were trying to for the first time really relate to political ideas and see what they could write in poetry and create new forms of poetry. And it was very important to speak the language of the community and speak to the people as the people spoke of the day, in that day, and not something that was very far away and long ago and all of that. I think today is different and I think that maybe if you want to talk about the rappers, if the rappers are trying to do something that they feel that they should be doing, which is not really a part of poetry except that it rhymes, but that it is a part of the pop music scene, which gives employment. And I think that that's, you know, very important. They've never tied themselves to any idea of like really this is poetry and blah-blah-blah-blah. They have their own agenda. And I think that's fine. It's not tied to a movement because there is no movement and they have made no real political movement for themselves within that mix. But it could still come, you know. But the thing is is that we're still here and we're still having to respond to what is happening today. And there are many things happening to our community and to our people and to African people all over the world today and we're still having to work on all fronts, and maybe just not one central thing but there are many things that we're involved in and we're working an all those fronts.

MORRIS: I think it depends on—it also depends on like hip-hop or anything, the time frames that the person is engaged in and what it emerged out of and whether—you know, even what you were saying about poetry was very much true of the origins of hip-hop. People are expecting to sell all these records and make all this money. It was actually, it wasn't really at the beginning conceivable in a way. This kind of configuration is fairly new. And I think that there's like different levels of politics and one of the levels of politics was the way that disco music and certain aspects of the music industry in the 1970s sort of prohibited people from creating live music, new music. It was all about the drum machine, the being in the studio. And I think that one of the ways they responded to like the pressure of not having access to live musical resources, including music programs in school and all that, was to construct new music out of music that was recorded. And that there's—I think that there's another kind of political discourse that happens in terms of how we get access to ways that we can make art and part of it might have been a response to—you know, I would say that that was part of that political response. But I know what you mean in terms of like overt political mass movements. But I think even some of them are involved with that. I know some of the rappers are very much involved with Mumia Abu-Jamal and, you know, a whole bunch of other issues. But in general I agree that this orientation that has shifted, like you said with the MTV and poetry and all of that, shifted towards the arena of pop music and entertainment as the resource that they're looking for as opposed to some other kind of community-based thing.

CORTEZ: Well, that's fine. You know, I think that the most important thing is to have a very high sense of awareness as a person. And I think that the rappers, like anybody else, will have to come to that. And when that happens, then whatever they're doing will reach another level. And that's—the most important thing is trying to get yourself, you know, into a higher intensity, a higher way of knowing what you should know. And, you know, poetry, all of this life is about knowledge, and just to try to get that into—get yourself into a position where you can think in a certain way.

You can keep it going because one thing goes after another and it's all related. But you have to start thinking like that. But if you're in a society that's always trying to capture your thoughts, there's so much propaganda and trying to tell you what to think and not to think, then you have a problem, so that you have to out-think that, you know what I mean, you have to think— these people are trying to tell me what to think so I cannot think like that, I have to try to find another way.

MORRIS: That's right. And you think about like the Stop The Violence movement that was a part of hip-hop and then all of a sudden it sort of got like washed away. Nelson George talked about this in one of his hip-hop America books. I think—and then all of a sudden there was gangsta rap and everybody forgot all about that or it wasn't just engaged in the same way. And like you said, it's like who's telling you what to think. It's not like either, you know, people didn't do that, but it's like—

CORTEZ: Evidently the record company is going to tell you O.K., we can sell this. But they didn't try to sell people from the Black Arts Movement because they would really be selling something. They couldn't sell it. So that you have a lot of artists who get together now, they're rappers or whatever, and they're doing little takeoffs on that. But that's not the real, real thing. So this can be sold, this can be sold and everybody in France and all over the world, in Senegal, everywhere that I go, they're rapping. O.K.? So it's fun, it's cute, everybody can do it. And that's why they can connect with each other because it's a way of communicating, and it's the same with poetry. Everybody writes poetry. Every time I go someplace there's some kid or somebody saying, oh, I write poetry too. I say uh-huh and, well, see that's why we can communicate, because you know what I'm talking about and I know what you're talking about. We're doing it on different levels, yes, but we can communicate.

EDITORS' POEMS

Erica Hunt

—for the missing

"Forty three percent of the people killed were not in the middle of committing a crime but were stopped for 'suspicious activity' "

A resting face.
She abandoned the cloud
and chose to go out on foot.
She was missing
a grin.
She knocked
at the wrong intersection.
He defeated a match
stick.
He crossed
diagonals.
They moved past
an uncovered spot.
They lost pump.
He was bowing in erratic directions.
She ran by spurious gloat.
They were potential trouble
makers who did not fit
the turn down-dressing of
the neighbor
hood who was speaking
in concealed carry
He bolted out cork dizzy
thinking free from the lockdown
She traced the body
that refused to fit a
grammar of disappearances.

She studied how Black
people getting excited in a
manner different than others
drives some people to
blunt displays of panic
and violence.

*(She studied how Black
people getting elected
with a coalition different from others
drives some people to
blunt displays of panic
and violence.)*

Lamenting in an
appropriate structure has
rendered her hoarse from
not screaming.

She is blind from reading
from inside her lids.
I would show you where it
happened on a map, but
the cursor of the public's
attention has vanished.

Erica Hunt

BROKEN ENGLISH

(*from* Veronica, a Lamentation)

Wound up in words
wounded
re-wounded
the beaten
bulleted body
repeats
wound
reads
into ache
stead
y
or not
ready
RED
already
or not
b/red
read
b/roken
syllab
les de
tachm
ent.

It's
not better
remember
red
It ren
ders
s
peechle
ss
tend
erness
it
strip
s

kin
dred
lik
e
ki
ndling
i/nto
bro
ken states
rende
ring
ileg
ible
and unintel
l
igible
wher
e
blac
kness sup
presse
d to laws
severed
tongu
to co
wer
us, and s/cowl
us de
ad
mute.

Yet she (I)
to speak
all at once
the thing
that has been on
her (my)
mind
which words
(verbs)
reco

ver
dignity?

restores
let

letters to the unm
uffled
(unmuzzl(ed))
full
-throated-sound as in
some-bodied?

the dead
lines (t)each
the proper order of time
scorch (ed)
zones of property,
propriety's
(in) tension
returns me
days after day
to variations of question:
how to breathe
freely
despite shackle-rattle and
pummeled jolts? Where does glare
concede to
the words we do,
walk past the edge of sight
and resist?

WILD SEED

The cat gets the lion's tongue
And all that the cat can do
Is SPEAK with its tail.
Its collar
Its cat food
Its cultured life of fur
And grooming.

The cat's got the lion's tongue
And gets lost in multiple claws
Nothing about slice and purr
Nothing about sir or gentle
Or quiet steps
That have a way of repeating

Cat stumbles through her lines
With the taste of blood on her tongue
A forgotten mouse
Fills her mouth
Doggereal

She holds the note
The thing in her paws, a
Parenthesis. Beast, beating,
heart—shaken
song stuck in her throat.

Show me a bird a cat doesn't know
when she hunts she is of two minds.
She makes a noise she doesn't understand
Somewhere between a purr and growl
When the bird takes flight.

WRITING *LIFE*

this labor is not silent
but requires collaboration between clamor and music
found in rustling. Not makeshift, you are its prototype
an advanced draft. Sense
applied to warm skin. Uncanned mannequin
against gun robot. Stand.
Tricks in a picture. Stand.
Name the ruse of normal in criminal bracket.
Stand. Duel with double optics, then
stand to its left. If the ground is too hot to tolerate long,
improvise and stand. But
stand.

Dawn Lundy Martin

PROLOGUE FROM *GOOD STOCK STRANGE BLOOD*

Q: If your book is a house, what does the foyer look like?

The book is a like a long, thin, wavy tendril stretched into the sky from a small spot at the top of my head. At the end of the tendril, somewhere far in the sky where I cannot see, is a mutilated black face. A little me is sitting on the top of my head, holding the tendril like the string to a balloon.

Q: Whose blood?

The blood is a corrupt(ed) document of one's fate. But when I am beautiful, and young, and open, with no features that distort or take away from, it's easy for the stranger to enter the space of the body like a god. Does the blood become a further stain on wet, light feet? I dunno. A psychic once told me that I would live a very long life—epic, she said, like in a Russian novel. Really, it's only blood. Very symbolic. So many days I spend in bed, bleeding out of my vagina, so hungry I'm distorted. I call people to my bed until I feel depleted enough to sleep.

Q: We are wondering why there is a small self. Maybe the prologue is your body.

Because the question at the center of the book is, *Why doesn't one just die?* And the little me is holding the thin line because there is a squashedness to existing in the present and I can't think about—

Q: What I like is that the little self is holding the tendril like a balloon, because it gives me the impression that you are letting this mutilated thing go.

—I can't think about how to exist now without pressing together big pasts and small pasts. Big pasts (like historical collective trauma) and the narrow self-indulgent past of personal invasion, self-configuration at the hands of another. The mutation of blood. The development of the multiple. Anyway, the little one holds the weight of the past. Maybe she's already dead as she sits. Who knows? But, then, as I was writing this book, it was the summer of Sandra Bland and then the summer of Freddie Gray, and then some cute kid was shot in a big-box store while holding a toy gun, and so many other of these deaths, unexplained in the logics of the rationality we hold so dear. And the white boys are hand-slapped for brutal rapes. Life just goes on. The past isn't the past but the present. It's all laid out in the same space / time plane; the tendril becomes like a reaching into another dimension. Its symbolism changes.

Q: Why exhale after the inhale? The breathing is the mantra. Could the trauma be keeping us alive?

What happens is: we walk through a door. On the other side of the door is a manifested future place. It's configured very differently from this one. Its shape is different. But we created it so we recognize it; we understand its workings, which are mostly based on intuition. In the book, what's keeping us alive is the ability to imagine something very other than what's been shoved down our throats, what's been taken up in our cells. To imagine something other is to leave the known world. No death. But, instead, the door. To place a body alongside the grubby stranger, and then the stranger in a lockbox, and then voilà: a self is three intentional selves. And, the three selves are like different manifestations of the thing we call "blackness."[1]

---

1 Some of the poems in this collection have been reconceptualized from their original context in the libretto Good Stock on the Dimension Floor, written for the HOWDOYOUSAYYAMINAFRICAN? global artists collective (the Yam Collective). The video installation piece of the same title, directed by the Yam Collective's Sienna Shields, premiered on Opening Nights at the Whitney Museum's Biennial Exhibition in 2015 but was withdrawn by the collective, in protest of the museum's racist and sexist curatorial practices, before the exhibition opened to the public.

Conceptually, the libretto was organized as follows:

The characters are no longer named in the poems that appear in this book, a gesture that takes its lead from the Yam Collective's interpretation of the text. In the text's enactment, multiple people inhabited and portrayed each body.

CAST:

LAND	The black embodied body
PERPETUUS	Reflection of LAND
NAVE	Plural

Nave has been born from the head of Sarah, the protagonist in Adrienne Kennedy's one-act play Funnyhouse of a Negro; she is continually peeling off her skin, only to find another layer beneath it. When Sarah, who is haunted and fractured by the blackness of her father, apparently (maybe) hangs herself at the end of Kennedy's play, Nave [I imagine] emerges in human form but with many arches and windows. She sings the problems of existence on earth. She sings from a deep memory and historical torment. Nave is both haunted and empowered by connectedness to ancestors and traditions.

Land is symbolic of the way the body can be trapped by racialized existence. Land exists in a perpetual state of longing, enclosure, and toil. (It should be noted that Land's utterances do not find their ways into this book.)

Perpetuus, Land's primary reflection, exists in a sphere of other kinds of knowing the black body. Perpetuus is untethered from the history of the body on Earth. S/he can weep without melancholy. S/he can sing through dimensions, through universes, and is unconnected to any sense of linear time. Though her/his skin is brown, s/he is without race boundary as s/he is without gender boundary.

Throughout the narrative, Land becomes more and more grief stricken until, at the end, speech is impossible. land resorts instead to moans, grunts, and muffled cries. These sounds cannot be written.

Perpetuus begins to transform into Land instead of being mere reflection.

THE NEGRO IN THE DESERT

Cattle land, I've never
        seen it, even in sleep,
break up the two-lane.
        Over there, he says,
        that's Juarez,
        just past the river.
"What goes ape in the night
        is a nigger with a fly
on his toe." Ever hear that one?

"That dirty N—
and his toes"
nobody thinking about
but I have seen them,
chaotic from labor,
the father's feet
got another foot
attached to them
got a leash around
their foot necks,
damn black stumps
and all over newspaper
he cuts 'em
and we run out
laughing cause
there's no foot like that
ever, black sentinel
knives, goddamn
this fortress undesired
because what desire
could live here?

I got another one,
        because why end there?
"Them old nigga fingers look
        like Slim Jims."

Dawn Lundy Martin

TOBACCO SHADE

She had been half made with real white blood. —Gertrude Stein

Or.
She been made
real with half
white blood.
In keeping
with tradition
sun blackening
continued, shoe
got nothing
on the field hand.
If there is a theme
it invades,
under our tongues
like poison seeds,
and we forget
our names.

OUR WANDERING

If they would only just beat or shoot me, but they wanted soul substance,
to harbor that like that, so I could never move from this place. So they
reached crackled hands inside and hold it open for raking. . .

We in a shit
             rustle, the way
in ramble and camaraderie,
brown hand of whose mother
makes its smooth noise
             over my mouth?

The burden of saying
             some *thing*, a head-
nodding, and I want to be in-
side of your knowing. Who
             lay their head
             on the disappeared's pillow?

             One minute a person licks your ear,
             the next, you cannot see your own white breath.

We gotta head
             on over to the party way
out in Bushwick because we're lost,

and our flesh in on fire. There's
a man walking behind us. And growing.

This is what I tell him:

             I am a not a boy in anyone's body.

             I am not a black in a black body.
             I will not kowtow inside your opposites.

How the world blisters you.
How hunger left you statued.

*   *   *

One falls past the lip of some black unknown, where time, they say, ends.

We got us a sugar-
            mouth, a bit feeding,
walk in circles in circular rooms
built so precisely for our shapes,
            hold the figure that is the body that is,
of course, me.

I stroke the feather that feeds me,
that lines my cage floor with minor luxuries,

I say "mama" into its wanting, sugary mouth.

What is the difference between ash and coal,
between dark and darkened, between love
and addiction on Dekalb at 2 a.m., and I fall
drunk from a ruinous taxi, already ruined
from *before* before, the absent weight screams
into your breath, *you are no good, no good . . .*

The space between *I* and *It*. Lolling.

The Ibibio man was not born in his cowboy hat.
Even *his* throat must ache like tired teeth.

TO BE AN ORPHAN INSIDE OF "BLACKNESS"

—is the condition of it (us). We can love it, sure, cradle its beautiful head, and eyes looking. It wants to be performed, leaping, but the *I* is not a good actor. The problem of the book is that it's never quite "black" enough. Language can perspire the thickest blackest blood but you are still the unheld nigger, the one inspiring the deadly shaking panicked rage. Your tennis shorts or salmon-colored pants will not help you. It's a good idea to have "black" in the title of the "black" book in case there are any questions as to its race. The "black" bits will be excisable, quotable in reviews. The book should be very interested in the thing you know as "blackness," all its clothes, its haberdashery. What the book actually wants, however, to know is the distance between the "I" and the "you," how it is drawn into space and action as when the white woman professor says you have written her a "vicious" letter and wants to know what's wrong with you. Claudia Rankine has reinvented this territory of the relation that is forever unrecognized in that relaxed [white] body. When one's actions have so clearly produced the interrogative text, the refusal to enter the text as subject. For you, the text lives in the floating unreal, a document that has nothing to do with you, but, my dear, it *is* you, the grotesque monument to the regime, so perfectly sculpted you cannot see yourself in the mirror.

OBITUARY

Plastic gaze into plastic coffin,
No calling up the wet stare
Of the wet mouth
Contorts into lie,
I love you like a saw
Into barely beating
Heart, my body hard
And flat against the coffee table
As dry blood,
Urgent wheeze
Girl splayed life anchor
But this is not what
The obituary says.
It says, *beloved husband,* says
Survived by, condolences,
Not *there were others.*

NO HUMANS INVOLVED

When I was a girl of 9 or 10
Anyone could have me
Any way they wanted
Because speech
Closed a blackness
in my throat
So cavernous and loud
The blackness,
A smoke so thick
Don't even think about
The procession on the body
All their maws loaded up

LOOKING PAST THE PAGES OF THIS BOOK

Tisa Bryant

from OUR WHOLE SELF[1]

AN INTRAVIEW OF BLACK WOMEN WRITERS' EXPERIMENTATION

ESSAY ON ELIDED AFRICAN DIASPORIC AESTHETICS IN PROSE

I always reach back—towards voices and thoughts gifted me in ink, pulp and pulse, from trees born in an air that no longer exists, through blood ties of cellular archives—to see forward. Divining fingers treble the web and call the spider, awakening words written on me so many times now, and they come forward in all their distinction, intoning and fiercely being and reminding me what I was born to, grown from. Black women's feminist writing. Black women feminists writing. Indexical. Notational. Intertextual. Letters to the future are always found there, in the overlaps and interstices of genres reshaped and invented to make a new clearing for the work. I did not say "experimental," though the writings that concern me here certainly experiment with the capacity of writing to express Black women's subjectivity, and necessarily flaunt convention and defy expectation in the process. To call their writing experimental puts something on it that doesn't belong there, a contextualization and a way of reading that may privilege a translated Eurocentricity. To not reckon with the experimental nature of their output excludes the work and the women who made it from critical consideration of their processes, which limits our appreciation and their inclusion to their valuable messages, but elides the fascination of their method, and perpetuates the false notion of Africans and African diasporic people as belated to formal innovation. So how do we name and champion, protect and propagate these formally inventive works of prose as part of the Tradition, as part of our whole self?

> Pinning things down is the way you claim them. When you claim them you empty them out of any past they had before and they begin with the name you've given them.[2]

Let's not decontextualize, defamiliarize, erase, diminish, bleach or blanch writing by Black women to make claims of canonical universality, or make of a Black woman's writing a theatrical repository for other people's projections, including my own. Let's revisit these works not as anthropology, or sociology, or psychology or ethnography, but as art. Rather than an emptying out of their pasts, let's call for a gathering of forces: Black feminist interventions, innovations with structure, layers of voice through address and register, (con)fusion of genre and normativity, refashioning of form. Their oppositional strategies of living thinking being in writing, are part of a continuum of Black women's prose, now and in the future. While a refusal to name these strategies using terms and methodologies from "outside" Black literature

---

1   A riff off of Gayl Jones' "from *The Quest for Wholeness: Re-Imagining the African-American Novel: An Essay of Third-World Aesthetics*," Callaloo, Vol. 17 No. 2, 1994.

2   Jamaica Kincaid, in conversation with Al Filreis, Kelly Writers House, March 20, 2007

and its theory is understandable[3], the seeming silence around Black women's work from the conversation experimental and innovative writing is untenable. I found that the silence isn't a silence at all but a refusal to see and hear. Even elision makes a sound.

> Questions form as you traverse the spaces. What can reach/touch us? Can we feel and think? Must we be bound and roped to feel? What is "we," "us," "I," or "you," any longer? What is the significance of any of these observations? How do these processes, conditions, or things in these spaces matter? Beyond what is to be done, what can matter? What basis is there for understanding beyond the lowest common denominator, i.e., we are alive?[4]

My sense of the experimental was first shaped through the indelible effect Gayl Jones' writing had on my mind. In her work's structure is voice, persona, character manifest through cadence, utterance and the unsaid. Dialogue of (mis)direction and slippage is atmosphere. Time is a tongue. Her writing is rightly called "psychological"; to which I would now add "haptic," for the sensation in her writing that activates sound into image. Her spare, precisely calibrated language intrigued and terrified, confirming that a vibrant energy had moved through my most private secrets and desires. Something ancestral. The promise of transcending trauma, embracing the sensual through voice and gesture, the behavior of language in the mindstate. I wanted to do *that*. The impression her work made on my earliest attempts at writing, "Light for Dark," and "Zoo Kid," is clear, but where I had imitation, she had methodology, "an all-inclusive structure"

> Which would theoretically include everything: experience and imagination, autobiography, history, legend, myth, ritual, metaphor, dream (essentially all forms both linguistic and experimental); it would make use of specifically black forms, both musical (blues, jazz, work songs, spirituals) and linguistic (the sermon, playing dozens, signifying, jive); it would see the erotic as an authentic method of expression.[5]

Imagine the sound. In grad school, I was told by a professor that, in writing nonfiction, I had to choose a single register, as if "voice" (like "audience") were a singular thing one must "find." I believe that let loose, the tongue is image and image maker, a seer of scenes unspoken, signified and speculated on. Is textual, visual, sonic, material. Visilingual. That is wet. Invented. Mine for the licking. I grew towards a method of fusing multiple registers (street, theory, inside, outside, masked, critical, true) of one tongue with the sound of many eyes. From this pleasure, character, reflection and psychic and erotic worlds are built. Gayl Jones' creative experiments

---

3   See Barbara Christian's "The Race for Theory," Feminist Studies, Vol. 14, No. 1, Spring 1988
4   Renee Green, *Other Planes of There: Selected Writings*, Duke University Press, 2014
5   Gayl Jones, "Toward an All-Inclusive Structure." Graduate dissertation, Brown University, 1973

with the psychology of speech, her "rhythmical flexibility, syntactical dislocation, forms of linguistic tensions"[6] completely changed the game of how novels about Black women could be written after 1975, making space for later experiments in narrative voice and structure like Carolivia Herron's *Thereafter Johnnie* and Yvette Christiansë's *Unconfessed*, a space not at all unrelated to the meticulously rendered (and erotic!) character, the *psyche* of Renee Gladman's sentences.

> People who allow themselves to understand that I'm involved in experimentation, in exploring black women and their sexuality, are far more open to examining the nooks and crannies of that experience as portrayed in my work. And that that people are seeing this has been very encouraging. I think the fiction has been better received than one or two of the theater pieces I've done. [...] And they [reviewers] expect a certain kind of theater, especially if it's black: it's got to be a "darky" musical or a kitchen drama, and it can't be experimental, and certainly it can't talk about themes they don't expect black people to address.[7]

Gayl Jones made explicit and theorized what earlier Black women writers, like Zora Neale Hurston, refused to squelch, opting instead to be everything. Her piece, "from *The Quest for Wholeness*," purports to be an excerpt from a longer work, the funky B-side oddity to her scholarly *Liberating Voices: Oral Tradition in African American Literature*. I consider "from *The Quest for Wholeness*" a *shadow book*,[8] following Kevin Young's conceptualization of the term and his taxonomy of the unwritten, removed or lost text. As an excerpt, Jones' text is uncannily complete; the desire for more swells from the pleasure of immersing further in the promise of the African-American novel's knowledge of self in relation to others, not from any sense of its being unfinished. Perhaps there is a fourth category of the shadow book: the *unfinishable*. As "from *The Quest for Wholeness*" maps its own continuum from its (our?) own point of view, perhaps it isn't, cannot be, a book at all. In its discursiveness, multiplicity, inclusive structure and ongoingness, we all write "from *The Quest for Wholeness*," forever. It's no surprise, then, that "from *The Quest for Wholeness*" contains several footnotes addressing experimentation within an African literary context: one being the lack of African publishers for experimental work; another, that the belief that Western critics were determined to deter experimental African writing and writers; yet another being that Jones's novel essay itself should be regarded as a revision of conventional fictional elements. See how she plays with the talking book? "from *The Quest for Wholeness*" encourages us to call in from isolation various like works of genre fusion, from Marie Vieux Chauvet's quasi-epistolary portrait in three acts, *Love, Anger, Madness (A Haitian Triptych)*, to Adrienne Kennedy's *Deadly Triplets: A Theatre Mystery and Journal*. These critical observations and their cited works invite inquiry specific to African diasporic women

---

6   ibid

7   Interview with Alexis De Veaux, *Black Women Writers at Work*, Claudia Tate, Continuum, 1989

8   *The Grey Album: On the Blackness of Blackness*, Greywolf, 2012

writers and experiments in writing, how they are/were supported and thwarted in expressing their whole creative and aesthetic selves, from the mid 1970s to today.

> BARNETT: What do you think about "Letter to My Students"? Do you consider that to be a play, a short story, a monologue? Is it supposed to be performed?
> KENNEDY: No, no. It's not a play. It's just supposed to be just nonfiction.
> BARNETT: Nonfiction? I'm confused. Nonfiction? Suzanne Alexander is fictional.
> KENNEDY: Well it's a blend of fiction and nonfiction. I really love doing that, obviously. It's a blend. It's a blend of part-truth and part-fiction. It's so obvious that I love to do that. I love to try to do that.[9]

Through the late '80s and '90s, with the Dark Room Collective and my own solitary wanderings I defined experimentation freely, intuitively sampling across disciplines. While the boundaries and dividing lines made themselves readily apparent (gender, sexuality, race and skin privilege, class, language), I was working with my new key words: paradigm, hegemony, generating recombinant codes for opening doors, a spell for haunting libraries and used bookstores, walking through walls with my mind. Imagining a promised totality. Textual orality as the mark of talking. It was here I made a discovery: I did not have to break to change. I could be here in writing as I am. And as I'm not. Telling the story of seeing through the body of text as speaker. Everything I was imprinted with, the singular and the shared. The quest for this, essaying into fiction, with poetry, with whatever I wanted, with everything I had and was given me. Material orality, what the tongue made me see to and remember. I sat on the floor at the Museum of Fine Arts Boston writing at the marble feet of dagger-eyed Medea, compressing her inanimate form over and over into active description, her terrified children behind her skirts. bell hooks' *Talking Back* in my bag, recalibrating my vision of critical sound, the cadence of conversation, rapping, dropping science, backing it all up, footnote free, against institutional cred. My notebook with capsule movie reviews, critiques of billboard advertisements, quotes from writers I loved, dreams and to-do lists, every crevice filled. Michelle Cliff's *The Land of Look Behind*: the plumage and distance between mother and daughter in the ekphrastic museum walk of "A History of Costume"; the match she strikes against colorism in "If I Could Write This in Fire, I Would Write This in Fire." The multivalent double helix. I shuffled, mindblown and scribbling, through an exhibit of Black women's conceptual art at Connecticut's Wadsworth Atheneum: Adrian Piper, Howardena Pindell, Alison Saar, Lorna Simpson and Carrie Mae Weems. The cinematic expressed through the citational body in transformation. The citational body becomes not typographically spectacular, but scopophilic spectacle. Squeezing margarine and annatto through hot brown fingers. Building up dark mileage in arthouse cinemas dreaming with independent Black women filmmakers: Julie

---

9   "An Evasion of Ontology: Being Adrienne Kennedy," Claudia Barnett, *TDR: The Drama Review*, Volume 49, Number 3, Fall 2005

Dash's *Illusions*, Camille Billops' *Finding Christa*, Zeinabu Irene Davis' *Cycles*. Seer seen seeing. Diegetic layers of sight, sounded through writing. The love of seeing (us) and the right to see differently—is sentinel in my sentences. The Unnamed Pointing Sister of *Unexplained Presence* retelling tales at the edge of the screen, and camera-eyed Iris of *The Curator*, detourning self and 'hood towards a missing auteur, are both born of these movements toward a method of voicing the visual of the unanticipated writing subject. Ancestral. Cinematic. Projection.

> Granny had a saying/without humps there'd be no getting over/you pay
> for what you get/and hardly ever get what you pay for/life's full of ups and
> downs/you got to find your own high ground/
> Mother Wit is your connection/use it for your protection.[10]

This is theory: Vertamae Grosvenor's *Vibration Cooking: Travel Notes of a Geechee Girl*. Cookbook, travelogue and a memoir. The song-tales, lived life and re-memories of Luisa Teish's *Jambalaya: The Natural Woman's Book of Personal Charms and Practical Rituals*. Adrienne Kennedy's deceptively simple scrapbook-cum-autobiography, *People Who Led to My Plays*. Self-making at the cusp between genres. The collected humor and wisdom of Zora Neale Hurston's *Tell My Horse*. Fran Ross' epic for the chile-woman in the promised land, *Oreo*, complete with farewell dinner menus, secret languages, signs and symbols for music making and butt-kicking. Ntozake Shange's *Sassafrass, Cypress & Indigo*'s spells, journal entries, potions, recipes and graphic affirmations. The novel as living subjectivity, and not without hilarity and sensual warmth. These women reworked and defied genre conventions, creating particular forms of commonplace books, compendiums of Mother Wit that reverberate with Old Country, up country, down home and new world everyday magic, specifically geared towards the survival of Black women's spirits and imaginations. The collectively compiled *Black Book*, usually attributed to Toni Morrison, is an ekphrastic archive of talking images, graphic texts and recovered subjectivity, stitched from bits of the I and the we of African diasporic history and culture, another *unfinishable* shadow book that continually writes itself as our knowledge of self is detailed and expanded. June Jordan's *Civil Wars* and Barbara Smith's *Home Girls* recalibrated the essay collection and the anthology by shape and content. Letters, reports, remembrances, dispatches, work histories, relationships, family albums, talks and critiques assembled against hegemony, from across the kitchen table, from out in front, from across the street. Lens of the eye, black and squinting.

> In a process that is central to African spirituality, her fixing ceremony
> is not merely that of remembrance for the sake of remembrance, but
> remembrance as the only way to begin the process of healing the psychic
> wound, which continues to have grave effects on the present. Those names
> we can no longer specifically call know that we have not forgotten them,

---

10 "Never Buy Texas From a Cowboy," The Brides of Funkenstein, Atlantic Records, 1979

that they are our "Beloveds," and that unless they release us from the wrath of the past, the future will be tormented and fractured.[11]

I'm dazzled by decolonizing structures, syncretic lure, and archival time travel of Erna Brodber's prose fictions *Jane and Louisa Will Soon Come Home*, *Myal* and *Louisiana*. She makes privacy for Black people an aesthetic imperative within her works, inna kumbla, with the healer, discovering an anthropologist's voice on a cache of found cassette tapes transmitting messages to her protégé from beyond the grave, each book crafted in a way I find radically innovative, and which she insists were written "for ordinary Jamaicans to understand."[12] The reader as seeker, the syncretic layered into the cut of the writing surface. M. NourbeSe Philip's *Looking for Livingston*'s traveling woman opening the way through time to the interior of the voices of ancestors, hiding in plain sight, making for an eternal apprenticeship in geography, language, naming and silence. Mother Wit here, too, is the connection and the protection guiding the code, the conjure and the study of relation. This isn't simply intuition. This is work.

> The shape of this anthology is incomplete and fluid—all collections are which purport to be fundamental. But the work is generically incomplete, for such are the lives of people, and Black women, among others in the First World, are people, creating and destroying with regular frequency ideas and even dogmas.[13]

The perpetual state of being and becoming, and being undone, redone, intrigues and frustrates. The Black feminist women writers I (re)turn to here didn't worry about being read, heard, seen by Black audiences, by other Black women. The difference between now and then is the project of the work. Or so it seems. It's (un)finished. This feminism. Their textual innovations and interventions made space and modes for generations of women, LGBTQIA folk of all colors and classes. Where did it lead for Black women writers in prose today? Where is it going? Have the moves they made been absorbed, subsumed, co-opted, reimagined or forgotten? Trace them. Parse it. Suss it out. Our urgency in telling our own stories is unchanged.

> In writing correct sentences, ending words with "ing" instead of "in," making my verbs agree with their subjects, I am choosing a certain tradition—that of John-from-Sussex. My audience, for the most part, is going to be a white audience, and possibly an educated Black Caribbean audience. However, in

---

11   Barbara Christian, "Fixing Methodologies: *Beloved*, Cultural Critique, No. 24, University of Minnesota Press, Spring 1993

12   Interview with Keshia Abraham, *BOMB* Magazine, No. 86, Winter 2004

13   Sturdy Black Bridges: Visions of Black Women in Literature, Roseann P. Bell, Bettye J. Parker and Beverly Guy-Sheftall, eds., Doubleday, 1979

order to keep faith with Abiswa, I must, within my writing self, constantly subvert the tradition of John-from-Sussex. This doesn't necessarily enlarge my audience to include the less formally educated speakers of nation language—on the contrary it probably reduces that segment of the audience since the work becomes more "difficult." It does, however, I hope, leave whatever audience there is less complacent and less comfortable with things as they appear to be.[14]

Some measure experimentation by duration. By frequency. As a sign. Of commitment. To experimentation in Black women's writing. It don't count if she only does "it" once, if her writing don't act up in the same or some kind of way, recognizably as such, every time. Like Charlotte Carter[15]. Or if they shift into another medium. Like Alison Mills[16]. Or most commonly, editors and agents insisting on narrow, off-the-shelf views of our existence. By these measures sisters can get discarded, dismissed and forgotten, those footpaths they trod into new territories choked by weeds, invisible from the main road…locatable only by guide possessing of a chipped and fading map… and we lose parts of ourselves.

This is not an exceptional story. It has to do with the limitations of publishing opportunities and also this straightjacket to be a "third world woman." The publishing world has a lot of negative control in the West, not only over "third world women" writers. The marketing side of publishing seems to be taking over other considerations entirely. The publishing houses want to make their money and they think they know what will sell, you know? This is what it's about and I think it affects all writing. Maybe with us the pressures are heavier because there are fewer publishing possibilities for "third world" writers. Someone can declare that your manuscript doesn't read like a manuscript from a third world person. I mean that's the trick! It seems incredible that one can encounter such reactions.[17]

14   M. NourbeSe Philip, *Frontiers: Essays and Writings on Racism and Culture*, The Mercury Press, 1992. "John-from-Sussex" represents the white colonial tradition, while "Abiswa" represents the typically ignored African-Caribbean context within colonial education as well as collective African memory.

15   Charlotte Carter is the author of two formally innovative collections, *Sheltered Life*, published in a limited edition of 350 in 1975 by the Poetry Project's Angel Hair Books, and *Personal Effects*, published in 1991 by United Artists. She now writes a successful mystery series.

16   See "Reader, I Married Him: An Interview with Alison Mills," *Callaloo*, Volume 27, Number 3, Summer 2004, and "Artistic Expression was Flowing Everywhere": Alison Mills and Ntozake Shange, Black Bohemian Feminists in the 1970s, *Meridians: Feminism, Race, Transnationalism*, Volume 4, Number 2, 2004. Both can be found in Harryette Mullen's collected essays and writings, *The Cracks Between Who We Are and Who We Are Supposed to Be*, University of Alabama Press, 2012

17   "A New Tail to an Old Tale": An Interview with Ama Ata Aidoo, Rosemary Marangoly George, Helen Scott and Ama Ata Aidoo, *NOVEL: A Forum on Fiction*, Vol. 26, No. 3, Spring, 1993. The interviewers recounted to Aidoo the plight of an African Indian writer whose work was refused publication because the publisher regarded her work as too experimental, not based solely in struggle and deprivation, hence inauthentic and unfit for the Heineman African Writers Series.

The women in this essay, among many others, make healing the African diasporic psyche through reparative, decolonial reading and writing an express objective of either their practice, process, content, or some combination therein. This may seem proscriptive, and not a project all self-identified Black women experimental writers, or Black women writers with experimental processes, would take on, much less pronounce. But when I consider all the possibilities for transformation and expansion for what an African or African diasporic reader, what any reader, really, imagines possible in the world through encounter with the experiments of Black women writers, the dimensions, structure and participants of such a healing project become excitingly unfathomable, free of binary, cliché, prescription, and free from the segregation among Black women writers these projections of binary, cliché and prescription tend to cause. From all these parts, fragments, assemblages and voices, a whole, perpetually being made. The power of change through limitless encounter. Healing in writing, in reading, being simply a way to make space for someone to be quiet with themselves, perhaps seen or felt, perhaps actualized or affirmed, or simply pleasured by play. It's no accident that the writers I've been gathering here are, for the most part, of a certain stripe, generationally, politically, as feminists, culture workers, radical dreamers of their own design, viewing the world, shapers and inheritors of so many Movements in language and story.

> So where do you go from here? Where do I go? And where does a committed woman writer go? Finding a voice, searching for worlds and sentences: say some thing, one thing, or no thing; tie/untie, read/unread, discard their forms; scrutinize the grammatical habits of your writing and decide for yourself whether they are free or repressed. Again, order(s). Shake syntax, smash the myths, and if you lose, slide on, unearth some new linguistic paths. Do you surprise? Do you shock? Do you have a choice? [18]

As experimental prose often resides very closely to if not *within* experimental poetry, is in fact often published by the same small and midsize presses that publish experimental poetry—the somatic labwork of Bhanu Kapil's notebook writing, the drawings, annotations, translations and counternarratives of John Keene, the incantatory provocation of Will Alexander's *Sunrise in Armageddon*, Renee Gladman's architectures of desire and apprehension, Bernadine Evaristo's novels-in-verse and experiments in prose, among recent happenings—there is engagement by dint of proximity with decolonization of literature for Black women experimenting in prose. This nonalignment with major mainstream presses and their general adherence to market-recognized forms makes sense. For Black feminist writers experimenting from the late 70s through the mid 90s, there was a similar nonalignment, as their independent presses were dedicated to women, to women of color, to lesbians, to Black women, across genre,

---

18 "Commitment from the Mirror-Writing Box," *Woman Native Other*, Indiana University Press, 1989. Trust, I know Trinh isn't a Black woman. I bring her forward because of what and who she brought and brings forward to me, in word deed and image, in her oppositional stance which continues to yield my (re)thinking and (re)writing. We loved the same people independent of each other; this discovery made her family: Toni Cade Bambara, Barbara Christian, hattie gossett, Gloria Anzaldúa, Achille Mbembe. And this quote from her is everything.

allowing women to name their destinies as they saw fit. When I cock my ear back to "Third World," I hear resonances of that nonalignment, that oppositional stance, echoing through today's conversations.

> They felt no need to worry over who should want them to be there eating. Why should they? Even if the world is rough, it's still fine to get paid to have an orgasm… or isn't it? Of course, later on when we have become
>
> Diplomats
> Visiting Professors
> Local experts in sensitive area
> Or
> Some such hustlers,
> We would have lost even this small awareness, that in the first place, an invitation was sent…[19]

I am curious about theories, prospects and actions for continued decolonizing of prose through various modes of experimentation, on the order that I experienced so thrillingly, so promisingly, in my 20s, in the vein and vibe of how we do that theorizing, in our stories, riddles, rhymes and dynamic language.[20] What is it that poetry allows for that the novel, that prose, doesn't, or won't? If we leave the surface theory that prose is the moneymaker and as its presumed impoverished opposite, poetry is more "free" out of it, and look instead at poetry and prose as *mediums* rather than as genres, might our sense of the stakes change? In terms of radicalizing gestures, is poetry to music what in world-building visions the novel is to film?

> There were two things that really got me interested in writing. One was a French film called *La Jetee*. It's very modernist and certainly avant-garde for its time. It's all still photographs, in black and white. […] I used to watch it over and over—I was incredibly moved by it. The idea of a story—or anything—being realistic, the idea of representing something as it is, was absurd. I could never even imagine doing that here. And then I read Alain Robbe-Grillet[…] it was some of his short stories. I cannot describe them except that they broke every rule. When I read them, the top of my head came off and I thought, "This is really living!" And I knew that whatever I did, I would not be interested in realism.[21]

---

19 Ama Ata Aidoo, *Our Sister Killjoy, or Reflections From a Black-Eyed Squint*, Longman, 1977. With its fusion of prose and poetry into a structure analogous to (ongoing) post-independence promise and discord in Ghana, between men and women, and between Africa and Europe, *Our Sister Killjoy* is one of the few formally innovative prose works (that I know of) from an African woman writer made available in the U.S. Unlike her more realist fictions, this book is out of print.

20 Barbara Christian, "The Race for Theory," Cultural Critique, No. 6, The Nature and Context of Minority Discourse, University of Minnesota, Spring 1987

21 "Jamaica Kincaid and the Modernist Project," *Caribbean Women Writers: Essays From the First International*

Decolonizing prose, making incursions against its conventions, experimenting with its forms and structures, with character, with plot and outcomes, certainly using the presence of Black and brown folks in unsanctioned, unanticipated, unaligned and unrecognizable narratives with defamiliarized techniques, is real subversion, and nothing new. The prose fiction of Jamaica Kincaid and Wanda Coleman are not commonly considered part of the currently popular "autofiction," yet critical engagement with fictions by Black women that hews very closely to lived experience would highlight and further expand existing possibilities for writing, teaching and scholarship. Nonalignment is not synonymous with nonexistence. Experimental and independent Black women filmmakers, past, present and future,[22] know this, make my brain shiver and prick. We keep writing up against the lie of the blank screen and the desiccated imagination. We pulse in the continuum. We conjure new senses of being.

> To be addressed as a writer, as an artist, still seems strange to me because despite *Jane and Louisa Will Soon Come Home* and *Myal* I still think of myself as a sociologist and my fiction writing as a part of my sociological method. My sociological effort and therefore the fiction that serves it, unlike mainstream sociology, has activist intentions: it is about studying the behavior of and transmitting these findings to the children of the people who were put on ships on the African beaches and woke up from this nightmare to find themselves on the shores of the New World. It is my hope that this information will be a tool with which the blacks and particularly those of the diaspora will forge a closer unity and, thus fused, be able to face the rest of the world more confidently.[23]

The trodden footpaths, the women I (re)turn to, who maps, who holds them? Who holds the women of this book, *Letters to the Future*, and will keep them, not just remember, but fix methodologies, create new and specific ways to critically engage the work without emptying it of its origins? Parentheses manifest in my writing, eyeing, mouthing, this anxiety of being held, and kept away. Absence and presence at once. Held in abeyance. (Un)explained. (Un)finished. (Un)resolved. (Un)explored. And the inverse, the active engagement, motorized wheel pushing against narrative stasis in the Imaginary. (Re)verb, happening in the continuum to (re)dress, (re)mix, (re)imagine, (re)visit and (re)view. The dream of an audience. (Cha) I've stopped trying so hard. I can't make you appear, to enjoy, to come and come back to these words. They are as they are. Black writers. Black audiences. Hold you in my sights then push the vision forward. Make it move.

Conference, Selwyn Cudjoe, ed., Calaloux Publications, 1990

22   For more, check out the L.A. Rebellion Filmmakers, the work of Akosua Adoma Owusu, Nijla Mu'min, Cauleen Smith and Mati Diop, and the traveling film exhibition, *The Black Radical Imagination,* curated by Erin Christovale and Amir George, among many others.

23   Erna Brodber, "Fiction in the Scientific Procedure," *Caribbean Women Writers: Essays from the First International Conference,* Selwyn R. Cudjoe, ed., Calaloux Publications, 1990

The most exciting writing that's going on right now is being done, for the most part, by people of color or Third World peoples, however you want to put it. We're able to be freer, more experimental because we're not faithful to Western forms as much as white, Western writers are. We have a different sense of time and space, and we have more access to a dream life. [...] The idea of literature in most white, Western European circles is as a discipline, and it's something that you're trained for, something that you fit yourself into as an artist. At least that's how I see it—that there is such a thing as the novel, such a thing as the short story. I think we are much more undisciplined, and therefore we have more access to our imaginations. That's a very prejudiced point of view, but that's how I see it.[24]

I teach in a creative writing program rooted in experimental practices, housed within a conceptual art school. In classes like "Hybrid Writing," "OutPosts" (a floating course name; subtitled "(Re)Constructions of Creative Practice," and "Experimental Writers of Color and the Status Quo," thus far), and in all my classes, generally, I teach Black women writers who experiment with form. I've been fortunate to have young Black women writers as students in these classes, and as mentees. I encourage them to go the way their blood beats (Baldwin) with their writing, to not worry about market, to trust in readers' willingness and ability to do some work as readers, to find pleasure in that, to want to be that engaged. To define experimentation on their own terms, and to always ask questions of all these received forms, both the so-called conventional and the so-called experimental. To want something from writing, to want it to do something, say something, be something, and to figure out how to get it.

I don't reject Western forms and visions but rather am trying to articulate my own style of self-expression with sensibilities that were born from my particular vantage point in the universe. My approach to playwriting is eclectic. The form and vision of Bertolt Brecht, the passion and lyricism of Federico Garcia Lorca, the scintillating surrealism of Adrienne Kennedy, Amiri Baraka or Sam Shepard. I like the surrealistic mode because of the unexpected juxtapositions, the symbolic objects and actions that emphasize the subconscious or nonrational imagery that is rooted in African American culture. I allow myself to be influenced by everything that concurs with my artistic vision no matter where it comes from. I do have a problem with imitating forms and perspectives because they are traditional.[25]

---

24 "An Interview with Michelle Cliff," Meryl F. Schwartz, *Contemporary Literature*, Vol. 34, No. 4 Winter, 1993, University of Wisconsin Press. As with Ama Ata Aidoo, Michelle Cliff's more formally innovative works, such as *The Land of Look Behind*, are out of print.
25 Aishah Rahman, "Tradition and a New Aesthetic", MELUS, Vol. 16, No. 3, Ethnic Theater (Autumn, 1989 - Autumn, 1990)

Here's what gives me life, la VIDA en mi vida: In the six years I've taught at this school, I've been fortunate to have worked with thirty-four of the young women of color grad students who have come to our program to write, fourteen of them from the African diaspora. The presence of these young African diasporic women, with their varying experiences, classes, subject positions, identifications and languages, is a gift and a spur; my teaching has become more grounded and fully expressed as a result. It's an extraordinary experience of ever renewing study and appreciation. Constant gathering and regroupings of collections of writings from the distant and recent past, documented attention, care, stewardship of intellect and aesthetics. Anthologies stay active and vital as long as they are returned to, revisited, folded into an ongoing retelling. Spiral back to move forward, always recursive, reflective, in review of what's still happening.

Sometimes in this work of teaching experimentation I wonder if I'm being irresponsible, but I am nothing if not honest about this business of writing, nonconformity and Black womanhood. I am serious in my ever-evolving feminism[26] and what it means to how I read and write, how I hope I, and they, will create pleasurable, unanticipated, transformative encounters with strangers through their writing, through a wide-ranging, inter- and transdisciplinary practice, a practice these young Black women bring their whole selves to. If they want to make money or be famous above all, they will figure it out and go do that; I support them in their efforts, regardless. My job is to create radical little monsters[27] (students? works?) that shapeshift and intervene to heal the world a fragment, a paragraph, a line, an image, a subjectivity at a time.

Dedicated to Candrice, Ebony, Kenyatta, Nijla, Djinji, Shana, Allison, Niela, Regine, Veronica, Jasmine, Jamila, Chelsea, and Amanda. For you here now and here before. And for you still to come.

---

26   While I have had the delight of working with trans and gender queer students in our program, I have not as yet had a Black or POC trans student. Soon come.

27   My homegirl scholar Ofelia Cuesiundiatvas said to me once that her research and teaching is for making radical little monsters of her Black and Brown students, so that they could go out into the world with tools for revolution, for healing, for life.

Notes

BETSY FAGIN "decolonized" and "indigenous silence" appeared in *All Is Not Yet Lost* (Belladonna, 2015). "crossroads and gates are movement (will work for food)" appeared in *Poverty Rush* (Three Sad Tigers Press, 2011). "eating ancient virtue" appeared in *The science seemed so solid* (dusie kollektiv, 2011).

LILLIAN YVONNE BERTRAM These pieces are an excerpt from the chapter "Knots, Near and Far," from *Lillian is the Site of a Fire* (*Puerto Del Sol*, 2015).

LATASHA N. NEVADA DIGGS "pidgin toe" appeared in Poem-a-Day (online), Academy of American Poets, July 30, 2014. "Son of a Negro Explorer (Not) at the North Pole (Colonel Platoff)" appears in the catalogue *Kehinde Wiley: A New Republic, Brooklyn Museum, 2015.* "nigga on a horse or metacomet (after Kehinde's Wiley's King Philip)" appears in the catalogue *Kehinde Wiley: A New Republic, Brooklyn Museum, 2015.* "Duck Season/Rabbit Season" appeared in *Art21 Magazine*, Sept/Oct "Publics" Issue, http://blog.art21.org/2014/10/17/duck-seasonrabbit-season/#.VgnWpouaKS0, 2015. "Trix are for Kids" appeared in SPBH Pamphlet Series; Self Publish Be Happy, March 2015, London, UK. "passing" was previously published in *Jubilat*, Issue 19, 2011.

TONYA FOSTER These pieces are an excerpt from "In/Somniloquies" in *A Swarm of Bees in High Court* (Belladonna*, 2001).

RENEE GLADMAN "Untitled Calamity" is an excerpt from *Morelia*.

DURIEL E. HARRIS These pieces are an excerpt from *No Dictionary of a Living Tongue* (Nightboat Books, 2017) and appear courtesy of the author and Nightboat Books.

"Decorus" and "Self Portrait with Black Box and Open Architecture" are two of a series of 3D poem-objects conceptualized as symmetrical light box cubes. For each piece, in one iteration of the exhibition, title, epigraph, and paratext would appear on a nearby wall or pedestal and the text would be engraved on the six symmetrical square panels of a light box displayed on a pedestal to be handled by attendees. In another iteration the title, epigraph, and paratext would appear on a wall outside of a square glass room. Text would be printed or engraved on the ceiling, walls, and floor of the room that attendees would enter to experience. The cube room would be illuminated by light panels from below and by natural light from overhead and side panels.

The graphotexts, or typographical representations, of the poems "Simulacra: Black Mary Integrates the School House" and "Simulacra: American Counting Rhyme" are designed by Emily Ching. The graphotext of the poem "Simulacra: Pretty Little WIC Check" is designed by Dawn M. Joseph. The graphotexts of the poems "self portrait with black box and open architecture" and "Decorus" are rendered by Steve Halle.

YONA HARVEY "The River Wanderer" appeared in *Fledgling Rag.* "Even Disasters" in *Hemming the Water.* "I worked hard so my girls didn't have to serve nobody else like I did except God" in

Spiral Orbit. "That," "Posting Bail," and "Q" appeared in *The Volta*. "Like A Magpie" in *The Los Angeles Review*, and "The Subject of Surrender" in *This Magazine.*

HARMONY HOLIDAY "You Hear With Your Bones," "Everything I Ever Wanted," and "A Woman Who is Not Interrupted" were published in *Hollywood Forever.*

ROBIN COSTE LEWIS These pieces are an excerpt from II. *Voyage of the Sable Venus* (Knopf, 2015).

DAWN LUNDY MARTIN These pieces are an excerpt from *Good Stock Strange Blood* (Coffee House Press, 2017).

HARRYETTE MULLEN These pieces are an excerpt from *Sleeping with the Dictionary* (New California Poetry, 2002).

ADRIAN PIPER "Why I'm Not Talking About My Artwork (2015)," "Table of Contents of Piper CV," and "Imagine [Trayvon Martin]" re-printed with permission from the Adrian Piper Research Archive Foundation Berlin. Adrian Piper in OPEN ACCESS. Second Wave Feminism: Unfinished Business, 2014. Lecture/Discussion delivered at the National Academy of Art, Oslo. DVD. 01:49:41. Collection of the Adrian Piper Research Archive Foundation Berlin. © APRA Foundation Berlin.

KHADIJAH QUEEN "The Dream Act" appears in *The Volta* (April 2017) and *Non-Sequitur* (Litmus Press, 2015). "When I met LL Cool J" appears in *Fence* (Winter 2016). "I want to not have to write another word about who the cops keep killing" was published by Lit Hub in August 2015.

CLAUDIA RANKINE This piece is an excerpt from *Plot* (Grove Press Poetry Series, 2001).

EVIE SHOCKLEY "at the musée de l'homme," "you can't deny it," and "never after," © 2011 by Evie Shockley. Reprinted by permission of Wesleyan University Press. "philosophically immune," "what's not to liken?," "topsy talks about her role," and "from *topsy in wonderland*," © 2017 by Evie Shockley. Reprinted by permission of the author.

KARA WALKER Artwork © Kara Walker, courtesy of Sikkema Jenkins & Co., New York. *Search for ideas supporting the Black Man as a work of Modern Art/ Contemporary Painting. A text work death without end: an appreciation of the Creative Spirit of Lynch Mobs -, 2007*
> Ink on paper
> 52 parts
> 22.5 x 28.5 inches (57.2 x 72.4 cm), each

"LUCILLE CLIFTON AND SONIA SANCHEZ: A CONVERSATION" BY ELISA DAVIS
Appears in *Callaloo*, Volume 25, Number 4, Fall 2002, pp. 1038-1074. Cave Canem Records.

James Weldon Johnson Collection in the Yale Collection of American Literature. Beinecke Rare Book and Manuscript Library. "Cave Canem Foundation Presents: Lucille Clifton and Sonia Sanchez in conversation with Eisa Davis," 2002. Sponsored by Cave Canem Foundation, Inc. and The Creative Writing Program at The New School, presented at The New School, New York, NY.

"WHAT SAVES US: AN INTERVIEW WITH WANDA COLEMAN" BY PRISCILLA ANN BROWN AND WANDA COLEMAN Appears in *Callaloo*, Vol. 26, No. 3 (Summer, 2003), pp. 635-661.

"CAVE CANEM LEGACY CONVERSATION WITH JAYNE CORTEZ AND SEKOU SIUNDIATA" MODERATED BY TRACIE MORRIS Lightly edited by Erica Hunt.
Cave Canem Records. James Weldon Johnson Collection in the Yale Collection of American Literature. Beinecke Rare Book and Manuscript Library. "Cave Canem Foundation Presents: Legacy Conversations with Jayne Cortez and Sekou Sundiata, moderated by Tracie Morris," October 24, 2002. Sponsored by Cave Canem Foundation, Inc. and The Creative Writing Program at The New School, presented at The New School, New York, NY.

Lillian-Yvonne Bertram

Lillian-Yvonne Bertram is the author of *Personal Science* (Tupelo Press, 2017), *a slice from the cake made of air* (Red Hen Press, 2016), *cutthroat glamours* (Phantom Books, 2013) and *But a Storm is Blowing From Paradise,* chosen by Claudia Rankine as winner of the 2010 Benjamin Saltman Award and published by Red Hen Press. The recipient of an NEA Poetry Fellowship, she received her MFA from the University of Illinois and her PhD from the University of Utah, and teaches at the University of Massachusetts Boston.

Photograph by Dennison Bertram.

Tisa Bryant

Tisa Bryant is the author of *Unexplained Presence* (Leon Works, 2007), a collection of fiction-essays on Black presences in film, literature and visual arts; co-editor, with Ernest Hardy, of *War Diaries*, an anthology of Black male desire and survival in the age of AIDS, and co-editor of the cross-referenced literary journal, *The Encyclopedia Project*, which released its final book, *Encyclopedia Vol. 3 L-Z*, in 2017. She was a commissioned writer/researcher for *Radio Imagination*, Clockshop's year-long Los Angeles celebration of science fiction writer Octavia Butler, in collaboration with the Huntington Library in Pasadena. In addition to recent conference presentations and live film narrations on Prince, her work has appeared or is forthcoming in *Body Forms: Queer Writing and the Essay*; *Brick*; *Flesh*; *I Stand In My Place In My Own Day*; and in *Sam Durant: The Meeting House/Build Therefore Your Own World*. She is working on *The Curator*, a novel of Black female subjectivity and imagined cinema, and on *Residual*, writings on grief, longing, desire and archival research, forthcoming from Nightboat Books. Tisa Bryant received her MFA from Brown University and is the Program Director of the MFA in Creative Writing at California Institute of the Arts, where she teaches fiction, nonfiction and experimental forms. She lives in Los Angeles.

Photograph by Paul Sepuya.

Lucille Clifton

Lucille Clifton was born in Depew, New York, on June 27, 1936. Clifton's work emphasizes endurance and strength through adversity, focusing particularly on African-American experience and family life. Awarding the prestigious Ruth Lilly Poetry Prize to Clifton in 2007, the judges remarked that "One always feels the looming humaneness around Lucille Clifton's poems—it is a moral quality that some poets have and some don't." In addition to the Ruth Lilly prize, Clifton was the first author to have two books of poetry chosen as finalists for the Pulitzer Prize, *Good Woman: Poems and a Memoir, 1969-1980* (BOA Editions, Ltd., 1987) and *Next: New Poems* (1987). Her collection *Two-Headed Woman* (BOA Editions, Ltd., 1980) was also a Pulitzer nominee and won the Juniper Prize from the University of Massachusetts. In 2010, Clifton was posthumously awarded the Robert Frost Medal for lifetime achievement from the Poetry Society of America. She served as the state of Maryland's poet laureate from 1974 until 1985, and won the prestigious National Book Award for *Blessing the Boats: New and Selected Poems, 1988-2000* (BOA Editions, Ltd., 2000). In 1999, she was elected a Chancellor of the Academy of American Poets. After a long battle with cancer, Lucille Clifton died on February 13, 2010, at the age of 73.

Photograph by Rachel Eliza Griffiths.

Wanda Coleman

Wanda Coleman—poet, storyteller and journalist—was born and raised in South Central Los Angeles. She is the recipient of grants from the Guggenheim Foundation and the National Endowment of the Arts. She was awarded the 1999 Lenore Marshall Poetry Prize for *Bathwater Wine* (Black Sparrow Press, 1998) and was a bronze-medal finalist for the 2001 National Book Award for Poetry for *Mercurochrome* (Black Sparrow Press, 2001).

Photograph by Susan Carpendale.

Jayne Cortez

Jayne Cortez is the author of eleven books of poetry and performer of her poems with music on nine recordings. Her voice is celebrated for its political, surrealistic, dynamic innovations in lyricism, and visceral sound. Cortez has presented her work and ideas at universities, museums and festivals around the world. Her poems have been translated into many languages and widely published in anthologies, journals and magazines. She is a recipient of several awards including: Arts International, the National Endowment for the Arts, the International African Festival Award, The Langston Hughes Medal, The American Book Award, and the Thelma McAndless Distinguished Professorship Award. Her most recent books are *The Beautiful Book* (Bola Press, 2017) and *Jazz Fan Looks Back* (Hanging Loose Press, 2002). Her latest CDs with the Firespitter Band are *Find Your Own Voice* (Bola Press, 2007), *Borders of Disorderly Time* (Bola Press, 2003), and *Taking the Blues Back Home* (1997), produced by Harmolodic and by Verve Records. Cortez organized the international symposium "Slave Routes: Resistance, Abolition & Creative Progress" (NYU) and directed the film *Yari Yari Pamberi: Black Women Writers Dissecting Globalization* (2007). She co-founded and acted as president of the Organization of Women Writers of Africa, Inc., and can be seen on screen in the film *Poetry In Motion* (1982).

LaTasha N. Nevada Diggs

A writer, vocalist and sound artist, LaTasha N. Nevada Diggs is the author of *TwERK* (Belladonna, 2013). Her interdisciplinary work has been featured at the Brooklyn Musuem, Museum of Modern Art, the Whitney Museum of American Art and the Walker Art Center. As a curator and director, she has staged events at BAM Café, Lincoln Center Out of Doors and El Museo del Barrio and is the co-founder and co-editor of *Coon Bidness/SO4* magazine. A native of Harlem, LaTasha is the recipient of numerous awards; of them include New York Foundation for the Arts, the National Endowment for the Arts, the Jerome Foundation Travel and Study Fellowship, the Japan-US Friendship Commission, Creative Capital and the Whiting Foundation Literary Award. She earned a BS at New York University's Steinhardt School of Education and an MFA at California College of the Arts. She lives in Harlem.

Photograph by Willy Somma.

r. erica doyle

r. erica doyle was born in Brooklyn to Trinidadian immigrant parents. Her debut collection, *proxy* (Belladonna* Books, 2013), won the 2014 Norma Farber First Book Award from the Poetry Society of America and was a Finalist for the Lambda Literary Award in Lesbian Poetry. Her work has been anthologized in *Best American Poetry, Our Caribbean: A Gathering of Gay and Lesbian Writing from the Antilles, Gumbo: A Celebration of African American Writing, Bum Rush the Page: A Def Poetry Jam, Gathering Ground: A Reader Celebrating Cave Canem's First Decade,* and *Voices Rising: Celebrating 20 Years of Black Lesbian, Gay, Bisexual and Transgender Writing.* Her poetry and fiction appear in various journals, including *Ploughshares, Callaloo, Bloom, From the Fishouse, Blithe House Quarterly,* and *Sinister Wisdom.*

Her articles and reviews have appeared in *Ms. Magazine, Black Issues Book Review,* and on the Best American Poetry and Futurepoem blogs. She has received grants and awards from the Hurston/Wright Foundation, the Astraea Lesbian Writers Fund, the DC Commission on the Arts and Humanities, the Humanities Council of DC and Poets and Writers, and she was a New York Foundation for the Arts Poetry Fellow. Erica is also a fellow of Cave Canem: A Workshop and Retreat for Black Writers.

Photograph by Laura Rubin.

Betsy Fagin

Betsy Fagin is the author of *All is Not Yet Lost* (Belladonna, 2015), *Names Disguised* (Make Now Books, 2014), and a number of chapbooks. She received degrees in literature and creative writing from Vassar College and Brooklyn College and completed her MLS degree in Information Studies at the University of Maryland. One of the librarians for the People's Library of Occupy Wall Street and a former editor of *The Poetry Project Newsletter*, Betsy's commitment to creating social justice through conscious, sustainable change centers on sharing the practices of mindfulness and creative expression. She teaches yoga and meditation in New York City and was awarded a 2017 NYSCA/NYFA Artist Fellowship in Poetry.

Photograph by Lisa Mackie.

Tonya Foster

Tonya M. Foster is the author of the bilingual chapbook *La Grammaire des Os* (Editions Joca Seria, 2016) and the poetry collection *A Swarm of Bees in High Court* (Belladonna*, 2015). A co-editor of *Third Mind: Creative Writing through Visual Art*, Foster has published poetry and essays in a range of publications. Born in Bloomington, Illinois, and raised in New Orleans, Louisiana, Foster earned a BA in English from Tulane University, an MFA in Poetry from the University of Houston, and is completing a PhD in English at the Graduate Center, CUNY. Foster has been a recipient of fellowships from New York Foundation for the Arts, the Macdowell Colony, the Ford Foundation, the Mellon Foundation, and the Graduate Center, CUNY, among others. She is an Assistant Professor of Writing & Literature and Creative Writing at California College of the Arts.

Photograph by Leah Souffrant.

Renee Gladman

Renee Gladman is a writer and artist preoccupied with lines, crossings, thresholds and geographies as they play out in the interstices of poetry and prose. She is the author of ten published works, including a cycle of novels about the city-state Ravicka and its inhabitants, the Ravickians, and *Calamities* (Wave Books, 2016), a collection of linked essay-fictions on the intersections of writing, drawing, and community. *Prose Architectures*, her first monograph of drawings, was released from Wave Books in summer 2017. Recent essays and visual work have appeared in *The Paris Review, Granta, Harper's, Stonecutter*, and *Poetry Magazine*. She earned a BA at Vassar College and an MA in poetics at the New College of California. A 2014-15 fellow at Radcliffe Institute for Advanced Study at Harvard University and recipient of a 2016 Foundation for Contemporary Arts Grant and a 2017 Lannan Foundation Writing Residency in Marfa, Texas. She makes work in New England.

Photograph by Danielle Vogel.

Adjua Gargi Nzinga Greaves

Adjua Gargi Nzinga Greaves (New York City, 1980) is an artist chiefly concerned with postcolonial ethnobotany working in mediums of scholarship, performance, corporeal wisdom, archival gesture and language. Greaves has been published in The Black Earth Institute's *About Place Journal, The Recluse, The Poetry Project Newsletter,* and *No, Dear.* In 2017, Belladonna* published her first chaplet—*Close Reading As Forestry.* She lives and works in New York City where she is Monday Night Reading Series Coordinator at the Poetry Project, a Wendy's Subway board member, and young mother of The Florxal Review.

On the 2012 autumnal equinox, Greaves began *unschoolMFA*—a durational performance of higher education culminating on the 2015 summer solstice in a comprehensive public reading and subsequent group discussion of her manuscript *The Bulletin of Wilderness and Academy: an introductory conclusion to unschoolMFA.* Galleries of her documentary photography and Afrofuturist dioramas are viewable on Instagram via @TerraBot and @SuperModelStudioPractice respectively.

Photograph by @TerraBot.

Yona Harvey

Yona Harvey is the author of *Hemming the Water* (Four Way Books, 2013), winner of the Kate Tufts Discovery Award in poetry. Her poems and essays can be found in *The Force of What's Possible: Accessibility and the Avant-Garde* and *Writing Away the Stigma: Ten Courageous Writers Tell True Stories About Depression, Bipolar Disorder, ADHD, OCD, PTSD & more.* She contributed to Marvel's *World of Wakanda*, a companion series to the bestselling *Black Panther* comic, and co-wrote with Ta-Nehisi Coates Marvel's *Black Panther and The Crew*. She earned an MFA from Ohio State University and is an assistant professor in the Writing Program at the University of Pittsburgh. She is the inaugural winner of the Lucille Clifton Legacy Award in poetry from St. Mary's College of Maryland.

Photograph by Yona Harvey.

Duriel E. Harris

Duriel E. Harris is a poet, performer and sound artist. She is author of three print volumes of poetry, including her most recent, *No Dictionary of a Living Tongue* (Nightboat, 2017), *Drag* (2003) and *Amnesiac: Poems* (2010). Multi-genre works include her one-woman theatrical performance *Thingification, and Speleology* (2011), a video collaboration with artist Scott Rankin. Appearances include performances at the Chicago Jazz Festival (with Douglas Ewart & Inventions), the Greenhouse Theater (Chicago), Naropa Capitalocene, The Votive Poetics Workshop (New Zealand), and Festival Internacional de Poesía de La Habana (Cuba).

Cofounder of the avant garde trio The Black Took Collective, Harris has been a MacDowell and Millay Colony fellow and has received grants from the Illinois Arts Council Agency, the Cave Canem Foundation, and the Rockefeller Brothers Fund. Her work has appeared in numerous venues, including *BAX, The &Now Awards, Of Poetry & Protest, Ploughshares, Troubling the Line,* and *The Best of Fence*; and her compositions have been translated into Polish, German, and Spanish. Harris earned degrees in Literature from Yale University and NYU, and a PhD from the University of Illinois at Chicago Program for Writers. The 2018 Offen Poet, Harris is an associate professor of English in the graduate creative writing program at Illinois State University and the editor of *Obsidian: Literature & Arts in the African Diaspora*.

Photograph by Gina Sandrzyk.

Harmony Holiday

Harmony Holiday is the author of *Negro League Baseball* (Fence Books, 2011), *Go Find Your Father/ A Famous Blues* (Ricochet Editions, 2014) and most recently *Hollywood Forever* (Fence Books, 2017). She is also the founder of Mythscience, an arts production house devoted to cross-disciplinary work that helps artists re-engage with their bodies, and the Afrosonics archive of jazz and everyday diaspora poetics. She worked on *The SOS, The Selected Poems of Amiri Baraka* (Grove Press, 2016), transcribing all of his poetry recorded with jazz accompaniment that had yet to be released in print. Harmony studied rhetoric UC Berkeley and taught for the Alvin Ailey American Dance Theatre. She received her MFA from Columbia University and has received the Motherwell Prize from FenceBooks, a Ruth Lilly Fellowship and an NYFA Fellowship. She is currently working on a book of poems, *Reparations and the body*, a collection of essays on the same topic, and a biography of jazz singer Abbey Lincoln. She lives in New York and Los Angeles.

Photograph by Harmony Holiday

Erica Hunt

Erica Hunt is a poet, essayist, and author of *Local History* (Roof Books, 1993) and *Arcade* (Kelsey St. Press, 1996), *Piece Logic* (Carolina Wren Press, 2002), *Time Slips Right Before Your Eyes* (Belladonna*, 2015), and *A Day and Its Approximates* (Chax Press, 2013). Her poems and non-fiction have appeared in *BOMB, Boundary 2, Brooklyn Rail, Conjunctions, The Los Angeles Review of Books, Poetics Journal, Tripwire, Recluse, In the American Tree* and *Conjunctions*. Essays on poetics, feminism, and politics have been collected in *Moving Borders: Three Decades of Innovative Writing by Women* and *The Politics of Poetic Form, The World*, and other anthologies.

Hunt has received awards from the Foundation for Contemporary Art, the Fund for Poetry, and the Djerassi Foundation and is a past fellow of Duke University/University of Capetown Program in Public Policy. Past writer in residence in the Contemporary Poetics/Creative Writing program at the University of Pennsylvania, and at Bard College's MFA program, Hunt has taught at Wesleyan University and was a repeat faculty member at Cave Canem Retreat, a Workshop for Black Writers from 2004 to 2015. She is the Parsons Family Professor of Creative Writing at Long Island University—Downtown Brooklyn.

Photograph by Erika Kapin.

Adrienne Kennedy

Adrienne Kennedy has been a force in American theatre since the early 1960s. She is a three-time Obie award winner, for *Funnyhouse of a Negro* in 1964, *June and Jean in Concert* in 1996 and *Sleep Deprivation Chamber* which she co-authored with her son Adam Kennedy. She is the winner of the 2008 Obie Lifetime Achievement Award. Among her honors are the American Academy of Arts and Letters award, a Guggenheim fellowship, an Anisfield-Wolf Lifetime Achievement Award in 2003 and a Modern Language Association Honorary Fellow in 2005. She has been a visiting professor at the University of California at Berkeley and Harvard University, among others, and has been commissioned by The Public, the Royal Court, Juilliard and by Jerome Robbins. Signature Theatre devoted its entire 1995-96 Season to her work, and in 2016 Kennedy closed out Signature Theater's 25th anniversary program. In 2016, a new staging of her one-act play *A Rat's Mass* (1967), directed and produced by Hilton Als, was staged at the Whitney Museum of Modern Art. Her memoir *People Who Led To My Plays* was recently reissued by Theatre Communications Group. She is a 2017 Hutchins Fellow at Harvard and in this 2017-18 season, her play *The Owl Answers* will be at Harvard in Farkas Hall and her play *He Brought Her Heart Back in a Box* will be at Theatre for a New Audience in New York City.

Photograph by Signature Theatre Mural NYC.

Ruth Ellen Kocher

Ruth Ellen Kocher is the author of seven books of poetry, including *Third Voice* (Tupleo Press, 2016); *Ending in Planes* (2014), winner of the Noemi Poetry Prize; *Goodbye Lyric: The Gigans and Lovely Gun* (The Sheep Meadow Press, 2014); and *domina Un/blued* (Tupelo Press, 2013). Her poems have been translated into Persian in the Iranian literary magazine, *She'r,* and have appeared in various anthologies including: *Angles of Ascent: A Norton Anthology of Contemporary African American Poets, Black Nature, From the Fishouse: An Anthology of Poems that Sing, Rhyme, Resound, Syncopate, Alliterate* and *Just Plain Sound Great, An Anthology for Creative Writers: The Garden of ForkingPath*. She has earned an MFA and PhD from Arizona State University, and grants and fellowships from the National Endowment for the Arts, Yaddo, and Cave Canem. She is a Professor of English and the Associate Dean for the College of Arts and Sciences at the University of Colorado at Boulder where she teachings Poetry, Poetics, and Literature in the undergraduate and MFA writing programs.

Photograph by Ruth Ellen Kocher.

Robin Coste Lewis

Robin Coste Lewis, the winner of the National Book Award for *Voyage of the Sable Venus* (Knopf, 2015), is the poet laureate of Los Angeles. She is writer-in-residence at the University of Southern California, as well as a Cave Canem fellow and a fellow of the Los Angeles Institute for the Humanities. She received her BA from Hampshire College, her MFA in poetry from New York University, an MTS in Sanskrit and comparative religious literature from the Divinity School at Harvard University, and a PhD in poetry and visual studies from the University of Southern California. Lewis was born in Compton, California; her family is from New Orleans.

Photograph by Guðbjörg Harpa.

Dawn Lundy Martin

Dawn Lundy Martin is a poet, essayist, and conceptual video artist. She is the author of four books of poems and three chapbooks, including most recently, *Life in a Box is a Pretty Life* (Nightboat Books, 2015) and *Good Stock Strange Blood* (Coffee House Press, 2017). She is currently at work on a memoir. Her nonfiction has appeared in *The New Yorker*, *Harper's*, and other magazines.

Martin is also a co-founder of the Black Took Collective, an experimental performance art/ poetry group of three, and a member of HOWDOYOUSAYYAMINAFRICAN?, a global arts collective. She has been awarded the 2015 Lambda Literary Award for Lesbian Poetry and a 2016 Investing in Professional Artists Grant from the Pittsburgh Foundation and the Heinz Endowments. Martin is Professor of English at the University of Pittsburgh and Co-director of the Center for African American Poetry and Poetics.

Photograph by Max Freeman.

Tracie Morris

Tracie Morris is a poet and vocalist who works in multiple media. She has performed extensively around the world. Her sound installations have been presented at numerous institutions, such as the Drawing Center, Ronald Feldman Gallery, Thomas Hirschhorn's Gramsci Monument presented by Dia Art Foundation, Jamaica Center for Arts and Learning, Dia: Chelsea, the Kitchen Performance Space, the Museum of Modern Art, the Silent Barn and the Whitney Biennial. Morris is the recipient of awards, fellowships, and grants for poetry and performance, including New York Foundation for the Arts, Asian Cultural Council, Franklin Furnace and Creative Capital fellowships as well as residencies at Millay, Yaddo and MacDowell colonies. Tracie's work has been extensively anthologized and recorded. Her most recent poetry collection, *handholding:5 kinds*, was published by Kore Press in 2016. She is co-editor of Best American Experimental Writing 2016 with Charles Bernstein, published by Wesleyan University Press. Tracie holds an MFA in poetry from Hunter College and a PhD in Performance Studies from New York University, has studied American acting technique at Michael Howard Studios and classical British acting techniques at the Royal Academy of Dramatic Art in London. She is a former fellow of Creative Writing at the University of Pennsylvania. Tracie has taught at many prestigious academies and is the founding Professor and Coordinator of Performance and Performance Studies at Pratt Institute, New York.

Photograph by Don Stahl.

Harryette Mullen

Harryette Mullen's books include *Recyclopedia* (Graywolf, 2006), winner of a PEN Beyond Margins Award, and *Sleeping with the Dictionary* (University of California, 2002), a finalist for a National Book Award, National Book Critics Circle Award, and Los Angeles Times Book Prize. A collection of essays and interviews, *The Cracks Between What We Are and What We Are Supposed to Be*, was published in 2012 by the University of Alabama. Her most recent book, *Urban Tumbleweed: Notes from a Tanka Diary*, was published by Graywolf in 2013. She teaches courses in American poetry, African American literature, and creative writing at UCLA.

Photograph by Hank Lazer.

Akilah Nayo Oliver

Akilah Oliver was born in St. Louis and grew up in Los Angeles. She received her bachelor's degree from New College and attended graduate school in New York, before moving back to Los Angeles and becoming a key figure in the multicultural arts movement. She was artist-in-residence at the Beyond Baroque Literary Arts Center and worked with the Los Angeles Prover Department (LAPD), a theater group that worked with the homeless. She also co-founded the avant-garde feminist performance group The Sacred Naked Nature Girls, whose work has been the subject of critical work by Coco Fusco, Meiling Cheng and others. She has taught at Naropa University, The New School, and The Poetry Project, among others, and after the death of her son, Oluchi, established permanent residence in New York where she taught and lived until her death in 2011. Her works include *The She Said Dialogues: Flesh Memory* (Smoke Proof, 1999), *An Arriving Guard of Angels: Thusly Coming to Greet* (Farfalla Press, 2004), *The Putterer's Notebook* (Belladonna, 2006), *A Toast In The House of Friends* (Coffee House Press, 2009), and *A Collection of Objects* (Tente Press, 2010).

Julie Patton

Julie Patton is a poet of paper as a form of connecting infinite thought planes and her inner pulpiness. The recent *Best American Experimental Writing 2016* (Wesleyan University Press) and *What I Say: Innovative Poetry by Black Writers in America* (University of Alabama Press, 2015) shows Julie at her inky best. Her site & time specific performances and collaborations with instrumentalists, dancers, bird sounds and other natural and man-made sources underscores the shape-shifting tendencies of paper dolls.

Julie is the founder of Let it Bee Ark Hives, an interspecies experimental housing project based in her former childhood neighborhood of Cleveland, Ohio. Julie is a 2017 Tamaas READ Translation Seminars in Paris invitee; a 2017 Maelstrom Festival (Brussels, Belgium) guest artist; a recipient of a Foundation for Contemporary Art 2015 Grants to Artists Award and Doan Brook Association 2012 Watershed Hero among other honors; and teaches at Naropa University's Jack Kerouac School of Disembodied Poetics Summer Writing Program on occasion.

Photograph by Harald Rumpf.

M. NourbeSe Philip

M. NourbeSe Philip is a poet, essayist, novelist and playwright who lives in the space-time of the City of Toronto. She practised law in the City of Toronto for seven years before leaving to write. She has published five books of poetry, including the seminal, *She Tries Her Tongue; Her Silence Softly Breaks* (Casa de las Americas, 1988), one novel and three collections of essays. Her most recent work of poetry, *Zong!* (Wesleyan, 2011), is a genre-breaking exploration of memory, history and the transatlantic slave trade. Among her awards are the Pushcart Prize (USA), the Casa de las Americas Prize (Cuba), the Tradewinds Collective Prize (Trinidad and Tobago), the Lawrence Foundation Prize for short fiction (USA), as well as the Arts Foundation of Toronto Writing and Publishing Award. Her play, *Coups and Calypsos*, was a Dora Award (Canada) finalist. She is a Guggenheim Fellow in Poetry (USA), a McDowell Fellow and a Rockefeller Foundation (Bellagio) Fellow.

Photograph by Gail Nyoka.

Adrian Piper

Adrian Piper is a first-generation philosopher and conceptual artist, working with artwork in a variety of traditional and nontraditional media, including photo-text collage, drawing on pre-printed paper, video installation, site-specific sculptural installation, digital imagery, performance and sound works. Her work explores the nature of subjecthood and agency, the limits of the self, and the continuities and discontinuities of individual identity in the metaphysical, social and political contexts. In 1970-73, her *Catalysis and Mythic Being* series introduced issues of race and gender into the vocabulary of Conceptual art. She has received Guggenheim, AVA, and NEA Fellowships and in 2012 received the College Art Association Artist Award for a Distinguished Body of Work, for having "since the late 1960s...profoundly influenced the language and form of Conceptual art." She has taught philosophy at Georgetown, Harvard, Michigan, Stanford, and UCSD, and since 2005 has lived and worked in Berlin, where she runs the APRA Foundation Berlin and edits *The Berlin Journal of Philosophy*.

Photograph of Adrian Piper: Adrian Piper in OPEN ACCESS. Second Wave Feminism: Unfinished Business, *2014. Lecture/Discussion delivered at the National Academy of Art, Oslo. DVD. 01:49:41. Collection of the Adrian Piper Research Archive Foundation Berlin. APRA Foundation Berlin..*

Khadijah Queen

Khadijah Queen is the author of five books, including *I'm So Fine: A List of Famous Men & What I Had On* (YesYes Books, 2017), and a verse play, *Non-Sequitur*, which won the Leslie Scalapino Award for Innovative Women Performance Writers. Fiona Templeton's The Relationship theater company staged a full production in December 2015 at Theaterlab NYC. Individual poems and prose appear in *Fence, Tin House, Gulf Coast, DIAGRAM, Fire & Ink: A Social Action Anthology,* and widely elsewhere. She is a doctoral candidate in English at the University of Denver, and is core faculty for the Mile-High MFA program at Regis University.

Photograph by Tariq Amari.

Claudia Rankine

Claudia Rankine is the author of five collections of poetry, including *Citizen: An American Lyric* and *Don't Let Me Be Lonely*; two plays including *Provenance of Beauty: A South Bronx Travelogue*; numerous video collaborations, and is the editor of several anthologies including *The Racial Imaginary: Writers on Race in the Life of the Mind*. Her most recent play, *The White Card*, will premiere in February 2018 (ArtsEmerson/ American Repertory Theater). Among her numerous awards and honors, Rankine is the recipient of the Bobbitt National Prize for Poetry, the Poets & Writers' Jackson Poetry Prize, and fellowships from the Guggenheim Foundation, the Lannan Foundation, the MacArthur Foundation, United States Artists, and the National Endowment of the Arts. She is a Chancellor of the Academy of American Poets and teaches at Yale University as the Frederick Iseman Professor of Poetry. In 2016, she co-founded The Racial Imaginary Institute (TRII). She lives in New Haven, Connecticut.

Photograph by Ricardo DeAratanha and Los Angeles Times.

Deborah Richards

Deborah Richards is the author of chapbooks, *Hide Me From the Day* (Bootstrap Press, 2001), *parable* (Leroy Press, 2001) and the poetry collection *Last One Out* (Subpress, 2002). Her work appears in *Encyclopedia Vol 1, I'll Drown My Book: Conceptual Writing by Women* and *What I Say: Innovative Poetry by Black Writers in America*. Deborah has work published in print and on-line journals including *Tarpaulin Sky, Chain, Pom Pom, Nocturnes, XCP: Cross Cultural Poetics* and *Callaloo*. Deborah is currently working on gustatory lacrimal reflex—crocodile tears—and other kinds of crying. Deborah earned her MA in English and Creative Writing from Temple University. She currently lives and works in London.

Photograph by Ravi Patel.

Metta Sáma

A 2016 co-winner of the Robert H. Winner Award from Poetry Society of America, Metta Sáma is author of the forthcoming poetry collection, *Swing at your own risk* (Kelsey Street Press, 2018), the chapbooks *the year we turned dragon* (Portable Press @ Yo-Yo Labs, 2016), *le animal & other creatures* (Miel, 2015), *After After/After "Sleeping to Dream"* (Nous-zot Press, 2014) and *Nocturne Trio* (YesYes Books, 2012). Her debut poetry collection, *South of Here* was published by New Issues Press (2005) under Sáma's legal name, Lydia Melvin. A literary scholar, prose writer, book reviewer, interviewer and poet, Sáma's work has been published in *Femininities and Masculinities in Action: On Theory and Practice in a Moving Field, Bluestem, Feminist Wire, Kweli, Fence, Prairie Schooner, The Volta, Literary Hub, Brooklyn Magazine, Puerto del Sol's Black Voices Series, Best American Experimental Writing,* and elsewhere. She is a co-editor of the critical, literary activism anthology, *Bettering American Poetry* and has guest edited several literary journals, most recently *North America Review* and *About Place Journal.* Sáma is a fellow of the Black Earth Institute and a member of Black Radish Books' Advisory Board.

Photograph by Stephanie Pruitt-Gaines.

Sonia Sanchez

Poet. Mother. Professor. National and International lecturer on Black Culture and Literature, Women's Liberation, Peace and Racial Justice. Sponsor of Women's International League for Peace and Freedom. Board Member of MADRE. Sonia Sanchez is the author of over 20 books including *Homecoming* (Broadside Press, 1969), *We a BaddDDD People* (Broadside Press, 1970), *Homegirls and Handgrenades* (White Pine Press, 1984), *Wounded in the House of a Friend* (Beacon Press 1995), *Does Your House Have Lions?* (Beacon Press, 1997), *Like the Singing Coming off the Drums* (Beacon Press, 1998), and most recently, *Morning Haiku* (Beacon Press, 2010). In addition to being a contributing editor to *Black Scholar* and *The Journal of African Studies*, she has edited an anthology, *We Be Word Sorcerers: 25 Stories by Black Americans*, and has been the recipient of many awards, including the 1985 American Book Award for *Homegirls and Handgrenades*, the National Visionary Leadership Award for 2006, and the 2009 Robert Creeley Award. Her book *Does Your House Have Lions?* was a finalist for the National Book Critics Circle Award. In 2011, Philadelphia Mayor Michael Nutter selected Sonia Sanchez as Philadelphia's first Poet Laureate, calling her "the longtime conscience of the city."

Photograph by Jim Alexander.

Evie Shockley

Evie Shockley is the author of several collections of poetry—most recently, *the new black* (Wesleyan, 2011), winner of the 2012 Hurston/Wright Legacy Award in Poetry, and *semiautomatic* (Wesleyan, 2017). She has also published a critical study, *Renegade Poetics: Black Aesthetics and Formal Innovation in African American Poetry* (University of Iowa, 2011). Her poetry and essays appear widely in journals and anthologies. Her other honors include the 2015 Stephen Henderson Award for Outstanding Achievement in Poetry and the 2012 Holmes National Poetry Prize. Currently serving as creative editor for *Feminist Studies*, Shockley earned her JD from the University of Michigan and her PhD from Duke University, and is Associate Professor of English at Rutgers University–New Brunswick.

Photograph by Nancy Crampton.

PHOTO UNAVAILABLE

giovanni singleton

giovanni singleton is the author of *Ascension* (Counterpath Press, 2011), winner of the California Book Award Gold Medal and the forthcoming *AMERICAN LETTERS: works on paper* (Canarium Books, 2018). She is founding editor of *nocturnes (re)view of the literary arts*, a journal dedicated to experimental work of the African Diaspora and other contested spaces. singleton holds the 2017-18 Holloway Lectureship in Poetry at University of California-Berkeley.

Kara Walker

New York-based artist Kara Walker is best known for her candid investigation of race, gender, sexuality, and violence through silhouetted figures that have appeared in numerous exhibitions worldwide. Walker's first large-scale public project, *A Subtlety: Or... the Marvelous Sugar Baby*, was displayed at the abandoned Domino Sugar refinery in Williamsburg, Brooklyn, during the spring of 2014. Commissioned and presented by Creative Time, the project—a massive sugar covered sphinx-like sculpture—reflected on and responded to the troubled history of sugar. The installation was seen by over 130,000 visitors over the course of 9 weekends that the exhibition was open to the public.

Born in Stockton, California, in 1969, Walker was raised in Atlanta, Georgia, from the age of 13. She studied at the Atlanta College of Art (BFA, 1991) and the Rhode Island School of Design (MFA, 1994). She is the recipient of many awards, notably the John D. and Catherine T. MacArthur Foundation Achievement Award in 1997 and the United States Artists, Eileen Harris Norton Fellowship in 2008. In 2012, Walker became a member of the American Academy of Arts and Letters.

Photograph by Ari Marcopoulos.

Wendy S. Walters

Wendy S. Walters is the author of a book of prose, *Multiply/Divide: On the American Real and Surreal* (Sarabande Books, 2015), named a best book of the year by *Buzzfeed, Flavorwire, Literary Hub, The Root,* and *The Huffington Post.* She has also written two books of poems, *Troy, Michigan* (Futurepoem, 2014) and *Longer I Wait, More You Love Me* (Palm Press, 2009). Her work appears in *Bookforum, FENCE, Harper's Magazine,* and elsewhere. She is a founding director of Essay in Public | A Humanities Project and a Contributing Editor at *The Iowa Review.* She earned her MFA and PhD at Cornell University, and works at The New School where she is Associate Dean of Art and Design History and Theory at Parsons and Associate Professor of Literary Studies at Eugene Lang College.

Photograph by Dan Charnas.

Simone White

Simone White is the author of three collections, *Dear Angel of Death* (Ugly Duckling Presse, 2017), *Of Being Dispersed* (Futurepoem Books, 2016), and *House Envy of All the World* (Factory School, 2010), the poetry chapbook, *Unrest* (Ugly Duckling Presse, 2013), and the collaborative poem/painting chapbook, *Dolly* (Q Avenue Press, 2008), with Kim Thomas.

Her poetry and prose have been featured in publications such as *Harper's Magazine*, *BOMB Magazine*, *Chicago Review*, and *Harriet: The Blog*, and her honors include a 2017 Whiting Award, Cave Canem Foundation fellowships, and recognition as a New American Poet for the Poetry Society of America in 2013. She works as Program Director at The Poetry Project and teaches writing and American literature at The New School, Eugene Lang College.

Photograph by Pat Cassidy Mollach.

Closing Words

BY ERICA HUNT AND DAWN LUNDY MARTIN

1.

This anthology is the convergence of many literary traditions, imaginational libraries, and artistic practices. I gratefully acknowledge my kinship and debt to Cave Canem, a Place for Black Poets, where I first met Dawn Lundy Martin, almost eighteen years ago. Our generative conversation and considered reading of each other's works has given the future a plausible horizon. Thanks also for the use of Cave Canem's Legacy Conversations, reprinted here, which capture some of the intellectual, emotional and poetic gambols of leading Black women writers. Cave Canem has truly been a home for Black poetry—of many practices and approaches, a hive, a haven, a gathering for fugitive writings.

I also gratefully acknowledge the contributions of all the writers in this anthology—a treasure box of unpublished plays, essays, emails, manifestoes, and experiments. Their generosity and willingness to step-up and address each other in the present and projected company is staggering and inspiring. I am particularly grateful for the contributions from Tisa Bryant, and also from M.NourbeSe Philip; their essays chart issues many writers will continue to explore fruitfully.

In closing, I am thankful for the companionship of Dawn Lundy Martin, my co-editor and co-conspirator, for the many hours of critical exchange, camraderie and intellectual adventure. The richness of Dawn's insights and strategies for getting it done more than made up for the hours of editorial toil that accompanied this undertaking.

Finally, a special thanks to my family, intimate and chosen—whose lives in the arts, and commitment to justice, provide constant encouragement to the notion that poetry and art is vital to the realization of a future we want to live in. Nowhere is the day to day more imaginable and renewed than in the creative exchange with Marty, my partner for 35 years, whose art and love sustains me.

—EH

2.

The days and days Erica and I spent inside of each other's heads thinking about the work included in this collection of extraordinary writing by Black women. We'd gather at my home in East Hampton for a weekend of work, reading and recording ourselves thinking through the impact of this work and the Blackness of it. Why now, we'd ask? Why women? What makes this possible in this moment more than any other moment? My partner Stephanie and I would roast chicken and in the evening we'd all drink wine pouring over the day. Sometimes I'd drive into the City at Erica's place in the East Village and we'd spend the day pulling books off the shelves in her library, moving our discussions from what was in front of us to the theorists, visual artists, and other creative people who might be in conversation with the work. At the end of the day, Erica would whip up, seemingly in an instant, a fabulous gourmet meal—and healthy to boot. I'm grateful to Erica Hunt for her generosity of spirit, her tireless energy, her unflinching intellect, and her wild imagination. I had been a fan long before we met in person, so to collaborate with her on *Letters to the Future* was a dream come true.

I am also deeply indebted to my partner, Stephanie Hopkins, and to my chosen family for their ongoing support of my work. Thanks to my mother for reading to me every night when I was a girl. Without all of you my imagination would cease to flourish.

Both Erica and I thank Lisa Bowden at Kore Press for inviting us to make this anthology in the first place, and for her undying patience. We're indebted to Lisa for having good faith in vision of this volume. Of course, a volume like this is deeply indebted to editorial assistants who transformed the gathering of pieces into the capacious dwelling that you, reader, hold in your hands. We thank Soham Patel, Gala Mukomolova, and Sarah Darwiche for administrative and editorial support on this project. We truly could not have done it without you. A special note of thanks is due Lorna Simpson for the visionary cover art of the volume. And, another special note of thanks is due to James Meetze and Mary Austin Speaker, who took on the interior book and cover design. We owe you big time.

Here's to the Future! Here's to everyone included in this volume!

—DLM

Colophon

Kore Press is an intersectional feminist arts organization founded by literary activists devoted to keeping the margins in the center through publishing, education, and programming that inspires public dialog. Since 1993, Kore has focused on the creative genius of women, writers of color, and queer artists, to deepen awareness and advance justice.

We thank the following individuals and entities for their intellectual, creative, moral, professional or fiscal support of *Letters to the Future:*

Ann Dernier

Dulce Botello

Niki Herd

Stephanie Troutman

Sarah Darwiche

Monica Casper

Tracie Morris

KXCI Community Radio

Joy Harjo

Lidia Yuknavitch

Brian Turner

Sarah Au

Anonymous

Alison Deming

Angela Patel

Soham Patel

Jacquelyn Jackson

Shirley Muney

Alison Deming

Emily Rothrum / Hauser & Wirth

Rachel Lowry